Authorised Lives in Early Christian Biography

What was distinctive about Christian biography in late antiquity? In this book, Dr Williams examines a range of biographies of prominent Christians written in the fourth and fifth centuries AD, and suggests that they share a purpose and function which sets them apart from their non-Christian equivalents. This was an age in which the lives of saints first emerged as a literary phenomenon, and a broad perspective on this developing genre is here complemented by close readings of more problematic works such as Eusebius of Caesarea's *Life of Constantine* and the *Confessions* of Augustine of Hippo. In including such idiosyncratic examples, the aim is to provide a definition of Christian biography which extends beyond mere hagiography, and which expresses a new understanding of the world and the place of individuals within it. It was a world in which lives might be authored by Christians, but could be authorised only by God.

MICHAEL STUART WILLIAMS lectures in Ancient History at the University of Cambridge.

CAMBRIDGE CLASSICAL STUDIES

General editors

R. L. HUNTER, R. G. OSBORNE, S. P. OAKLEY,
W. M. BEARD, M. MILLETT, D. N. SEDLEY,
G. C. HORROCKS

AUTHORISED LIVES IN EARLY CHRISTIAN BIOGRAPHY

Between Eusebius and Augustine

MICHAEL STUART WILLIAMS

University of Cambridge

CAMBRIDGE UNIVERSITY PRESS
Cambridge, New York, Melbourne, Madrid, Cape Town, Singapore, São Paulo, Delhi

Cambridge University Press
The Edinburgh Building, Cambridge CB2 8RU, UK

Published in the United States of America by Cambridge University Press, New York

www.cambridge.org
Information on this title: www.cambridge.org/9780521894906

First published 2008

Printed in the United Kingdom at the University Press, Cambridge

A catalogue record for this publication is available from the British Library

Library of Congress Cataloging in Publication data
Williams, Michael Stuart, 1977–
Authorised lives in early Christian biography: between Eusebius and
Augustine / Michael Stuart Williams.
p.   cm. – (Cambridge classical studies)
Includes bibliographical references (p. 236) and index.
ISBN 978-0-521-89490-6 (hardback)
1. Christian biography.   I. Title.   II. Series.
BR1690.W55   2008
270.2092'2 – dc22   2008007561

ISBN 978 0 521 89490 6 hardback

BR
1690
.W55
2008

CONTENTS

PREFACE

The title of this book deliberately refers to 'Christian biography' for a number of reasons, but above all because I wish to make the claim that such a category exists as a distinctive form of writing, with its roots in late antiquity. It is to be distinguished therefore from the tradition of classical biography represented by such works as Xenophon's *Cyropedia*, Suetonius' *Lives of the Caesars*, and (above all) Plutarch's *Parallel Lives*; it is also, however, to be distinguished from biographies of pagan philosophers and miracle workers such as Philostratus' *Life of Apollonius of Tyana*, Porphyry's *Life of Plotinus* and Eunapius' *Lives of the Sophists*. At the same time, the term 'Christian biography' is intended to connote a particular subset of early Christian writings: one which excludes the gospels (which I take to be in a category of their own) and early martyr acts (which I shall argue are not to be considered true biographies), but which is broader than the class of writings usually considered under the term 'hagiography'. The lives of the saints that begin to appear in the fourth and fifth centuries AD are certainly worthy of study, and much work has been done to advance our understanding of the genre in the last few decades in particular. I have preferred a different term not because I feel that this work has been lacking – and on the contrary, I have derived great profit from much of it – but because I feel that a different perspective on the genre might bring new insights. My claim in this book is that our understanding of hagiography – and of the world in which it was written – can be improved by paying close attention to those texts traditionally considered to occupy the fringes of the genre.

This book thus concentrates on those biographies which are not straightforwardly accounts of saints or miracles; works which may include elements of imperial panegyric or speculative philosophy or pilgrimage narrative or autobiography; but which nevertheless seem to deploy many of the narrative techniques and presuppositions that have been recognised as appropriate to hagiography. Some of these works have been studied in detail before, although others remain remarkably underexploited, and a few are yet to be translated into English. My aim here has been to bring them together and situate them as part of an ongoing Christian discourse about the relationship between the Bible and the post-biblical world, and between the lives of individuals and their implications for the wider Christian community. I hope that in my various close readings of these texts I have managed to enlarge the scope of their possible functions and meanings; but I hope too that the works I have focused on will be recognised as sharing rather more than an accidental similarity. The juxtaposition of these texts is a significant part of the argument: that although they may derive from distant corners of the empire, and may have been composed originally in Latin, Greek, Syriac or Coptic, they reveal a consistent set of attitudes and assumptions which can only enhance our awareness of how the Christians of late antiquity understood and experienced the world around them.

A brief comment may be helpful in order to explain how I have used the Bible. When referring to or quoting the original texts I have generally not specified an edition, with the exception of when it proved necessary to note an unusual or variant reading. In providing English translations I have used a number of different modern versions, chiefly the King James or Authorised Version [AV], the Revised Standard Version [RSV] and the New English Bible [NEB]. In each case I have chosen the translation that seemed best to bring out the meaning I wished to emphasise, and have noted its source in the footnote. Consistency, in this instance, has therefore been sacrificed in favour of clarity of interpretation.

This book has its origins in a Ph.D. thesis written in Cambridge under the supervision of Christopher Kelly. He has since guided it through to its present form, and his close reading supplemented by detailed and constructive criticism has been invaluable. His influence is inscribed in this book from the title onwards, and I am very grateful. My thanks also go to Peter Garnsey and Gillian Clark, who examined the original Ph.D. thesis, and who have since offered me no end of support on this venture and on others; and to Robin Osborne, who has been interested and engaged from the start and who has shown remarkable good humour and willingness to help as I struggled to complete it at a desk ten feet away. Among those who have helped me with my thinking on various matters I should especially like to acknowledge the contributions of Claudia Rapp, Mark Humphries, David Scourfield and Mark Vessey. Too many others have listened to me express – or fail to express – my ideas for them all to be thanked individually; but I would especially like to thank my former colleagues in Maynooth and in Salem, and the fellows, faculty, staff and graduates in Corpus Christi and in the Faculty of Classics here in Cambridge. I should also thank Michael Sharp at Cambridge University Press for overseeing this book from inception to conclusion.

Nothing I write here will adequately capture the debts I owe to my friends and family, and to name names seems invidious. All the same, I would like to mention Ann Fielding and Rachel Smith, who have probably had to bear with me more than most; and of course my parents, who have had to witness me disappear for months at a time as I tried to devote some time to writing. I hope it will suffice to say that support can come in many guises, and that many people have contributed to this book without reading a word of it. With that in mind, I should like to dedicate this book to my grandparents.

ABBREVIATIONS

Many of the primary sources are referred to in the footnotes in abbreviated form: a list of these abbreviations is given below. Full details regarding published editions and translations of these texts are provided in the bibliography – translations in this book are my own except where specified.

C.Th.	*Codex Theodosianus*
Conf.	Augustine of Hippo, *Confessionum*
De ciu. dei	Augustine of Hippo, *De ciuitate dei*
De uera rel.	Augustine of Hippo, *De uera religione*
De util. cred.	Augustine of Hippo, *De utilitate credendi*
De uir. ill.	Jerome, *De uiris illustribus*
Doct. christ.	Augustine of Hippo, *De doctrina christiana*
HE	Eusebius of Caesarea, *Historia ecclesiastica*
HM	*Historia monachorum in Aegypto*
HR	Theodoret of Cyrrhus, *Historia Religiosa*
In Bas.	Gregory of Nyssa, *In Basilium fratrem*
Io. eu. tr.	Augustine of Hippo, *In Iohannis euangelium tractatus*
OC	*Oratio Constantini ad sanctos*
Pan. lat.	*XII panegyrici latini*
Retr.	Augustine of Hippo, *Retractationes*
VA	Athanasius of Alexandria, *Vita Antonii*
VC	Eusebius of Caesarea, *Vita Constantini*
VGThaum.	Gregory of Nyssa, *Vita Gregorii Thaumaturgi*
VHil.	Jerome, *Vita Hilarionis*
VMac.	Gregory of Nyssa, *Vita Macrinae*
VMalchi	Jerome, *Vita Malchi*
VMoys.	Gregory of Nyssa, *Vita Moysis*
VP	*Pachomii uita prima*
VPauli	Jerome, *Vita Pauli*

Abbreviations are also used in the notes to refer to the two main collections of sources edited by J. P. Migne – the *Patrologia Latina* [*PL*] and *Patrologia Graeca* [*PG*] – and to the series of English translations of ancient patristic texts published as A Select Library of the Nicene and Post-Nicene Fathers of the Christian Church [NPNF].

INTRODUCTION:
BIOGRAPHY AND TYPOLOGY

And so was God here then, but now has gone on a journey? God can always do these things.

> (Apa Apollo, quoted in the *Historia Monachorum in Aegypto* 8.47)

Living Scripture

In 1897, the State of Massachusetts took possession of the original manuscript of what was inaccurately described as the log of the Mayflower – it was in fact, the seventeenth-century history *Of Plymouth Plantation* by William Bradford, who had rapidly established himself as leader of the Plymouth pilgrims and who spent much of his life as Governor of the new colony. In his speech on the occasion, Senator George F. Hoar welcomed the acquisition and declared that there had been nothing like this history of the early American colonists 'in human annals since the Story of Bethlehem'.[1] In making this grand claim the Senator was only following the example of the Pilgrim Fathers and indeed of Bradford himself, for whom parallels were easy to draw between their own age and the age of the first Christians in the New Testament, or else between the predicament of the new arrivals and the travails of the nation of Israel in the Old Testament. As Bradford looked back in his history on the arrival of the Mayflower at Cape Cod, he asked:

May not and ought not the children of these fathers rightly say: 'Our fathers were Englishmen which came over this great ocean, and were ready to perish in this wilderness; but they cried unto the Lord, and He heard their voice and looked on their adversity' etc.[2]

---

[1] Bradford 1952; the text was completed in manuscript around 1650, and a first full printed edition was published at Boston in 1912; I am using the 1952 revised edition by Samuel Morison, with Hoar's comment quoted at Morison 1952: xxxviii.

[2] Bradford 1952: 63; cf. Deuteronomy 26:5–7.

I

Like the others who would come to refer to the new colony and its surroundings as the 'New English Israel' or the 'New English Canaan', Bradford found his parallel with the Israelites who could say, 'the Lord brought us out of Egypt with a mighty hand and an outstretched arm, with great terror, with signs and wonders; and he brought us into this place and gave us this land, a land flowing with milk and honey'.[3]

It is perhaps not unexpected that someone such as Bradford should see around him the 'signs and wonders' of Deuteronomy, and the 'mighty hand and outstretched arm' of God guiding the settlers, but it is important to note that for these seventeenth-century Puritans this was not simply a matter of literary allusion; rather it reflected a genuine belief about history. The evident connection between their own escape from persecution and entry into the Promised Land and that of the Israelites as recorded in Scripture was not to be considered merely a product of the author's rhetorical skill; rather, it was to be supposed that God Himself, as the divine author of events, had arranged them in precisely this way. The belief was that 'God had commissioned this small band of colonists to fulfil the special mission of creating a new Jerusalem in a barbarous land.'[4] The biblical parallels in works such as Bradford's *Of Plymouth Plantation* were therefore an indication of the pilgrims' true place as successors to the nation of Israel in God's divine plan:

Between Israel and Plymouth exists more than a parallel, more than an analogy; for when God's chosen peoples go in search of Canaans, the ancient lives are reenacted. The past lives again in the present.[5]

Thus the Pilgrim Fathers imagined themselves to be a new chosen people, watched over and directed by divine providence; and they found proof of this in the similarities between the events and personalities of their own time and those recorded in the authoritative accounts of God's work as set out in the scriptures. They believed themselves to be pioneers not only in a new land but of a new

---

3 Deuteronomy 26:8–9 [RSV]; Cotton Mather would later proclaim 'Good News for the *Israel* of God, and particularly for His *New English Israel*' in his *Wonders of the Invisible World* (Boston, 1692), quoted at Lowance 1977: 245; Thomas Morton had already published his account of the *New English Canaan*: Morton 1637.
4 Elliott 1977: 206–7.   5 Rosenmeier 1972: 99.

biblical age, such that the 'contemporary events' of their own lives 'formed part of sacred history'.[6]

Yet this willingness on the part of the Plymouth pioneers to see themselves in such terms should not be dismissed as 'mere sectarian extravagance': indeed, 'there was nothing extraordinary or perverse' in their understanding of Scripture as providing both a pattern for events of their own time and a guide to their interpretation.[7] Their attitude was not universal among Christians, but it was not unprecedented; and if seventeenth-century Protestantism was a 'golden age' for this kind of interpretation, nevertheless it may also be recognised as a prominent feature of Christian thought in the later Roman empire.[8] There too a formerly persecuted sect had found itself suddenly presented with a world in which it was now the dominant party, and with an opportunity to build for itself a new relationship with that world. The guiding hand of divine providence could easily be seen in the conversion of the Emperor Constantine; and like William Bradford, many Christian authors turned to the scriptures as a means of interpreting that and subsequent events.[9] The Bible was an obvious recourse in the face of the apparent intervention of God. It offered not only a historical precedent for strange and marvellous events, but also a structure and narrative within which they could be located and rendered meaningful. For many in late antiquity, the understanding of contemporary history came to be predicated on, and structured by, the re-enactment of Scripture.

There is evidence of such an attitude among the explicit doctrinal statements of many late-antique theologians; but as a theory of history, it is manifested above all in contemporary historical writings.[10] The church histories and chronologies composed

---

[6] Zwicker 1977: 116.   [7] Fabiny 1992: 113.

[8] Fabiny (1992: 10) does indeed pick out these two periods as successive 'golden ages'.

[9] It is notable too that Bradford locates a parallel with the post-Constantinian church at the beginning of his history, quoting a passage from the fifth-century historian Socrates to help paint his picture of contemporary Europe; Bradford's history, which was unusual in including 'letters and even long official documents' (Morison 1952: viii), may even have taken some inspiration from Eusebius of Caesarea.

[10] For the traditional theological approach to ideas of biblical typology and re-enactment, see especially the works of de Lubac (1947 and 1959), and Daniélou (1960); more recent works have engaged with the implications of particular late-antique approaches to biblical exegesis, as for example Dillon (1983) and Dawson (1992).

3

by Christians in this period show a certain development of this approach, not least in the revealing attempts to combine history sacred and secular into a single universal narrative.[11] Yet the beliefs and assumptions which underlay Christian historical thinking in the later Roman empire may also be effectively approached through another literary form which developed in the wake of Constantine's conversion in the fourth century AD: one which also involved the relationship between the present and the past, and between the world of the Bible and the lives of contemporary Christians. Biography in the ancient world has at times been considered a poor relation of history – less ambitious in its scope, and often more various in its structure and style. It is one of the most self-effacing of literary genres, in which content has traditionally seemed to take priority over form, and so it has often resisted satisfactory definition: perhaps the best that can be said, at the risk of tautology, is that a biography provides an account of an individual life.[12] Christian biography presents further problems, and I intend to focus on the most problematic examples. Yet despite these difficulties of definition, or perhaps precisely because of them, the study of Christian biography can offer a valuable insight into an attitude to the world which was shared among a variety of different authors in the century after Constantine.

Christian biography

Insofar as it can be defined as a phenomenon in its own right, Christian biography can be said to have its origins in late antiquity. Of course, biographies – even biographies of Christians – were known before the conversion of Constantine. The written life had long been a significant part of Graeco-Roman culture, reaching perhaps its most lasting expression in the *Parallel Lives* of

[11] The contours of the Christian understandings of history were famously set out in Momigliano (1963), which remains the best introduction to the problem; more recent accounts of Christian attempts to write universal and sacred histories include Mortley (1996) and Inglebert (1996).

[12] See, for example, the discussion in Heffernan 1988: 38–54.

Plutarch; and late-antique examples of the form can be seen as continuing some important aspects of this tradition.[13] At the same time, biography had been employed as a Christian mode since that faith's very foundation in the gospels, and can be traced further back into the Hebrew scriptures.[14] Attempts have been made to combine Christian and non-Christian biographies, under the early Roman empire especially, into an over-arching genre of 'aretalogy' defined by the inclusion of miraculous events.[15] Even when this 'hypothetical genre' is rejected, however, studies of biography in the Roman empire have tended to concentrate on the similarities between Christian and non-Christian lives, and implicitly to regard them as comprising a common tradition.[16] Yet there are also significant differences between pagan and Christian lives – in form and content, and in the underlying assumptions of the authors – and these differences are equally worthy of study.[17] Thus without wishing to deny the possibility of non-Christian influence on Christian writings, it may reasonably be maintained that 'l'*homme de Dieu* biblique et hagiographique est autre chose que l'*homme divin* antique'.[18] Christian and non-Christian biographies can perhaps be usefully thought of as siblings: as interesting as what they share is what they also fail to share.

---

[13] For ancient biography in general, the best introduction is Momigliano (1993); from a vast amount of literature on Plutarch, one particularly interesting study is that of Duff (1999). The development of biographical literature from a late-antique viewpoint is discussed in Cox (1983) and in Edwards and Swain (1997) – and particularly in the contributions of Edwards and Swain themselves. See also the review of this collection by Fox (2000). The collection edited by Hägg and Rousseau (2000) provides alternative perspectives on the issue of Greek biography in late antiquity.

[14] Burridge 1995; cf. Edwards 1997: 228–33.

[15] Aretalogy is the concept used in Hadas and Smith 1965, and is further explained in Smith 1971.

[16] Cox (1983: 1–4) provides a useful account of the problems of what she calls the 'hypothetical genre' of aretalogy, noting that the need for miracles would exclude such notable pagan and Christian lives as the *Life of Plotinus* by Porphyry and the so-called 'Life of Origen' – in fact one chapter of a larger work – by Eusebius of Caesarea. Cox nevertheless goes on to consider Christian and non-Christian lives as engaged in a common biographical enterprise.

[17] For Momigliano, indeed, Christian biography was a very different enterprise from its ancient model, and Christianity 'influenced ordinary biography less than we would expect': Momigliano 1963: 88.

[18] Van Uytfanghe 1985: 566; cf. the account of hagiography and aretalogy in Van Uytfanghe 1993.

Elsewhere, a similarly fraternal relationship has been suggested between Christian biography and the acts of the Christian martyrs, as produced or set in the persecuted church of the first few centuries AD.[19] It is again undeniable that there are many things that the two forms have in common; yet it seems reasonable to exclude the acts of the martyrs from the present study of Christian biography. Certainly by late antiquity there had been a noticeable shift away from martyr narratives and towards biography, so that Constantine's conversion coincided with the development of 'a very different narrative framework'.[20] Defining this new structure is notoriously difficult, but it seems intuitively appropriate to limit biographies to those works which present 'an account of a life'.[21] While vague enough to include a range of works on the margins of Christian biography, such a definition would, I think, have to exclude martyr acts.[22] For even when providing an unusually detailed account, martyr acts were concerned with portraying only a tiny proportion of human experience.[23] They offered an account of a death rather than an account of a life.

Thus distinguished on the one hand from the acts of the martyrs, and on the other from its non-Christian counterparts, a case can be made for late-antique Christian biography as a suitable object of study in its own right.[24] It will also be useful to maintain a distinction between 'Christian biography' and the more familiar, but also rather narrower, generic term 'hagiography'. Historically, studies

---

[19] Bowersock 1995: 24. They 'constitute a twin literary offspring of early Christianity'.

[20] Wilson 1988: 109. This is not to say that martyrs lacked importance in the post-Constantinian church, and the various roles they played are ably demonstrated in Tilley 1997 and Grig 2004.

[21] Burridge (1995: 93) notes the view that biography 'is more than just an account of a life', but seems to disagree; Dihle, whom Burridge was citing as a supporter of this maxim, in fact wished merely to make a distinction between 'die spezifisch griechische Kunst der Biographie', exemplified by Plutarch, and a looser conception of biography in general: Dihle 1983: 406, quoted at Burridge 1995: 92. See also Edwards 1997, including criticism of Burridge, and Fox 2000 on the difficulties of definition.

[22] Swain (1997: 22–3) is prepared to label martyr narratives as in some sense 'hagiographical', but this seems to fall short of considering them to be full-blown hagiographies.

[23] Brown 2000: 159. '[M]artyrdom, the impending climax of their lives, had caused their past to pale into insignificance'; see also A. G. Elliott 1987: 11–19 and esp. 45: 'a very different narrative structure'.

[24] A case also made at Stancliffe 1983: 86–102, on the context of the *Life of Martin of Tours*.

of the latter have often focused on formal and generic aspects, and have usually preferred the more obviously fictional or 'artificial' examples; even going so far as to exclude the work of writers from the fourth and fifth centuries AD – 'the last representatives of classical antiquity'.[25] This is to recognise the fact that the first century after Constantine produced many more problematic texts – Delehaye calls them 'shot through with art and life' – which would inevitably complicate such studies.[26] These texts have instead been quarried for the historical facts they may accidentally preserve or, in more sophisticated terms, for the evidence that they can supply concerning social relations in late antiquity.[27] Yet the variety of unusual forms and approaches taken by texts from the fourth and fifth centuries has more recently been understood as recommending them for closer and more detailed literary and historical study in their own right.[28] My intention is to extend this approach to

[25] Delehaye 1998: 49. Here he specifically excludes Sulpicius Severus and Hilary of Arles, preferring to concentrate on 'the artificial productions of later epochs which sometimes affect to be inspired by them'. Similarly, A. G. Elliott wishes to emphasise the 'generative narrative matrix' (1987: 10) underlying hagiography, and so chooses to study only the most obviously fictional examples of the form. Her study connects directly to the fourth century only through her use of Jerome's *Life of Paul the First Hermit*; but her examples, and her broadly Proppian account of the genre's conventions, are confined to a particular variant of hagiographical narrative as exemplified by the *Life of Onophrius*.

[26] Delehaye 1998: 49. Indeed, it is not clear that a formalist approach is even productive with later medieval hagiography: so that Delehaye, having excluded fourth-century texts, must admit that hagiography 'may take any literary form suited to honouring the saints' (1998: 4). A more attractive approach is provided by Heffernan, who emphasises historical contexts rather than formal literary analysis; but his focus is on medieval biographies such as the twelfth-century *Life of Aelred* (1988: 74–87).

[27] The emphasis on facts may be considered the traditional approach of the Bollandists; their work has been fundamental to any consideration of hagiography, but for some of its limitations see the discussion in Menestò and Barcellona (1994). The second model is perhaps most associated with the work of Peter Brown, although it captures only a part of his broad programme; for the potential difficulties of this approach, see Hayward and Howard-Johnston (1999), and especially the discussion at 16–20 (Howard-Johnston) and 32–43 (Av. Cameron). Brown himself has reflected upon the presuppositions of his study of hagiography in a number of places: see especially the third essay in Brown (1995); the debate and discussion in Brown *et al.* (1997); and the retrospective in Brown (1998) with the companion essays of Elm (1998) and Vessey (1998).

[28] Averil Cameron has frequently pointed out the need for such an approach to the biographical texts of the late-antique period, as at Cameron 1991: 2ff.; elsewhere she explicitly demands that biographies be considered not as 'innocent histories', but as 'didactic and apologetic works': Cameron 2000: 83. In recent years, scholars have taken up this challenge, often following on explicitly from the work of both Brown and Cameron, and of others such as Philip Rousseau and Elizabeth Clark. A particular concern with

a broader category of late-antique Christian biography, of which hagiography may be considered a special case, and so to include a number of awkward texts which appear sufficiently complex to resist any simple conception of their literary genre.[29] These works may be thought of as taking part in what may be considered a Christian biographical discourse – a shared network of concerns and approaches, both literary and historical, which binds together a range of late-antique texts.[30]

There are, then, numerous texts in this period which seem to exist on the margins of the more familiar genres of biography and hagiography, or which seem to found (or attempt to found) new genres of their own. Among these are some of the most famous works of the period by some of the most celebrated authors: it will suffice here to mention only the *Life of Constantine* by Eusebius of Caesarea and the *Confessions* of Augustine of Hippo. Precisely because these works so conspicuously fail to conform to received expectations of content and form, they promise to be all the more useful in clarifying the character of Christian biography in the later Roman empire. If they are indeed to be established as contributing to a single, unified discourse, then it will not be through identifying any generic similarity but instead by demonstrating the

hagiography as a literary phenomenon can be recognised in Clark (1986) on Melania the Younger; a comparable approach is also evident in Brock and Ashbrook Harvey (1987) and in Ashbrook Harvey (1990), although in the latter examples there is a continuing focus on the historical figures obscured by the hagiographer's art. By contrast, and in line with the reflections in Brown (1995), the discussion of the *Life of Antony* in Brakke (1995) focuses (as does the rest of the book) on the hagiographer himself. Such an approach to hagiographies as revealing primarily the interests of the author is characteristic of much subsequent engagement with the form. Thus Cooper (1996) offers a reading which seeks to align hagiographies with the ancient novel; the 'fictional' aspects are foregrounded too in Coon (1997), who in addition seeks to demonstrate the theological and cultural revisionism of many of the works; most prominent in this respect among recent works have been Krueger (2004), which is devoted to Christian conceptions of authorship, and Burrus (2003), which focuses on issues of gender and sexuality. It will be noted that much of the work discussed here has taken for its subject the portrayal of holy women in late antiquity; that my own account discusses almost exclusively male authors and subjects should be seen not as a repudiation of this tradition but as a recognition of its great merit.

[29] Hagiography is acknowledged as a special case of biography (both Christian and non-Christian) at Brock and Ashbrook Harvey 1987: 14; but the Christian biographies I shall be discussing here seem resistant to a neat inclusion in either category.

[30] I am here adapting the term 'discours hagiographique' from Van Uytfanghe 1993: 148–9, where he in turn credits it to de Certeau 1975.

existence of a consistent set of assumptions about the writing of a life and its implications. For a biography – at least, a significant biography – can claim to be more than an account of a life. In addition, it can claim to be revealing some truth about the world, about lives and about life in general.[31] Christian biographies in the fourth and fifth centuries AD were set apart by the nature of the truth they revealed, one unavailable to works written in any rival tradition: it was a truth bound up with a Christian interpretation of the world and its history – one expressed above all in the canonical scriptures.

Typology and history

The most significant factor which served to unify late-antique Christian biography was a collective engagement with the biblical tradition. The Old and New Testaments had formed the foundation of an unusually literary religion, and any new writings had first to negotiate a relationship with the authoritative biblical text.[32] The importance of this scriptural tradition marked off Christian biography from its pagan counterpart; it was no mere window dressing, but was crucial to the conception, purpose and function of these Christian lives. Late-antique Christians possessed a canonical account of their own past, and it inevitably affected the way in which they viewed their present. They lived in the shadow of Scripture, in a world in which the most important events had already happened. The development of Christian biography in late antiquity can therefore be seen as a specific, polemical intervention – an attempt to redraw the familiar pattern of life in the later Roman empire. In contrast to secular and pagan approaches to biography and history, a close engagement with the Bible allowed the articulation of a distinctively Christian view of the world.[33]

---

[31] As noted by Goldberg 1981.   [32] As recognised at, for example, Cameron 1991: 5–7.
[33] See, for example, the remarks of Reydellet (1985: 433) on the world-view of Ambrose of Milan: 'L'écriture lui fournit les éléments d'un théorie de pouvoir, elle lui inspire des comparaisons entre des situations contemporaries et des épisodes de l'Histoire sainte, elle lui propose des archétypes qui s'imposent à son imagination.' Cf. also Auerbach 1953: 156 on medieval mystery plays.

Christian biographies from the century after Constantine can thus be understood as efforts 'to continue, develop and adapt' the conventions of the Bible.[34] As with William Bradford in the seventeenth century, this engagement frequently manifested itself in claims regarding the 're-enactment' of Scripture in the contemporary world: claims which are bound up very closely with the concept and practice of 'biblical typology'. These terms, and their assumptions and implications, will be important throughout my discussion of late-antique Christian biography. Nevertheless, it must be noted that there has been frequent disagreement about the right use of the term 'typology', whether referring to a hermeneutical method or to a literary strategy, and some of the difficulties must first be dealt with here.[35]

One major problem in using the term is that, in the various ancient discussions concerning the interpretation of Scripture, a consistent technical distinction seems not to have been made between typology and allegory.[36] This in turn has led to the proposal that modern accounts should conform to the practice of antiquity, so that both typological and allegorical exegesis are subsumed under the blanket term of 'spiritual' or 'figurative' interpretation.[37] Yet although this may allow some insight into the way ancient authors explained their own practice to others, it is relatively simple from a modern vantage point to distinguish at least two different

---

[34] Penco 1968: 2. Hagiography 'ha inteso continuare, sviluppare ed adattare . . . [la] . . . Sacra Scrittura'.

[35] These difficulties are well explained in the introduction to Charity 1966: 1–9. Interested readers are directed to Charity for a more complete account of the value of this understanding of 'typology'. I should here like to acknowledge the contribution made to my thinking on the subject by a number of excellent works, among which the most notable have been Charity (1966), Frye (1982), Fabiny (1992), Barr (1966), Markus (1996), Irvine (1994) and Auerbach (1959). Not all of these writers have agreed with one another, and perhaps none of them would agree with me. I must therefore take full responsibility for the presentation of typology here and throughout this study.

[36] A difficulty pointed out most recently at Clark 1999: 74, citing de Lubac 1947. Much of my discussion below will be framed as a response to the comments of Clark, who has conveniently collected the critical work of many of her predecessors in her discussion at 70–8.

[37] Notably, again, by Clark 1999: 74–8. Such language may well correspond rather better to the ideas of many readers in the ancient world, although perhaps not to all: Augustine, for one, seems to have had strong ideas about the kinds of readings that were and were not permissible, which to a large extent correspond to what are nowadays labelled 'typology' and 'allegory': Markus 1996: 1–11 and *passim*.

modes of interpretation. That such a distinction was not made in antiquity is no reason to refuse to make one now – especially when it is a useful distinction to make.[38] For while a self-conscious choice was rarely made between typology and allegory, and while it would be a misrepresentation to understand them as two mutually exclusive alternatives, these two approaches to the interpretation of Scripture imply radically different assumptions about world and text.[39]

Perhaps the simplest distinction between typology and allegory is one that has been attributed to Jean Daniélou: that 'allegory is concerned with *words*, typology with *events*'.[40] Allegorical exegesis typically provides the words of a text with a non-literal meaning: for example, arguing that when Scripture describes the Garden of Eden, it is in fact referring not to a real garden but to the human soul.[41] This is not necessarily incompatible with the idea that an actual garden is also being referred to, but this literal understanding of the text is not required for the allegory to succeed.[42] In typological interpretation, by contrast, the words of a text can have only a single, literal meaning: the description of the Garden of Eden refers to an actual garden, and to nothing else. Nevertheless, typology does allow for other, hidden meanings, but it is not true that the biblical text refers to two things at once; rather, 'it is what the text is literally referring to that itself has a further meaning'.[43] The thing

---

[38] Thus the modern distinction is maintained at, for example, Dawson 1992: 16, in which typology is considered 'simply as one species of allegory', subject to certain additional constraints.

[39] A point recognised in the very title of Markus (1957), emphasising the 'presuppositions of the typological approach to Scripture'.

[40] Louth 1983: 118, characterising the view of Daniélou; emphasis is in Louth's original. Note that Daniélou in his own studies seems not to have maintained this distinction: Daniélou 1960, although it specifies 'biblical typology' in its subtitle, appears instead to defend 'allegorical procedures under the name of typology': described thus by Dawson 1992: 255 n.53.

[41] This is the reading set out in his *Legum allegoriae* 1.56–9 by the first-century Jewish exegete Philo of Alexandria. See Dawson 1992: 99.

[42] Markus 1996: 11. It is unclear how far Philo himself wished always to maintain the literal sense of Scripture; Hanson (1959: 63) suggests that for him it had 'no profound significance', a view also put forward at Dillon (1983: 79–80). Dawson (1992: 100–2), however, argues that Philo sought to maintain both literal and allegorical meanings simultaneously; yet he too allows (103) that specific literal meanings were dispensed with when they appeared 'quite out of keeping with the facts'.

[43] Markus 1996: 10; see also the explanation (with diagrams) at Irvine 1994: 262–3.

to be explained is not a word but an historical event. And in turn, it signifies other historical events.[44]

Typology may thus be said to concern itself with 'historical recurrence' – with the repetition in history of previous historical events.[45] The aim is to identify 'something real and historical' which corresponds to something else 'real and historical'.[46] Of course, these historical events were mainly to be found in written history: and so typology cultivated a distinctive approach to literary and historical texts.[47] For Jews, these parallels between the various books of the Old Testament confirmed the essential unity of the scriptures, and in particular the active presence of God, who had so disposed events that they referred to one another. Such links between figures and events were common throughout the Old Testament – the golden calves set up by Jeroboam, for example, quite clearly recalled the cult established by Aaron in Exodus, generations before.[48] Indeed, it was rare that any significant event could not be seen as providing an image of a previous one – a distorted or inverted image, perhaps, but an image nonetheless. In the same way, each event provided an image for the next, offering a succession of types in which each event reinstantiates the tradition and simultaneously develops it further.[49] Applied to individual figures, the Old Testament could be interpreted in part as a series of exemplary lives, in which each significant life could be understood to have provided a pattern for the next.

But when Christians added the New Testament to the corpus of the Holy Scriptures, the use of typology took on a new importance. To suggest that events in the Old Testament might correspond to events in the New was to present the Old and New Testaments as

[44] The importance of the historical nature of the 'resultant system' in typology is emphasised at Barr 1966: 108–9; cf. Auerbach (1959: 54), for whom typology depends on 'the historicity of both the sign and the signified'.

[45] The term 'historical recurrence' is taken from Hollander 1977: 6ff.; cf. his examples of 'improper typology' at 10–12.

[46] See Auerbach 1959: 29, where this phrase is used to describe the exegetical practice of Tertullian in the second century AD.

[47] Noted at Barr 1966: 115, and at Louth 1983: 118.   [48] 1 Kings 12.28; cf. Exodus 32:4.

[49] See Frye 1982: 106, where his account of the Bible's phases of revelation can effectively be applied (as here) to smaller events; see also his reference there to Kierkegaard 1983.

part of the same tradition, and therefore to suggest that the same God was responsible for both. The typology practised in the early church accordingly focused on 'the demonstration that certain figures in the two Testaments corresponded to one another'.[50] That this was a central tenet of Christian belief is made clear in what came to be the opening verse of the New Testament, in which the Gospel of Matthew announces itself as 'The book of the genealogy of Jesus Christ, the son of David, the son of Abraham'.[51] There are various historical relationships in play here. The subsequent string of names identifies Jesus as a direct descendant of Abraham and David, and so at a simple level ties together the Old and New Testaments as part of the same ongoing historical narrative. At the same time, this genealogy presents the claim of Jesus to be the Messiah foretold by the prophets: a descendant of David but also his successor, ready to revive the Old Testament tradition and re-enact the achievements of his ancestors. In these first few lines, then, Jesus is established as another significant figure in the development of the biblical story, taking his place in the tradition while simultaneously revising and reinterpreting it.[52] From the beginning, the New Testament asserts itself to be not only a continuation but a fulfilment of the Hebrew scriptures.

Yet this was an idea to which many forcefully objected – not least the Jews, whose sacred texts were co-opted for the new religion, and in such a way as to render their own interpretations generally invalid. Within Christianity, too, there were those (such as the Marcionites) who wished to separate the Old Testament and the New Testament.[53] Such arguments therefore sought to present Christianity as a complete departure from the traditions of Judaism, whether in order to present it as spurious and illegitimate, or else (as Marcion believed) as an entirely new and more valuable set

---

[50] Charity 1966: 88–9.
[51] Matthew 1:1–4 [RSV]; cf. also the remarks of Hopkins 1999: 302.
[52] For this reading of the New Testament's rhetorical purpose and function, see especially Kermode 1968; cf. also Reinhard Lupton 1996: xvii. '[T]ypology describes the exegetical relationship between the Old Testament and the New, in which the prior text forms both the hallowed origin and the superseded beginnings of the latter work'.
[53] For Jewish opposition, see Hopkins 1999: 221–6, 234–44; for Marcion and his supporters, see Knox 1942 and Blackman 1948, esp. 113–24.

of insights. For many others, however, the antiquity of the Christian message mattered: for without its links to the Hebrew scriptures, the new religion did indeed risk seeming rather *arriviste*.[54] Typological interpretation, then, stood opposed to this separatist approach: it was intended to bring the two narratives together. It asserted, against Jews and Marcionites alike, that the New Testament described the works of the same God who had worked in the Old; and it purported to prove this by identifying correspondences between events in the two traditions. The New Testament could therefore be claimed to have a share in both the divine and the cultural authority of the Hebrew scriptures.

The existence and prominence of such debates concerning the relationship between the Old and New Testaments can only have increased the value of typological interpretation. The argument from typology was a genuine argument, conducted in the face of real and open opposition. Moreover, it was an increasingly important one, as the historical continuity which typology implied was rapidly becoming fundamental to Christian orthodoxy.[55] For Christians the most important figure was naturally Christ himself, and Christian typology was devoted above all to identifying events in the Hebrew scriptures which had 'prefigured' events in his life.[56] The life of Christ could thus be fitted into a traditional pattern, and could be seen to be encoded in the whole of biblical history. Indeed, his life could be seen as the single, crucial event of which all the rest had been merely 'sub-fulfilments'. From a Christian perspective, the only true and perfect fulfilment of the pattern of Scripture was to be found in the Incarnation.[57] It was the defining event of Scripture as a whole.

Nevertheless, although Christ was in this way the proper culmination of the Christian tradition, that tradition did not come to end with his death and resurrection. Christian history continued and, for instance, in the Acts of the Apostles the life and martyrdom of

---

[54] On the importance of the Hebrew scriptures as a 'Christian prehistory', see esp. Mortley 1996: 120ff., and Kofsky 2000: 100–14.

[55] Christian orthodoxy might even be defined by a concern with history: Mortley 1996: 131 n. 234.

[56] For a sense of how widespread this practice was in the New Testament, see Charity 1966: 112–29.

[57] Charity 1966: 60.

Stephen can easily be recognised as corresponding to the life of Christ.[58] It is important to note, then, that typological interpretation did not necessarily require any commitment to a chronological progression towards perfection. Stephen was not 'prefigured' by Christ in the sense that the martyr 'fulfilled' or 'perfected' his model: Christ, after all, was perfect already. Once again, and this time within the New Testament itself, the use of typological parallels could be used to express a profound continuity between what might otherwise seem a series of unconnected events. Nor was it the case that Christ had to feature in every typological relationship. Correspondences might be recognised between other, secondary figures, as in the connections made between John the Baptist and Elijah.[59] It is perhaps best, then, to replace such terms as 'fulfilment' or 'prefiguration' – or indeed, 'postfiguration' – with a broader and less technical language dealing with repetition and recapitulation.[60] The significant relationships identified between distinct historical events might thus be characterised in terms of 'correspondences' and 're-enactments'. Stephen's life may be seen as a 're-enactment' of the life of Christ, in the same way as Christ's life re-enacted the life of Moses. Much as with coins, successive lives will turn out to be indifferently superior or inferior; and from time to time, a perfect example might appear.

Thus practised, Christian typological exegesis was a means of establishing the unity of the Bible, by showing that the actions and presence of God might be recognised throughout the canonical scriptures. Yet it took on a whole new importance with the identification of correspondences between the scriptures and historical

---

[58] See Charity 1966: 150–3.
[59] Matthew 17:13; Mark 9:11–9:13; see also Charity 1966: 124–6.
[60] 'Postfiguration' is the term suggested at Fabiny 1992: 112. For similar reasons I am avoiding the term 'antitype', which can suggest a single, unique fulfilment – although see Frye 1982: 8off., where he suggests that a single event may be both antitype (of an earlier event) and type (of a future one). The idea that typology is a 'diachronic' method of interpretation, ordained towards a particular end, is the primary objection to the use of the term put forward by Clark (1999: 74–8), following on from the earlier discussion by de Lubac. Clark prefers instead to focus on the dynamic of circularity or repetition: Clark 1999: 74 n.13. Yet it is possible to argue that these are compatible, and the combination of apparent progression and essential circularity may indeed be said to represent the unique contribution of typology to the understanding of history: for its view of the world may be captured in the image of a wheel rolling along a road, in which the same familiar features recur in constantly new situations.

texts beyond the canon. For Christian history, which did not end with Christ, failed also to end with Acts, or with the sending of the last canonical letter. Christians continued to live on in the ensuing centuries, at an increasing distance from the biblical world; from the world, that is, in which God was an active participant. The gradual closing of the canon effectively limited the scope of God's activity to the biblical past – along with, at least in those versions of the Bible which included the book of Revelation, the hopeful prospect of an equally 'sacred' future.[61] What remained less securely sacred was the present, that awkward time excluded from the Bible's confidence about the 'already' and the 'not yet'.[62] Early Christians living after the time of the New Testament thus found themselves inhabiting a 'narrative gap'. Members of a minority and persecuted church, they might justifiably have felt themselves to have been abandoned by God. The situation was perhaps comparable to that encountered by the Pilgrim Fathers, or by the first Christians in Judaea: and the answer might once again have been to interpret the events and achievements of their own time as partaking of the authoritative tradition set out in the scriptures.

Contents and approach

Thus it is easy to imagine the impact that must have been made by the conversion of the Emperor Constantine to Christianity. This astonishing event coincided with a rapid rise in the popularity of works centred on the lives of individual Christians, and the century after Constantine is characterised in part by the development of Christian biography as a distinctive literary form. This change must owe something to the ending of the great persecutions of the third century and a corresponding decline in martyrdoms and martyr accounts; and yet it is significant that so many late-antique Christian writers should have turned to biography as a form through

---

[61] If indeed it was understood at the time as a prophecy of the Last Judgement. The inclusion of the book of Revelation in the New Testament canon was by no means universal in the early church: see Kyrtatis 1989: 155.

[62] Markus 1990: 87–9.

which their own times might be approached and understood. Christian biography was able to offer a response to their new position in the world, and a recognition of the divine guidance which had presumably brought it about. It was a form in which a contemporary life could be defined in relation to the new Christian empire and to the course of Christian history as a whole. Thus it is hardly surprising that a consistent and unifying theme of late-antique Christian biography was a devotion to the discovery of 'elaborate correspondences' between past and present persons and events – above all, between the contemporary world of the later Roman empire and the divinely authorised world of the scriptures.[63] The effect was to portray modern Christians as living under a new dispensation: like the Plymouth pilgrims, late-antique Christians would emerge as re-enacting the figures and events set forth in the scriptures.

Attention must be paid, then, to those texts which seem to have played an especially prominent role in developing and articulating this understanding of the later Roman empire. My first chapter therefore takes for its subject one of the most significant – and also one of the most problematic – Christian biographies of the period: Eusebius of Caesarea's *Life of Constantine*. Eusebius was the author of perhaps the first example of a genuinely Christian historiography, in his *Ecclesiastical History*; and the so-called 'Life of Origen', which constituted a single chapter of that history, has been suggested as the foundation of late-antique Christian biography.[64] Yet the status of the 'Life of Origen' as part of a larger work makes it difficult to treat as a contribution specifically to the genre of biography; and there are other reasons too for picking out the independent *Life of Constantine* as pioneering a new and distinctive approach. Quite apart from Constantine's obvious prominence as the first Christian Roman emperor, it is significant that here Eusebius has set out – unlike in the 'Life of Origen' – to describe a contemporary, and therefore to render an account of the world in which he and his immediate readers now lived. Most important, therefore, are the terms in which Eusebius chooses to

---

[63] Hollander 1977: 5.
[64] On Eusebius as pioneer, see especially Momigliano 1963: 80–1. On the 'Life of Origen' treated as a biography, see Cox 1983: 69–101.

INTRODUCTION: BIOGRAPHY AND TYPOLOGY

present the emperor, praising him not with reference to his imperial forebears but in terms of the heroes of Scripture, associating him with Moses and even Christ. The traditional history of the Roman empire was elided, indeed largely ignored. Eusebius' Constantine took his place not among the Roman emperors, but among the biblical prophets and patriarchs.

In its independence, its contemporary focus and its consciously Christian concerns, the *Life of Constantine* can be considered the founding work of Christian biography in late antiquity. Its unconventional structure may make it an awkward fit for traditional literary genres; but as 'part panegyric, part biography [and] part moral lesson' it conforms to at least one prominent characterisation of later hagiography, and it has accordingly been identified as offering a 'prototype for a saint's life'.[65] It must be admitted, all the same, that the *Life of Constantine* remains at the margins of what might be described as conventional Christian biography, and it is difficult to demonstrate any direct literary influence on subsequent historical or biographical writing.[66] Yet not every pioneer is imitated in every detail, and the influence of the *Life of Constantine* seems to me more evident in the assumptions it implies about history, and about the relationship between the contemporary world and the Bible. In this sense its themes and concerns were taken up throughout the following century, whether in the popular lives of contemporary holy men and women, or in the more unusual products of the late-antique engagement with biography and its relation to Scripture.

Thus my second chapter seeks to identify and further define this engagement in the works of another eastern bishop and writer, Gregory of Nyssa. That a similar habit of mind may be found in Gregory as in Eusebius should stand in the first place as evidence that a concern with typology and the re-enactment of Scripture was widespread in this period. In addition, however, Gregory of Nyssa can be set apart by his active involvement as an author of

[65] Delehaye 1998: 54; Cameron 1997: 173. For further discussion of the generic status of the text, see Chapter 1, below.
[66] Momigliano 1963: 94; but see also the comments of Cameron 2000: 85 on a possible connection to the *Life of Antony*.

18

Christian biography, most famously in the portrait of his sister as an icon of feminine holiness in his *Life of Macrina*. This biography of his sister certainly reveals some aspects of Gregory's attitude and approach to the wider world, but its contribution may be supplemented by two more awkward biographical works which might be contrasted with it, and coupled with each other: his speech in praise of his late brother Basil, and his exegetical *Life of Moses*.[67] The latter is not a biography of a contemporary, and the former is at least in part a panegyric; and yet they can usefully be considered as important contributions to late-antique biographical discourse preoccupied with problems of biblical precedent and authority. For in conjunction with one another, they provide a neat expression of the late-antique approach to interpreting both Scripture and the contemporary world.

In relating the life of his brother, then, Gregory adopted the example of Moses as a scriptural model – another example of a Christian author presenting his world in terms of the re-enactment of Scripture. Moreover, he took the complementary step of also applying this parallel in his efforts to describe and explain the world of the Bible. Thus his *Life of Moses*, while in many ways an allegorising account, shows the influence of typology in an unexpected way by portraying Moses both as a man and as a Christian leader in terms borrowed from the career of Basil. The scriptures are thereby understood by Gregory to represent a world not only historically continuous with Christian late antiquity but operating, as it were, under the same assumptions. Once again the distinction between the past and the present is elided, with the Bible now available to be interpreted according to the conventions of late-antique piety. The world of late antiquity and the world of the Bible now stood separated by very little of consequence. Just as the composition of the New Testament had forced a reassessment of the Old, so the portrayal of Basil in biblical colours demanded a new understanding of familiar biblical characters and events. Not

---

[67] For a contrast between Gregory's accounts of Macrina and Basil, in terms similar to those employed here, see Momigliano 1985a; the *Life of Macrina* has most recently been discussed in Krueger 2004, and interested readers are directed there for a more detailed account than I shall be able to provide.

only was Basil identified as a re-enactment of Moses, but Moses himself became a kind of proto-Basil.

This alignment of present and past had implications too for authors and readers. If Basil were established as a re-enactment of Moses, it was at least possible for Gregory to begin to think of himself in the guise of Moses' brother Aaron. Similarly, readers now found themselves confronted with a world which contained such modern avatars of biblical heroes, and it must only have been the most unimaginative who failed to reconsider their own place in such a world. The development of these ideas in the course of the rise of late-antique Christian biography, and especially through the lives of the desert saints, is briefly sketched in my third chapter. This part of the study is kept intentionally brief: the lives of the desert saints, like hagiography in general, have been dealt with in depth elsewhere, and the texts are often familiar, and in some cases over-familiar. What may now seem to represent an obvious and indispensable feature of the Christian saint's life – the imitation of Elijah in withdrawing to the desert, or the performance of miracles in imitation of Christ – may perhaps instead be seen as a series of attempts to wrestle with the same concerns of Eusebius and Gregory with regard to the contemporary re-enactment of Scripture. As a result, these lives may come to seem more of a challenge to the conventional understanding of the world and also, in some respects, more influential than is often thought to be the case. Those late-antique saints who struck out for the desert were more than straightforwardly exemplary: their lives might also be recognised as indicative of certain disturbing realities.

The third chapter therefore begins with the *Life of Antony* ascribed to Athanasius of Alexandria, and traces not only the relationship of the figure of Antony to the ascetics and prophets in Scripture, but also to his successors in late-antique Christian biography. Antony enjoyed an extended literary afterlife, brought on for cameo appearances in later biographies by authors who most likely wished to trade on his authority as a genuine and orthodox ascetic hero. At the same time, the presence of Antony in these subsequent texts helped to promote the sense of an ongoing ascetic tradition, so that even when an author such as Jerome sought to correct or enlarge the focus of Antony's asceticism, his own heroes nevertheless took their places in a defined and coherent world. The desert was not just a city: it was a cosmopolis, populated by a consistent cast of characters linked to the Bible, to each other, and – above all – to the familiar world of their readers. Antony's Egypt may have been exotic to the foreign monks who were the intended recipients of Athanasius' biography, but it was firmly a part of their world; and as saints' lives began to situate their heroes in the heartlands of the Roman empire, so the lives of the saints became the lives of one's friends and neighbours. The Bible had been a distant example; so too had the solitary life of the desert. Now, surrounded by a new breed of prophets and apostles, readers in late antiquity might easily come to look on the re-enactment of Scripture as a challenge to be taken up in their own lives.

With this as the centrepiece and the turning point of the study, the fourth and fifth chapters go on to look at the ways in which Augustine of Hippo engaged with this tradition in his life and writings. Augustine is one of the few late-antique figures who can be witnessed reading and reacting to a contemporary Christian biography, and his encounter with the *Life of Antony* plays a defining role in the conversion described in his *Confessions*. My fourth chapter therefore provides a close reading of Augustine's own account of his conversion, paying particular attention to his engagement both with the lives of his contemporaries and the scriptural tradition that seems to have lain behind them. Antony was for Augustine an example of the biblical world brought up to date, and his life therefore presented a more convincing and more accessible demonstration of the possibilities of conversion. It offered both an exemplary way of life and an example of a contemporary response to Scripture; and it allowed Augustine to engage with the Bible as something other than a collection of beliefs and precepts wholly alien to the contemporary Roman world. Augustine would not imitate Antony directly, nor would he be drawn to re-enact any element of Scripture in his own life. Yet the *Life of Antony* provided a prism through which he might view the readings in Matthew and Paul with which he had found himself struggling. In displaying an attitude towards the biblical world which firmly connected that world to the more familiar world of its readers, the *Life of Antony* played a vital role in setting out the terms in which Augustine could define and explain his own conversion to Christianity.

It is equally important, however, to recognise that Augustine's ideas concerning these issues were subject to change over time, and that the Augustine who converted in 386 was not the same man who wrote the *Confessions*, and who revised his views further in his magisterial *City of God*. Even in looking primarily at these two works, the two most familiar monuments in his career, it appears that there was a definite development with regard to the specific question of the relationship of biography and Scripture. Despite his enthusiastic response to the *Life of Antony* at his conversion, as seen in the *Confessions*, Augustine seems later to have developed doubts concerning the implicit assumptions made there and in other late-antique Christian biographies. To present the contemporary world as offering numerous opportunities for the re-enactment of Scripture was to assert a continuity not only in the realm of historical events but also in their interpretation: Christian biography, that is, claimed implicitly to have recognised the presence of God in the world, and to have reliably recorded His actions and interventions. For Augustine, at least by the time of the *City of God*, this was to claim for Christian biography the guaranteed accuracy and the divine authority which by right belonged only to Scripture itself. It was unacceptable for contemporary authors to feel capable of adding to sacred history. The biblical canon was closed; and as Paul had said, man could do nothing more than descry the things of God through a glass, darkly.

Authorised lives

This book therefore aims to provide, at the very least, a coherent account of the context in which this attitude of Augustine's was able to develop. The world presented in Christian biography between Eusebius and Augustine had as much in common with the Bible as with the world of contemporary experience. By combining the two in a single continuous pattern, it allowed its readers to shift between them: to realise that modern heroes could be singled out as participants in an ongoing 'sacred history', and to believe that the same might apply to themselves. In effect, these biographies offered a literary portrayal of the later Roman world which promoted a change in the way their readers understood their own place in that world. It may be understood then, how a text such as the *Life of Antony* could play so important a role in the conversion of Augustine when his philosophical speculations and the guidance of the Milanese clergy, and even the reading of Scripture itself, had not succeeded in forcing the change. Christian biography in the later Roman world showed its readers a vision of modern life governed by the conventions of the Bible, and overseen by the continued presence of the Christian God. In the process, it encouraged them to adapt their own lives to it.

An account of the 'biblicising' approach typical of late-antique Christian biography can therefore help to reveal the attitude of Christians in the later Roman empire to the present and the past. Like all historical writing, these biographies expressed a philosophy of history – which for Christians especially, amounted to nothing less than a philosophy of life.[68] They represent not only a chronological progression between the times of Eusebius and Augustine, but also a point of genuine divergence between their respective understandings of history and Scripture: an understanding of Christian biography in this period, therefore, can shed light on the assumptions of some of the most important writers and thinkers in early Christianity. In addition, however, these Christian lives were important as a means by which contemporary Christians could write, read and think about themselves. As 'singular or striking lives' which were nevertheless established as part of their own community, they serve 'to disclose and perhaps to correct or enlarge the community's moral vision'.[69] Thus Christian biography may help to reveal a typically late-antique habit of mind, as a constituent element in what might be called the late-antique 'representation of reality'.[70]

At stake, then, were issues of narrative and history, belief and interpretation, and authorship and authority. Christian authors

[68] Momigliano 1963: 832–5.   [69] McClendon 1990: 22.
[70] The latter was the project famously undertaken in Auerbach 1953; the idea of a society's exhibiting idiosyncratic 'habits of thought' is owed in my case to the example of Shuger 1990.

naturally looked to the Bible for inspiration, but it remained open to dispute exactly how far their own writings could be considered inspired. It is perhaps true that 'the unity of the biblical plot' is a product of this period of intense controversy; if so, it is arguable that it was owed largely to Augustine's intransigence in denying the 'imperial theology' of Eusebius (and its claim be able to interpret the 'pattern, progress and meaning' of contemporary history) in favour of 'the unfathomable workings of divine providence and grace'.[71] Between these extremes, and these two ancient authorities, there was space to create, assay and dispute interpretations of the present and the past; and for authors and readers alike to recognise 'a broad range of connections between the texts they read and the lives they led'.[72] But above all, these discussions were grounded in history: in individual contemporary lives, whether authored or authorised by God or by man. Lives of emperors, saints and selves were written down so as to fit into a conception of the world at large; and readers were challenged to live up to the world they implied.

[71] Vessey and Pollmann 1999: 7; Harrison 2000: 205. For a preliminary consideration of the shift in attitudes to the Roman empire between Eusebius and Augustine, see Markus 1963, of which a number of themes are expanded in Markus 1988 and Markus 1990. My debt to Markus, as well as our differences, should become obvious throughout the following chapters.

[72] Stock 2001: 18.

CONSTANTINE: THE AUTHORISED LIFE

Never, perhaps, were coincidences in character and fortune, between any two illustrious men who have lived, so numerous and striking as between MOSES AND WASHINGTON.

(Jedidiah Morse, *A Prayer and a Sermon on the Death of George Washington*. London, 1800: 28)

Eusebius of Caesarea has long been considered the founder of 'a new kind of history', a form characterised 'by the importance attributed to the more remote past, by the central position of doctrinal controversies and by the lavish use of documents'.[1] His *Ecclesiastical History* thus rejected the narrow focus and the invented speeches of the existing secular tradition in favour of a universal history of Christian salvation – but which nevertheless allotted to the Roman empire 'a clear and necessary place in the story of man's redemption'.[2] In supplementing his *Ecclesiastical History* with a *Life of Constantine*, Eusebius continued to pursue this approach, both in his historiographical style – so that he continued to incorporate original documents, for example – and in his concern for the unfolding of God's providential plan in the history and politics of the Roman empire. Inevitably, however, the shift in his focus from a universal history of the Christian church to the life and achievements of a single contemporary figure, and a Roman emperor at that, required Eusebius to present these matters from a very different perspective. The *Life of Constantine*, even when it borrows or adapts remarks and vignettes from the earlier work, must therefore be seen as rather more than merely an updating of the *Ecclesiastical History*: it was a reconsideration of the nature of Christian

[1] Momigliano 1963: 90, 91.
[2] Markus 1963: 343. Precedents for a universal history are proposed in Mortley 1990 and expanded in Mortley 1996, although this should not be taken to detract significantly from the originality of Eusebius' historiography in general.

25

history as it found expression in the life and achievements of the first Christian emperor.

The *Life of Constantine*, in focusing on a single protagonist, could thus hardly avoid making him into a hero. Merely as the object of a biography, Constantine's life was evidently to be understood as in some sense exemplary; but in addition, by what has been called 'the royal metaphor', it was possible to see the emperor as summing up the whole of his society.[3] For Eusebius, Constantine represented 'the culmination of all God's purposes' in establishing and perpetuating the Roman empire, and with his conversion and his subsequent success the emperor proved himself a sign and an example of 'God's direct intervention in history'.[4] This interpretation of the emperor's role can be recognised throughout the *Life of Constantine*. In its presentation of the first Christian emperor, however, it allowed him to represent not only the history of the Roman empire as a whole, but also to stand for the new Christian world in which he governed. The *Life of Constantine* is therefore a work which engages deeply with questions of authority and authorisation: the authority which the Christian God could grant; the authority which Constantine as emperor could exercise; and the possible authority which might underpin the lives of more ordinary Christians.

It is important to note, however, that the *Life of Constantine* must be understood as primarily representing a Eusebian view of the emperor. It was a partisan and polemical work, and in developing parallels with biblical figures such as Moses and Christ, it anticipates an audience which would recognise and appreciate the rhetorical and literary strategies of the Christian scriptures. This, then, is the context in which Eusebius chose to set the emperor: not as the latest in a long line of imperial predecessors, but as a revival of heroes from the Old and New Testaments. That may not have been a manner in which Constantine would often have chosen to present himself to his subjects, even to those of them that were Christian; and it is to be noted that the *Life of Constantine* was finished only after the emperor's death. And yet Eusebius perhaps sought to address this concern in deciding upon the final form in

[3] Frye 1982: 87.　　[4] Markus 1963: 343.

26

which his work was to be offered to the public. For he appended to his *Life of Constantine* a speech or two on a similar theme that he had given in the presence of the emperor – and which might therefore imply imperial approval for the interpretation he proposed in the *Life* – and, more impressive still, a further speech delivered by Constantine himself.[5] Eusebius was no doubt showing off his access to imperial documents and his closeness to the emperor – but at the same time, he was seeking to prove the truth of his interpretation of the emperor's role. Whether or not Constantine would in fact have adopted this mode of presentation, Eusebius at least sought to suggest that his *Life of Constantine* was in this sense too an authorised life.

The emperor speaks

It is reasonable to begin, then, by reading these works in conjunction with one another, and by examining the way in which the emperor's speech draws attention to some of the central themes of the *Life of Constantine*. Ostensibly the occasion for including this speech was Eusebius' passing comment that the emperor would often choose to occupy himself in addressing ecclesiastical and lay audiences on matters of religion.[6] In order to support this claim, and to demonstrate the emperor's rhetorical skill, Eusebius thus appended to the *Life of Constantine* a sample of Constantine's preaching in the form of a speech he refers to as 'About the Assembly of the Saints'.[7] In this speech, presented in some manuscripts as

5 For Eusebius' own speeches, and their relationship to the material appended to existing manuscripts of the *Life of Constantine*, the most complete account is Drake 1975; an alternative approach is taken in Barnes 1977, and later contributions may be found at Drake 1988: 22–5, Barnes 1989: 101, and Cameron and Hall 1999: 331. The authenticity of the speech attributed to Constantine was long in doubt, although for my purposes here it only matters that Eusebius should have presented it as genuine; in any case, it is now generally accepted to be genuine, and the most comprehensive account, including the relevant bibliography, is given in Edwards 2003. The date is still in question: Edwards 2003 prefers an earlier date than Bleckmann 1997, who is followed in most details by Barnes 2001.
6 *VC* 1.44.1.
7 *VC* 4.32: τῷ τῶν ἁγίων συλλόγῳ. In Latin the work is often known as the *Oratio ad sanctos*, and in English as the *Oration to the Assembly of the Saints*; however, in Edwards 2003, followed here, the text is labelled the *Oratio Constantini* [*OC*] and translated as the *Oration to the Saints*.

'the fifth book' of Eusebius' biography, Constantine can be found to indulge in a certain amount of doctrinal speculation, which for some modern readers has raised the suggestion that either Eusebius or the emperor himself took a position suspiciously close to Arianism.[8] The main emphasis of the speech, however, was not on the details of doctrine but on a 'more conventional' defence of Christianity and an attack on the fallen ideologies of its enemies.[9] Thus:

Memphis and Babylon have received the fruit that was proper to such worship [i.e. of idols], having been laid waste and left uninhabited along with their ancestral gods. And this I say not from report, but I myself have been present to behold it, and have been an eye-witness of the miserable fortune of the cities. Memphis is waste, where Moses in accordance with the decree of God shattered the arrogance of Pharaoh, the greatest potentate of the time, and destroyed his army.[10]

Thus after speaking in theological and philosophical terms about the Father and the Son, here Constantine offers himself as a witness to the modern fulfilment of the biblical prophecies.[11] Yet the appearance of Moses in this passage seems unwarranted: the destruction of Memphis had indeed been prophesied in the scriptures, but by Jeremiah and Ezekiel.[12] No doubt the story of the Jewish exodus will have come naturally to mind given the theme of the destruction of Egypt; but at the same time it allows the emperor to associate himself with Moses, united by their association with Memphis and their victories over an established pagan order.[13] Constantine, moreover, goes on to devote more time to a

---

[8] For the manuscripts, see Edwards 2003: xvii; for Arianism, see Barnes 1981: 271, followed by Lane Fox 1986: 644. Such hints (here and elsewhere in Eusebius) form the basis for the extreme position put forward in Kee 1982, which attributes a far more radical theological position to Eusebius and to the emperor than is required by my argument here.

[9] Lane Fox 1986: 644; a full introduction to the speech is given in Edwards 2003; Drake (2006: 126–9) sees the speech as above all a statement of Constantine's sincere commitment to the Christian faith.

[10] *OC* 16: translations of this text are taken from Edwards 2003.

[11] Drake (2006: 127) sees the oration divided into three parts along these lines.

[12] Jeremiah 46:14–19; Ezekiel 30:13.

[13] There is no other evidence that Constantine ever in fact visited Memphis, but it is certainly possible that he had accompanied the Emperor Diocletian to Egypt in 301/2: Lenski 2006b: 60, and for a fuller reconstruction of Diocletian's movements see Barnes 1982: 49–56.

panegyric of his illustrious predecessor, who is described in revealingly practical terms:

> What could one say about Moses to match his worth? Leading a disorderly people into good order, having set their souls in order by persuasion and awe, he procured freedom for them in place of captivity, and he made their faces bright instead of blear.[14]

This Moses is not the visionary shepherd but the military and political leader, who has freed his people from a pagan tyranny and restored them to their true exalted position. He appears not only as an ethical and religious exemplar but also as a political and secular one.[15] It is difficult to read this as anything other than a kind of idealised portrait of the first Christian emperor – that is, as a portrait of Constantine himself. At the very least, his audience were being invited to make such a connection.

Yet Constantine's evocation of the biblical past in his *Oration to the Assembly of the Saints* does not stop with the figure of Moses. He immediately goes on to discuss two further items which proved the triumph of Christianity over paganism: the famous Christian acrostic, attributed to the Erythraean Sybil, foretelling the birth of Christ and the death of the pagan oracles; and Virgil's 'messianic' *Eclogue*.[16] These texts gathered together a valuable set of themes for Constantine, both in terms of his immediate agenda in his oration and also in terms of his broader ideological self-presentation. In particular, a complex web of connections lay behind his use of the passage from Virgil: written, as it is now supposed, as a mythicised account of the birth of an anticipated child of Antony and Octavia in the first century BC, the poem's prophetic manner led it to be continually re-evaluated as circumstances changed.[17] By the fourth century, a tradition had developed connecting Virgil's fabulous child with the Emperor Augustus.[18] In an earlier oration given in the presence of Constantine, the poem had been

---

[14] *OC* 17.

[15] For the value of Moses as model in secular terms – as 'a legislator, a philosopher, an inventor, and a general' – see Hollerich 1989: 84.

[16] Virgil, *Eclogues* 4: the most complete account of the poem is Van Sickle 1992, but cf. also the contributions of DuQuesnay 1976 and Clausen 1994.

[17] Clausen 1994: 121–2.

[18] MacCormack 1998: 23, citing Servius, *In Vergilii Bucolica* IV.1, 11, 13; see also Carcopino 1930: 195–201.

used as a device to link the emperor to the long-awaited child, here apparently identified as Apollo; and a similar conceit was later revived in 324 in a poem by the exiled Porfyrius.[19] Thus when the emperor, in his own *Oration*, refashioned Virgil's poem so that it referred to the birth of Christ, he was implicitly inviting an association of Christ with Augustus, Apollo and himself. This is not to say that the identification was uncertain: the Greek translation which Constantine quotes made the Christian meaning plain, and the emperor indeed denied that Virgil could have been speaking of any mortal.[20] Nevertheless, the evident ambiguity of the poem was only emphasised by this further reinterpretation, and the familiar historical and divine associations of the central figure will have benefited the emperor. Christ, as the Sybil made clear, had taken over the functions of Apollo; and what Apollo had formerly been for Augustus and even for Constantine himself, Christ might now be for Constantine under the new regime. This divine child was both a historical ancestor and a divine patron, and perhaps at the same time an alter ego.

Thus Constantine's oration was in some ways as vague and inoffensive as might be expected from a relatively new Christian on such a public occasion, but it also reveals a clear fondness for biblical and prophetic allusion and association. The speech presents Constantine as looking to the Bible for parallels and precedents for his own career, and it demonstrates his success in finding them. It is possible to argue that these are the aspects which led Eusebius to choose this particular speech as his example of the emperor's rhetoric, and to append it to his *Life of Constantine* – for Constantine's oration sketches out an approach to scripture and history more fully developed by Eusebius in the *Life*. In that work he set out to provide 'a philosophical, historical and apologetic exposition of Constantine's special position in God's plan', which at a basic level was achieved through the insistent use of parallels between the emperor and his alleged scriptural predecessors – most obviously Moses, but also Christ.[21] Indeed, the *Life of Constantine*

---

[19] *Pan. lat.* VII.21.5; Porfyrius, *Carmina* 14.3ff., cited in Lane Fox 1986: 661. For Porfyrius, see Barnes 1975. Barnes (1981: 36) also suggests that the presence of Apollo might again have recalled Augustus, whose patron the god had been.

[20] Lane Fox 1986: 649–53; *OC* 21. [21] Cameron 1997: 166; cf. Barnes 1989: 95.

can be shown to have been structured around the emperor's recapitulation of these two lives, successive centrepieces of the Christian tradition. Constantine's allusions to Moses and Christ in his oration thus fitted in well with Eusebius' portrayal of a ongoing Christian narrative in which the familiar fourth-century world could be transformed into a new biblical era, a world illuminated and structured by the conventions of Scripture. Eusebius appropriated both the emperor's authority and the authority of Scripture for his own historiographical purpose: to reveal the continued fulfilment of God's plan in the life and works of the Emperor Constantine.

Reconstructing a life

Eusebius therefore sought to establish himself in the *Life of Constantine* as 'the authoritative interpreter of the Constantinian empire'.[22] Yet despite his eagerness to provide his credentials – or perhaps because of it – the reliability of the *Life* has remained a matter of controversy.[23] There is now little doubt about the authenticity of the documents that Eusebius quotes; but there are certainly still questions to be raised about his level of access to information and documents other than those presented in the *Life*. Moreover, even if his information could be shown to have been accurate and complete, it would be possible to remain suspicious about his posture as a privileged insider. At one extreme, therefore, it is possible to caricature the Bishop of Caesarea as an upstart easterner whose access to the emperor was occasional and brief – and the *Life* as an attempt to hijack Constantine's fame for his own agenda. At the other, he might be represented instead as an imperial lapdog, a conduit for the emperor's propaganda. The result in each case would be to cast doubt on the value of the information contained in the *Life of Constantine*, by portraying Eusebius as either an ill-informed outsider or else, as Burckhardt notoriously dismissed him, 'the

---

[22] Barnes 1981: 271.
[23] I am accepting Eusebius as the author of most – if not necessarily all – of the *VC*. For details and arguments, see Cameron and Hall 1999: 4–6 and works referred to there, especially Tartaglia 1984: 13–14 and Winkelmann 1975: lvii–lxiv; and cf. especially Barnes 1981 and 1989.

most objectionable of all eulogists, who has utterly falsified his [subject's] likeness'.[24]

Although these two extremes appear equally unsustainable, it is unnecessary to deny that Eusebius' portrayal of Constantine was influenced by the bishop's own positions, interests and aspirations, and by the circumstances in which (and *for* which) the work was written. It makes sense, therefore, to establish what can be known or guessed about Eusebius' procedure and about the context of the *Life of Constantine*.[25] Thus it can plausibly be argued that the *Life*, or what would turn into the *Life*, was begun as early as 325, quite conceivably as a sequel to Eusebius' own *Ecclesiastical History*.[26] It must nevertheless have reached its final form between 337 and 339, during the uncertain years following Constantine's death and the bloody succession of his three remaining sons.[27] In the work as it survives, reference is made to this situation, and the *Life* is offered to the sons of Constantine as a means by which to understand and perpetuate the success of their father.[28] Of course, this allowed Eusebius not only to recommend to the new regime continuity with Constantine's policies; but with Constantine dead, he was also in a position to define what those policies were.[29] Whatever else the *Life* may have been, then, it was certainly an opportunity to influence the new regime and to present a distinctively Eusebian view of the recent past.

If his presentation of Constantine's policies were to seem reliable, therefore, it was important for Eusebius to advertise his close association with the emperor, and in the *Life* he accordingly included several references to occasions on which the two of

[24] Burckhardt 1949: 260. The perils of such positions are effectively laid out in Cameron 1983.

[25] Much of what follows draws in particular on the work of Averil Cameron, T. D. Barnes, and H. A. Drake; most of the arguments and opinions involved can be found expressed in more detail in their cited works. Their most recent and comprehensive treatments of this specific issue are Barnes 1989, Cameron 1997 and Drake 2000: 355–92 more recent accounts of Constantine in general may be seen in Cameron 2005, Lenski 2006a and Hartley 2006.

[26] Barnes 1989: 114. Yet despite Barnes (1981: 265), it is possible to imagine such a sequel taking a form distinct from that of the earlier work. See also Drake 1988: 31, on the *VC* as the culmination of 'an idea Eusebius had carried around in his head for several years'.

[27] Cameron and Hall 1999: 10; Tartaglia 1984: 15.

[28] See *VC* 1.1.3, 4.69.2. The *VC* contains no references to Constantine's eldest son, Crispus, who had been executed long before 337: Barnes 1981: 270.

[29] Cameron and Hall 1999: 12.

them had met and conversed. In this way he could claim to have been a close confidant of the emperor, his information acquired either as an eye-witness or, if at second hand, direct from Constantine himself.[30] Nor, indeed, would such a claim have been entirely implausible: Eusebius had certainly delivered speeches in Constantine's presence, and at such times had perhaps had the opportunity to see and speak further with the emperor.[31] These occasions, however, seem to have been rare. Eusebius was hardly a particular favourite of Constantine, who had refused to transfer him to the more prominent see of Antioch when that became vacant, and who even appears to have sought to dissuade him from visiting the imperial capital too frequently.[32] Perhaps the bishop's orthodoxy remained suspect – for Eusebius had been regarded as an Arian sympathiser until he finally subscribed to the doctrinal formula proposed (under Constantine's guidance) at the Council of Nicaea.[33]

Whatever the cause, it seems unlikely that Eusebius enjoyed much intimacy with the emperor. The information he evidently gathered at court, along with the stuff of his anecdotes and reminiscences, need suggest at most only four or five visits there – and those mostly on episcopal business at various councils.[34] The letters from the emperor from which the bishop so often quoted would likewise generally have reached him in his official capacity.[35] Eusebius, it can be agreed, 'was never close to Constantine: he was a provincial bishop who saw and admired from afar'.[36] This distance from imperial affairs suggests that the view of Eusebius as a court propagandist is unlikely, if not unsustainable.[37] He was

[30] For a clear example, see VC 1.28–31.
[31] As argued in Drake 1988: esp. 23–31, and reiterated at Drake 2000: 368–77.
[32] VC 3.60.3; 61.1; 62.1; with Barnes 1981: 228 and Drake 1988: 34.
[33] Cameron and Hall 1999: 3; Barnes 1981: 266. Eusebius never subscribed wholeheartedly to the Nicene creed, and he seems to have retained markedly Arian views until his death: Barnes 1981: 277.
[34] Four listed by Barnes 1981: 266, another suggested by Drake 1988: 25–7, 29.
[35] Barnes 1981: 267; Cameron and Hall 1999: 16–17.
[36] Barnes 1992: 637. This need not rule out the possibility, of course, that Eusebius was able to acquire accurate information courtesy of contacts in the imperial administration: Warmington 1986: 93–8 and Barnes 1989: 113. Yet this seems to apply only in the case of the document quoted at VC 4.9–13 – none of the other documents quoted in the work require such an explanation.
[37] Barnes (1989: 114) ascribes this view to, among others, Peter Brown and Arnaldo Momigliano, who may both be seen (at times) to have presented Eusebius as a 'shrewd

certainly an effective rhetorician and apologist, as his occasional invitations to speak at court might suggest, but there is little sign that he followed anything that might be called a 'Constantinian agenda'. The Bishop of Caesarea was simply too far removed from the imperial throne: a scholar known to Constantine and doubtless well regarded, but by no means solely a vehicle for his master's voice.[38] The *Life of Constantine* was no official imperial (auto-) biography, but rather an unofficial Eusebian work.

Nevertheless, this distance from the emperor and from imperial affairs is no proof of objectivity on the part of Eusebius, and if he was not a propagandist we need not therefore conclude that he was conscientious and reliable.[39] The sources he cites seem to have been authentic, but it is impossible to speak for his interpretations and conclusions; and at best, as in the generous assessment of Franchi de' Cavalieri, the *Life of Constantine* emerges as 'tendentious, passionate, partial, deliberately lacunose, [albeit] not knowingly mendacious'.[40] Thus although the *Life of Constantine* is not to be dismissed as an imperially sponsored falsification of history, its interpretations and conclusions remain those of Eusebius himself.[41] The bishop may have been independent of the court, but he retained a mind of his own. His distance should not be mistaken for disinterest.[42]

Doubts have been raised too over whether the *Life of Constantine* was ever presented in the form Eusebius intended. There is certainly some evidence that the work remained incomplete at the time of the author's death: chapter headings and addenda appear to have been supplied (sometimes incompetently) by a later editor, and there are occasional doublets and infelicities to be found in the text.[43] In addition, that Eusebius was apparently collecting

and worldly adviser' (Momigliano 1963: 85), who 'placed his pen at the emperor's disposal' (Brown 1971: 86).

[38] Barnes 1981: 267; cf. Drake 1988: 37.

[39] That this distance from the imperial court makes Eusebius 'reliable' seems to be implied at Barnes 1989: 114 and at Barnes 1992: 637.

[40] As quoted with apparent approval at Barnes 1994: 11.

[41] For a general defence of this approach, see Cameron 1989: 1–13; for Eusebius in particular, see also Drake 2000: 368–71.

[42] Drake 1988: 21; see also Drake 2000: 371.

[43] Barnes 1989: 98–102, following Pasquali 1910, and summarised at Barnes 1994: 1; the work's unfinished state is accepted (with some reservations) by Cameron and Hall 1999: 6, 10, but see also Cameron 1997: 146 and her n. 5.

material for the work as early as 325 might also suggest that he engaged in a certain amount of rewriting, whether on two separate occasions (adding new material to an already extant work) or as part of a longer process involving more numerous successive drafts.[44] On this basis, it has been argued that the *Life* represents a conflation of a 'historical' work and a 'panegyrical' work, and that Eusebius never intended it to be published in its present 'transitional' state.[45] The 'problematical' structure and genre of the *Life* can then be explained by the death of the author in the middle of the process of moving from one defined genre to another – so that what remains is essentially a panegyric which contains interpolated passages of history, or else is essentially a history preserving some remnants of an 'abandoned panegyric'.[46] Consequently, it is argued, the *Life of Constantine* cannot and should not be read as a coherent whole; and the implicit suggestion is that any tendentiousness in the work can be limited only to those passages which may be assigned on some basis to this putative panegyric, leaving the more 'historical' aspects as a source of reliable evidence.[47]

This explanation, however, is unconvincing. The argument that the structure of the *Life of Constantine* demonstrates that it was left unfinished at Eusebius' death can rest only on 'subjective judgements' as to what Eusebius intended.[48] There is nothing to suggest that Eusebius planned to make substantial changes to the text which survives, and little evidence that later editorial intervention extended beyond the addition of chapter headings and addenda.[49] Indeed, the evidence is stronger that the work was close to complete by the time of the author's death, since it was supplied by Eusebius with a preface and a conclusion, each relating to the work as a whole.[50] The infelicities and doublets that remained can quite plausibly be explained as the result of authorial inattention.[51] And although the very presence of such errors might

---

[44] Barnes 1989: 97 (and *passim*); compare Cameron 1997: 145–6, and Cameron and Hall 1999: 29.
[45] Barnes 1981: 265; 1989: 102–10; 1994. Barnes' argument is again adapted from Pasquali 1910, differing mainly on the supposed order of composition.
[46] Barnes 1989: 95; the alternatives are the respective versions of Pasquali and Barnes.
[47] Thus Barnes 1989: 97.   [48] Cameron 1997: 150.
[49] Barnes 1994: 1, with Cameron and Hall 1999: 8–9.   [50] Cameron and Hall 1999: 30.
[51] Authorial inattention is suggested both by Barnes 1989: 99, and by Cameron 1997: 146 n. 5.

perhaps imply a process of multiple drafts, these may just as easily be explained as representing successive drafts of a single, unitary work.[52] The structure and genre of this work would, admittedly, have been unusual; but there is nothing to prevent us from believing that this was deliberate.[53] Eusebius, as the *Ecclesiastical History* proves, was certainly capable of historiographical innovation.

The *Life of Constantine*, as it survives, can therefore plausibly be regarded as the product of repeated redrafts of an unusual and innovative work. There is little reason to regard it as anything other than tendentious, flattering, unbalanced and misleading, as much as any other historical or biographical work; but there also seems little reason to deny it the virtue of consistency, if only insofar as it was all of these things in equal measure throughout. Above all, there is little reason to suspect that it misrepresents the intentions of its author. In his *Life of Constantine*, Eusebius presented a clear and coherent image of the emperor. The work he produced was perhaps not polished to perfection; but it is unnecessary to assume that it was therefore incompetent or incomplete.

Constantine as Moses

The image of Constantine that Eusebius put forward in his *Life* showed the extent to which the author was 'immersed in the Bible and in biblical ways of historical and quasi-historical thinking'.[54] Constantine was to be understood in terms borrowed from biblical and Christian history, and this was made most evident by the persistent and explicit parallel drawn in the *Life of Constantine* between the emperor and Moses.[55] The choice of Moses was no doubt in part a pragmatic one, since of all Old Testament figures he was especially appropriate as a model for those 'who are not only distinguished by their exemplary lives of piety, but who also occupy

[52] Cameron 1997: 145–6; Cameron and Hall 1999: 29–30.
[53] Cameron and Hall 1999: 27–34. In fact, the *VC* is perhaps not as unusual as it might seem. It shares many features with hagiography, and if the *VC* requires to be assigned to a particular category, then it might best be considered part of that genre – see also Barnes 1989: 110, Cameron 1997: 150, Cameron and Hall 1999: 30–1.
[54] Barnes 1981: 97.
[55] On the presence of the Old Testament in general and on Moses in particular, see especially Cameron and Hall 1999: 20–2, 35–9; Mortley 1996: ch. 5; and Hollerich 1989.

positions of responsibility'.[56] Thus the same features which had made Moses an attractive forebear for Constantine himself in the *Oration to the Assembly of the Saints* now recommended him to Eusebius – and the shared appeal to Moses suggests that it was no idle or incidental comparison. Indeed, it has been argued that the parallel is 'fundamental to the organisation' of the *Life of Constantine*, and that for Eusebius 'the whole of Constantine's life . . . is now to be read in terms of the figure of Moses'.[57]

The example of Moses was particularly suited to the young Constantine's spectacular and warlike early career.[58] The patriarch's life was traditionally constructed on the basis of three distinct and consecutive roles: as an innocent child amongst tyrants; as the subsequent avenger of his ancestral faith; and as a lawgiver on behalf of God.[59] This same outline can be seen to have been reapplied by Eusebius to Constantine; and the running parallel with Moses begins where the narrative itself begins. Before he starts on Constantine's story, Eusebius refers his readers to the Old Testament:

An ancient report relates that terrible generations of tyrants once oppressed the Hebrew people, and that God, disclosing Himself as gracious to the oppressed, provided for Moses, a prophet still in his infancy, to be reared in the heart of the palace and family circle of the tyrants . . . When the passage of time summoned him to manhood . . . it was time for the Prophet of God to leave that home of the tyrants and . . . [to acknowledge] as his own those who were his true kith and kin. God then raised him up as a leader of the whole nation, and he liberated the Hebrews from bondage to their enemies, while through him He pressed the tyrannical race with the torments of divine pursuit.[60]

This brief summary of the life of Moses offers all the essential elements with which Eusebius will seek to structure the remainder of his account of the emperor. The shortage of specific historical details – the naming of Moses and the Hebrews aside – only

---

[56] Rapp 1998: 290 – reiterated in Rapp 2005: 125–31. The same point about the value of Moses as a paradigm for Christian leaders is made at Hollerich 1989: 81.

[57] Wilson 1988: 116; Cameron and Hall 1999: 35–6; the Moses comparison in the *VC* is also pointed out in Hollerich 1989 and at Rapp 2005: 130.

[58] Hollerich 1989: 82; see also Drake 2000: 376, arguing that the early career of Christ or Paul would have offered too 'passive' an example.

[59] Cameron and Hall 1999: 36; see also Harl 1967: 407–12. Note that, along with the Bible, Eusebius' sources almost certainly included Philo's *Life of Moses*: Cameron and Hall 1999: 193. Indeed, Philo's *Life* has been tentatively suggested as a possible model for the *VC* as a whole: see Tartaglia 1984: 10 and Drake 2000: 376.

[60] *VC* 1.12.1.

helps to prepare the way: it becomes a universal story of freedom from oppression which readers can more easily apply to their own times. Tyrants and leaders were already familiar in the world of late antiquity; God and his prophets would, in Eusebius' work, soon take their place alongside them.

For Constantine too had spent his youth under the care of his enemies – in this case his father's colleagues in the imperial tetrarchy, whom Eusebius names tyrants for their persecution of Christianity.

Tyrants who in our time set out to make war on the God over all oppressed His Church, while in their midst Constantine, soon to be the tyrant-slayer, still a tender young boy and blooming with the down of youth, like that very servant of God, sat at the tyrants' hearth.[61]

The link with Moses is thus explicitly made, and is reiterated throughout the account of the emperor's early youth: so that Constantine continued to conduct himself 'in the same way as that ancient prophet of God', until at last he recognised that his apparent protectors were in fact plotting against him, and took flight – 'in this also', as Eusebius did not neglect to point out, 'preserving his likeness to the great Prophet Moses'.[62] This initial, childhood phase ended as Constantine chose to ally himself with the religion of his ancestors, represented by his father Constantius I, whom Eusebius had previously sought to establish as a devout monotheist and effectively a Christian.[63]

In due course, Constantine succeeded his father to become a leader in his own right; and, in the process, he adopted his father's faith and subsequently had its true nature revealed to him.[64] Having rediscovered his religious identity, then, the stage was set for Constantine to turn liberator. The persecuting tetrarchs of his youth were now mostly retired or dead, but their pagan heirs could still be portrayed as tyrants from whose oppression Constantine could seek to free his new co-religionists. What might have appeared nothing more than civil war was established as a battle of gods, with Constantine overcoming terrible odds against an enemy whose

---

[61] VC I.12.2.   [62] VC I.19.1; I.20.2.

[63] VC I.21; I.27. For the most recent comments on the religion of Constantius I – which largely leave the matter open – see Cameron 2005: 91 and Lenski 2006b: 68.

[64] VC I.27–32. For further allusions to Moses in this section, see also Cameron and Hall 1999: 205.

offences were not limited to paganism but included adultery, murder and even witchcraft.[65] Yet Constantine, like Moses, could count on divine aid:

> Maxentius put his confidence more in the devices of sorcery than in the loyalty of his subjects, but fortified every place and territory and city which was under his dominion with an immense number of soldiers and countless military units. But the emperor who relied upon the support of God attacked the first, second, and third formations of the tyrant, overcame them all quite easily at the very first onslaught, and advanced to occupy most of the land of Italy.[66]

Thus Maxentius, the tyrant, played Pharaoh's part; and Constantine's victories were to be compared to the victories of Moses in leading the exodus from Egypt.

Conveniently for this presentation of events, Maxentius' final defeat was to come in 312 at the battle of the Milvian Bridge. The possibility of connecting this watery defeat with the defeat of Pharaoh's forces at the Red Sea had previously been recognised and exploited by Eusebius in the account in his *Ecclesiastical History*.[67] This parallel he duly reappropriated for the *Life of Constantine*, no longer as an isolated allusion but instead as a crucial episode in a prominent and carefully developed thematic structure. Thus the parallel was reworked and slightly expanded. Maxentius was again compared to Pharaoh, his followers to Pharaoh's army:

> Accordingly, just as once in the time of Moses and the devout Hebrew tribe 'Pharaoh's chariots and his force he cast into the sea, and picked rider-captains he overwhelmed in the Red Sea', in the very same way Maxentius and the armed men with him 'sank to the bottom like a stone', when, fleeing before the force which came from God with Constantine, he went to cross the river lying in his path.[68]

Constantine's followers, similarly, were described as recalling 'those who accompanied the great Servant Moses'.[69] Eusebius went further than in his original account, however, in reaffirming the direct relationship between Moses and Constantine, making clear that in this action as in others the emperor had been acting 'in the same way as the great Servant'.[70] It was therefore especially

---

[65] *VC* 1.33–6.   [66] *VC* 1.37.2.   [67] Eusebius, *HE* 9.9.
[68] *VC* 1.38.2; the quotations are from Exodus 15:4 and 15:5.   [69] *VC* 1.38.5.
[70] *VC* 1.39.1; see also Cameron and Hall 1999: 36.

convenient that Constantine, too, in his official propaganda, was eager to present his victory over Maxentius as the final liberation of the oppressed 'from the tyrant's yoke'.[71] Such a portrayal of one's enemies had a history stretching at least as far back as the *Res Gestae* of the Emperor Augustus; but Eusebius here could exploit it to fit in with the language of his retelling of the story of Moses.[72]

Thus although too much of Constantine's story remained for the parallel with Moses to be maintained in such detail, Eusebius' initial summary of the Old Testament story allowed his readers to interpret the emperor's actions as consistent with the apparent biblical model. Certainly Eusebius draws no further explicit comparisons in the remainder of the *Life*, but it is perfectly possible to identify subtle and scattered hints as to the similarity of Constantine and Moses. In the account of Eusebius, then, once Moses was established as 'leader of the whole nation' and had 'liberated the Hebrews from bondage to their enemies', then through him God had 'pressed the tyrannical race with the torments of divine pursuit'.[73] This vague reference is primarily no doubt to the plagues inflicted on Egypt, but it can describe too the emperor's pursuit of his imperial rivals, and even the suggestion of divine vengeance in their deaths.[74] It might also be taken to refer to the measures taken by Constantine to stamp out certain pagan practices: Eusebius, for example, quotes a decree of the emperor outlawing the worship of idols in Egypt and other regions, and it is perhaps not unreasonable to see in this a revival of Moses' fear that the Israelites would relapse into idol worship.[75] The point might even be pressed to include the familiar idea of Moses as the paradigmatic lawgiver; and for Eusebius, Constantine too was notable for his interventions in legal and religious affairs, and he takes the trouble to quote in the *Life* examples of his hortatory letters and 'countless decrees'.[76]

[71] *VC* 1.40.2, quoting from the inscription on the Arch of Constantine.

[72] For the connection with the Augustan programme in general, see Elsner 2000a: 177–8. For the *Res gestae* itself, see Brunt and Moore 1970, with the retranslation and discussion in Eck 2003.

[73] *VC* 1.12.1.

[74] Thus the death of Maximin Daia, who had supported Maxentius, is described as divine judgement in Lactantius, *De mortibus persecutorum* 49.

[75] *VC* 4.25, 26–7: cf. Tartaglia 1984: 10 on a possible parallel here with Philo's *Life of Moses*.

[76] *VC* 4.27.3; and see, for example, the documents quoted at *VC* 1.44–5, 2.24–42 and 2.45.1.

In any case, the sheer insistence on the parallel with Moses at the start of the work must have encouraged the drawing of such general connections.

Thus the explicit comparisons in the early narrative gave way to, and were reinforced by, a more shadowy long-term presence: a consistent range of acts and imagery which could not help but bring Moses to mind.[77] As examples, Averil Cameron has proposed 'the account of Licinius as idolator [2.5] and of Constantine's campaign against him', noting 'the detail of the latter's prayer-tent on the field [2.12–14], which explicitly recalls the actions of Moses in Exodus 33'.[78] Similar allusions can be detected in Eusebius' presentation of the *labarum* – the 'cross-shaped trophy' shown by God to Constantine, and which the emperor later adopted as his standard.[79] Eusebius' description of the object's manufacture – and, in particular, the very instruction to Constantine to produce a replica of the object revealed in his vision – might easily allow it to be compared to the Ark of the Covenant; at the same time, the *labarum*'s miraculous powers might suggest an alternative or additional parallel in Moses' rod or staff.[80] If any of these parallels were indeed recognised, then the prominence of the standard in Constantine's career and in his later imperial imagery offered an opportunity for Eusebius to maintain an association between the emperor and Moses even in the absence of explicit comparisons.

This connection between Constantine and Moses might therefore be seen to emerge as the work's 'leitmotif'.[81] It seems clear that, as a worldly leader and a spiritual benefactor, the Old Testament patriarch provided Eusebius with a valuable precedent for the novel experience of life under a Christian emperor. Yet there is perhaps more at stake than just the exploitation by Eusebius of a model and a story familiar to him and to his Christian readers. Constantine does not only adopt the outward appearance of his Old Testament predecessor, nor does he merely recapitulate his role as a leading man in the community of the faithful: as Constantine's own oration seems to suggest, he also took over something of the patriarch's providential role in Christian history. Whether or not

---

[77] Wilson 1988: 117–20.   [78] Cameron 1997: 158.   [79] *VC* 1.29–31.
[80] Cameron and Hall 1999: 209; cf. Exodus 25:9; Wilson 1988: 116.
[81] Rapp 2005: 130.

this was in fact Constantine's own understanding of his reign – and Eusebius will of course have taken great care in choosing appropriate documents to include and to quote from in his *Life* – it seems to be that put forward by his biographer. Constantine was worth writing about at all because he was not just another Christian leader: he was one who had overcome the old order and led his people into a world they seemed set to dominate. He had done for the Christians of late antiquity what Moses had done for the Jews: his actions were to be seen as equally significant for the development of history – and sacred history at that. It should be no surprise, then, to find that Moses was not the only biblical figure with whom Eusebius chose to associate Constantine. His life, in re-enacting the Old Testament, also went some way towards re-enacting the New.

Constantine as Christ

Alongside the explicit comparison of Moses and Constantine, then, and very often closely bound up with it, much of the *Life of Constantine* also evokes an implicit, but no less insistent, association between Constantine and Christ. There was of course an inevitable overlap between roles that Moses and Christ might be taken to personify, so that for example Constantine could combine the roles of lawgiver and evangelist: as when in instructing the churches of their legal responsibilities, he also 'urged them to conduct all their business for the honour of the divine Word'.[82] Whether in these instances Constantine was imitating any particular figure is difficult to confirm; and whether on such occasions he is considered to have been acting as a bishop or as an apostle, as an Old Testament patriarch or as a messianic preacher, is to some extent a matter of personal preference. Yet a genuine ambiguity is surely to be recognised in the emphasis on the emperor's *labarum* or standard: a 'cross/sign/trophy' which recalls not only Moses but more directly the crucifix.[83] That allusions to Moses and Christ might overlap in this way is only to be expected from the well-established association of Moses and Christ as parallel figures in conventional typological interpretation. This was a link of which

[82] *VC* 3.63.1.   [83] Cameron and Hall 1999: 39.

Eusebius was well aware, having expounded upon it in his earlier *Proof of the Gospels*, while in the process identifying as many as sixteen distinct parallels between the two figures.[84]

Just as in the comparison with Moses, then, the language in which Constantine is described in the *Life* also consistently recalls the presentation of Christ in the gospels; and taken together with Eusebius' exposition of the emperor's historical and cosmological role, these persistent allusions seem to add up to a portrait of Constantine in the guise of Christ. This is not to say, however, that Constantine was to replace Christ in his own or in Eusebius' theological understanding.[85] This Eusebius seems explicitly to deny, reporting that even in the face of pagan opposition the emperor 'continually announced the Christ of God with complete openness to all, in no way concealing the Saviour's title, but rather taking pride in the practice'.[86] But this teaching in itself might only seem to connect Constantine with Christ's own ministry – a link visible also in his status as an apparent amateur among professionals, recalling the young Jesus disputing in the temple, and in his willingness to extend the boundaries of conventional religion to appeal to a wider audience: for just as Christ took his message to the people, so too did Constantine in his stated eagerness to act as a bishop to those outside the church.[87] The emperor was thereby established as a preacher pushing Christianity forward through sheer charismatic authority, a man whose 'marvellous' virtue alone appeared sufficient 'to counter the hordes of the godless'.[88] Constantine was not only proclaiming the name of Christ, but was in some ways reprising his role.

The defining episode in the life of Christ was of course his death and resurrection, and the parallels between Constantine and Christ become most evident as the *Life* begins to focus on similar themes. As the death of the emperor came nearer, Eusebius established him to have been in excellent health, 'sound and unimpaired, free from any defect and [his body] more youthful than any young man's'.[89]

---

[84] Eusebius, *Demonstratio Euangelica* 3.2.6; Hollerich 1990: 318–22; on the association in general, see Cameron and Hall 1999: 37; Wilson 1988: 109.

[85] That Constantine in effect superseded Christ in the emperor's own theology is argued in Kee 1982; it is not my intention to make the same claim here.

[86] *VC* 3.2.2; and more generally, 3.1–3. [87] *VC* 1.44.1; 4.24. [88] *VC* 3.2.2; 3.1.8.

[89] *VC* 4.53.

His death was not a matter of human infirmity, nor did his body suffer any indignity; it seems that God had simply chosen an appropriate time to 'translate him to higher things'.[90] Constantine even voiced the regret that he could not further imitate Christ before his death by being baptised in the River Jordan.[91] No doubt Eusebius was constrained by his audience's knowledge of the timing of the emperor's death, but his account is still remarkably suggestive: for Constantine's final illness fell in the midst of the Easter celebrations – not on Good Friday, but on the Day of Salvation itself.[92] From that point on, at least until Pentecost, the emperor gave up the purple and wore only white clothes 'which shone like light' – as was traditional for the newly baptised, but which might also recall the grave clothes of the risen Christ; and again like the resurrected Christ, Constantine departed the world on Ascension Day.[93] Even the emperor's mausoleum in Constantinople fitted into the general pattern, for it followed on from and mimicked Constantine's design for the Church of the Holy Sepulchre in Jerusalem: in Eusebius' description, the emperor's tomb lay surrounded by representations of the twelve apostles.[94] If Constantine and Christ were not therefore 'interchangeable magnitudes', it seems evident enough that they were presented as 'parallel figures'.[95]

The death of Constantine is a scene which exemplifies Eusebius' approach in the *Life*, for it brings together not only the more straightforward instances in which Constantine could be seen to have imitated Christ – in his (thwarted) desire to be baptised in the Jordan, or in the layout of his mausoleum – but also the more subtle suggestions of a link made through the use of biblical language. Both techniques had been used too in the comparison of Moses and Constantine, although in that case Eusebius was prepared to

---

[90] *VC* 4.60.5; cf. John 19:36 (with Psalms 34.20) – 'not a bone of his body shall be broken' – and note also the miraculous preservation of Moses in old age in Deuteronomy 34:7 [LXX].

[91] *VC* 4.58–60; 4.62.2; and see Cameron and Hall 1999: 342.

[92] *VC* 4.60.5; and see Cameron and Hall 1999: 339–40.

[93] *VC* 4.64; Cameron and Hall 1999: 343.

[94] *VC* 4.60–3; for arguments over the layout and meaning of the tomb, see especially Mango 1990, Krautheimer 1983: 59–66 and Leeb 1992; additional commentary may be found at Elsner 1998: 164, Rebenich 2000c, Dagron 2003: 138–41 and Johnson 2006: 294.

[95] Krautheimer 1983: 66.

make explicit statements.[96] The parallel with Christ was more tentative, perhaps, but is easily seen for example in the reaction of Constantine's friends and companions to his death:

> Immediately the praetorians and the whole company of personal guards tore their clothes, threw themselves on the ground, and started beating their heads, uttering wails of lamentation with groans and cries, calling him Master, Lord and King, not so much Master as Father, just as if they were trueborn children. Tribunes and centurions wept aloud for their Saviour, Protector and Benefactor, and the rest of the troops suitably attired mourned like flocks for their Good Shepherd.[97]

The association of Constantine with Christ in this passage is so strong as to be unmistakable; and Eusebius could hardly have been unaware of it, for as Christian bishop and scholar he would have been steeped in the language of the Bible. The epithets given here to Constantine are all familiar from biblical descriptions of Christ: Lord (κύριος); Master (δεσπότης); Saviour (σωτήρ); Shepherd (ποιμήν).[98] Elsewhere, he is called 'Blessed One' (μακάριος), another of Christ's familiar titles.[99] Thus Eusebius chose to draw upon conventional biblical imagery of Christ in his account of the death of Constantine. There need not have been any doubt that Eusebius was writing primarily about the emperor; but the language he used still spoke recognisably of Christ.

Nor did Constantine's story end with his death. Eusebius concluded the death-scene with a description of a coin struck to mark the occasion.[100] The coin portrayed Constantine rising in a chariot, and being reached for by a hand from heaven: a not uncommon image of imperial apotheosis, but one that also carried relevant Christian connotations.[101] Alongside those resolutely pagan figures, such as Hercules, who had traditionally ascended to the gods, the image of the ascending chariot inevitably recalls the bodily ascent to heaven of the prophet Elijah, conventionally

---

[96] Thus compare the explicit statements of the connection with, for example, *VC* 1.38.2, where the parallel is implicitly made by reapplying direct quotations from Scripture.
[97] *VC* 4.65.1–2.
[98] These epithets can be found referring to Christ at, for example, Ephesians 6:9 (κύριος); 2 Peter 2:1 (δεσπότης); Luke 2:11 (σωτέρ); John 10:14 (ποιμήν).
[99] On the significance of this epithet, see Tartaglia 1984: 10.
[100] *VC* 4.73.
[101] See Cameron and Hall 1999: 348–9 and references there, esp. MacCormack 1981: 119–20 on the ceremony surrounding the death and funeral of Constantine.

associated with the apotheosis of Christ.[102] In Constantine's case there was no bodily ascent into heaven, as Eusebius was prepared to make clear.[103] Yet the emperor had been reborn in a specifically Christian – indeed, specifically Christ-like – sense: he was not like the phoenix, which defeats death but only 'turns into what it was before'.[104] Rather, Constantine 'is more like his Saviour'.[105] His soul had ascended into heaven. Thus Eusebius sums up the emperor's career in the light of his afterlife:

> Alone among Emperors and unlike any other he had honoured by acts of every kind the all-sovereign God and his Christ, and it is right that he alone enjoyed these things, as the God over all allowed his mortal part to reign among mankind, thus demonstrating the ageless and deathless reign of his soul.[106]

Constantine had enjoyed divine favour in his lifetime, and he enjoyed it too in death. He did not have to wait for the resurrection of the dead: he was immortal in heaven already.[107]

This image of Constantine in heaven might seem at first to be serving merely an obvious apologetic purpose: as an upfront demonstration of the benefits to be gained from pursuing a pious Christian life.[108] Constantine's spectacular successes on earth could be seen to have been all of a piece with his reward in heaven: here, then, were the fruits of piety; here was proof of God's existence, and of the truths of the Christian faith. Yet the message is surely more complicated: not every Christian could hope to become emperor, nor indeed be expected to reach heaven before Judgement Day.[109] But the extent to which Constantine was a special case goes deeper than his status as emperor or as an especially favoured worshipper. Eusebius' account of the emperor's eternal and immortal reign in heaven seems to imply that a more ambitious claim is being made. Constantine's soul now reigned in heaven alongside the Father and the Son: he seems to be no mere favoured courtier to the heavenly throne, but a full participant in the administration of divine power.

---

[102] 2 Kings 2; MacCormack 1981: 122–4.
[103] *VC* 4.64.2: 'he bequeathed to mortals what was akin to them'.
[104] *VC* 4.72.   [105] *VC* 4.72.   [106] *VC* 4.67.3.
[107] Some of these points are also made in Rebenich 2000c, where Constantine's death and resurrection is defined not as an ἀνάστασις but as an ἀναβίωσις, but is considered no less significant for that.
[108] Heim 1992: 90–1.   [109] See MacCormack 1981: 120.

In fact, here at the end of the *Life of Constantine* we are returned to its beginning. There too Eusebius had presented an image of this 'great Emperor' who was 'recently visible in a mortal body', now residing in heaven 'in the very presence of God, stripped of all mortal and earthly attire, and brilliant in a flashing robe of light'.[110] The emperor's soul, he made clear, was 'no longer confined in mortal occupations for long periods of time, but honoured with the ever-blooming garland of endless life and the immortality of a blessed eternity'.[111] And although Constantine had departed the world, he was nevertheless still present and still somehow able to intervene:

[For] today our thought stands helpless . . . Wherever it casts its gaze, whether east or west, whether all over the earth or up to heaven itself, every way and everywhere it observes the Blessed One present with the Empire itself. On earth it perceives his own sons like new lamps filling the whole with his radiance, and himself powerfully alive and directing the whole government of affairs more firmly than before, as he is multiplied in the succession of his sons.[112]

In one sense, perhaps, this is a particularly flowery way of asserting the persistence of the emperor's memory and the continuation of his imperial legacy. And yet it literally presents Constantine as presiding over the empire, authoritative and omnipresent, his soul translated into heaven where he rules more powerfully than he did in his time on earth. He has become, it seems, more significant than ever, and at last is in his rightful place. His new status, in other words, seems remarkably reminiscent of that of the risen Christ.

By beginning with this description of the state of the empire soon after the death of Constantine, and by combining it with this vision of the emperor in heaven, Eusebius is able to establish from the start an eschatological focus to his *Life of Constantine*. His subject is not merely a Christian emperor, but an emperor whom he portrays as representing God's own example to humanity. Indeed, the central figure is not so much Constantine as God – or, at least, what has been aptly characterised as 'God's achievement in Constantine'.[113] It was God, according to Eusebius, who provided in Constantine 'a foretaste of His rewards, somehow guaranteeing immortal hopes to

---

[110] *VC* I.1.1; I.2.1; I.2.2. [111] *VC* I.2.3. [112] *VC* I.1.2–3.
[113] Cameron and Hall 1999: 69, referring to *VC* I.4–6.

mortal eyes'.[114] This divine intervention he continually reaffirmed: Constantine was 'set up' by God, 'established' by Him as a beacon to mankind.[115] God it was who had made Constantine a monarch on his own model, and who had 'appointed him victor over the whole race of tyrants'; and it was he who supplied Constantine (and therefore mankind) with 'convincing proofs' of the Christian religion that he practised.[116]

Moreover, it was through Constantine's life and death that God had 'now proved the promises of His own words to be unfailing'.[117] The emperor was a special case, perhaps, in the same way that Christ had been; Constantine, it appears, was a new guarantor of God's covenant with his people. After all, 'God's achievement in Constantine' is a barely disguised recapitulation of his achievement in Christ:

By him He cleansed humanity of the godless multitude, and set him up as a teacher of true devotion to Himself for all nations, testifying with a loud voice for all to hear, that they should know the God who is, and turn from the error of those who do not exist at all.[118]

Constantine here is a prophet and teacher, but also an effective agent of change: through him God had converted the world to His worship. This does not make Constantine a replacement for Christ, nor indeed even a direct equivalent, but it certainly gives the emperor a significant place in the interpretation of Christian history.[119] Constantine, at the very least, is placed in the tradition of Moses and Christ as a historical figure through whom the Christian God can be shown to have intervened in the world, with the three of them thus 'linking the biblical past to contemporary history'.[120] The *Life of Constantine* therefore offers an image of the emperor as a quasi-biblical figure transplanted to the modern age. Moreover, it implies that it was not only Constantine's story which began and ended with God: for Eusebius, the history of his own times could best be understood within the overall context of Scripture.

---

[114] *VC* 1.3.3. [115] *VC* 1.4.1; 1.3.4. [116] *VC* 1.5.1; 1.4.1.
[117] *VC* 1.3.1. [118] *VC* 1.5.2.
[119] Hollerich (1990: 310) notes the presentation of the emperor in biblical terms, but discounts the idea that Constantine's position was such as to 'rival' or 'supplant' the Incarnation or Parousia.
[120] Hollerich 1990: 323–4.

Converting the world

The final paragraph of the *Life of Constantine* is dedicated to showing, in the words of the chapter heading assigned by the fourth-century editor of Eusebius' text, 'that Constantine was more pious than the Roman emperors before him'.[121] This of course was only a matter of reminding his readers what they will already have known: that Constantine was 'the unique emperor' insofar as he was 'the only one of the widely renowned emperors' to have adopted the Christian religion.[122] This, for Eusebius, was his defining feature:

He alone of all the Roman emperors has honoured God the All-sovereign with exceeding godly piety; he alone has publicly proclaimed to all the word of Christ; he alone has honoured his Church as no other since time began; he alone has destroyed all polytheistic error, and exposed every kind of idolatry; and surely he alone has deserved in life itself and after death such things as none could say has ever been achieved among either Greeks or barbarians, or even among the ancient Romans, for his like has never been recorded from the beginning of time until our day.[123]

Yet this brief contrast with his imperial predecessors falls far short of the kind of extended comparison recommended in the rhetorical handbooks, and so characteristic of (for instance) the *Parallel Lives* written by Plutarch in the early second century AD.[124] Certainly, aside from these few brief mentions, Eusebius seems to have been notably uninterested in comparing Constantine to Roman emperors before him. Thus in this life of a later Roman emperor, the Roman imperial past is conspicuous by its absence.

The omission comes to seem all the more pointed as it becomes clear that Eusebius did indeed include at least one passage of conventional rhetorical comparison. Instead of a previous Roman emperor, however, the chosen figures were Cyrus, the king of

---

[121] Cameron and Hall 1999: 52, 66.
[122] Cameron and Hall 1999: 182; *VC* 1.4.1; *VC* 4.67.3.　　[123] *VC* 4.75.
[124] Such comparison –σύγκρισις – can be recognised as a prominent feature of the classical panegyric (or βασιλικὸς λόγος), at least as laid down in the handbook of *Menander Rhetor* 2.376.31–377.9; see also Cameron and Hall 1999: 31–2, and bibliography there. Plutarch's biographies were not only structured as a series of parallel lives, but often also featured some form of σύγκρισις within an individual *Life* – as, for example, in the *Life of Caesar*, where an explicit comparison with 'numerous past and contemporary Roman generals' is included alongside the more formal parallel with the *Life of Alexander*: see esp. Duff 1999: 249–52.

Persia, and Alexander the Great. The comparison with Cyrus was cursory, with the king's 'shameful' death confirming him as Constantine's inferior.[125] Alexander, too, was criticised for his early death, and indeed for its manner – the Macedonian having apparently been 'carried off by revelry and drunken orgies'.[126] The recklessness and haste of this 'man like a thunderbolt' were also condemned by Eusebius; and, at rather greater length, were contrasted with Constantine's popularity, and his 'mild and sober injunctions' to his men.[127] All of this, of course, was designed to bring Constantine credit: for Cyrus and Alexander were traditional model rulers. Alexander, in fact, as Eusebius noted, for his dubious deeds and achievements 'is hymned in choruses'; yet Constantine 'began where the Macedonian ended, and doubled in time the length of his life, and trebled the size of the Empire he acquired'.[128]

In its approach, this passage conformed entirely to conventional practice. The choice of Alexander and Cyrus as exemplars could hardly be called eccentric, and it was only to be expected that this modern hero should be seen to have surpassed them. Nevertheless, both of these figures represent non-Roman societies pre-dating the days of the empire. They not only fail to relate directly to the history of imperial Rome, but might seem to have been selected specifically to exclude it. Thus in the closing paragraph of the work, Eusebius makes the grandiose claim that nothing to match Constantine's achievement has been recorded 'from the beginning of time until our day', naming (in addition to Cyrus the Persian and Alexander the Macedonian) the 'Greeks', 'barbarians' and 'ancient Romans' – from a fourth-century perspective, presumably intending only those of the Republic.[129] These he surpassed in virtue; with other Roman emperors he did not even compete. The result is that Constantine is divorced almost entirely from the society which seemed to have produced him. None of these examples did anything to place Constantine in the Roman imperial tradition.

There are exceptions: this reluctance applied only to the few positive examples which the empire might have furnished. The tetrarchs appeared, who as contemporaries and rivals of Constantine could hardly have been ignored. Yet their role in the *Life* was

[125] *VC* 1.7.1.   [126] *VC* 1.7.1.   [127] *VC* 1.7.2–1.9.1.
[128] *VC* 1.7.2; 1.8.1.   [129] *VC* 4.75.

as adversaries showing up Constantine in stark relief: they were not to be considered in terms of their virtues but overcome on the battlefield for their vices. Indeed, the tetrarchs were so thoroughly condemned in the *Life* as such contemptible tyrants that formal comparison was entirely unnecessary.[130] A similar case might be made for dismissing (for present purposes) a paragraph towards the beginning of the *Life*, in which Eusebius contrasted his own project with the numerous accounts of 'vicious and godless tyrants' such as the Emperor Nero.[131] No doubt the virtues of Constantine were implicitly to be contrasted with Nero's tyranny; but there is no comparison between Eusebius' hero and such a proverbial villain. The presence of Nero and the tetrarchs is thus far less remarkable than the absence of others: the traditional model emperors of the principate, Trajan, Hadrian, Marcus Aurelius – all of whom routinely featured in late-antique panegyric, even to Christian emperors – never appear.[132]

This silence regarding the history of the Roman empire seems to have been a choice made by Eusebius himself. It is certainly not representative of Constantine's own practice. For one thing, the emperor's victory at the Milvian Bridge had been commemorated by the erection of the Arch of Constantine, a new monument ostentatiously designed to locate the new emperor as an heir to those same exemplary predecessors. Whether this was a decision of Constantine or of the Senate, it seems unlikely to have misrepresented Constantine's own preferred public image.[133] Similarly, Constantine at other times encouraged the suggestion that he was descended from the rather obscure, but generally reputable, third-century emperor Claudius Gothicus.[134] All of these claims made by the emperor himself served a traditional purpose of imperial propaganda, tying Constantine firmly into the institutional history of the Roman empire. They helped to bolster his authority,

---

[130] *VC* 1.12.2; 1.26; 1.33–6; 1.37.2, etc. [131] *VC* 1.10.2.

[132] Compare, for example, the 389 panegyric of Pacatus to Theodosius I, which provides a substantial roll-call of worthy imperial models: *Pan. lat.* 2.11.6.

[133] On the design and meanings of the Arch of Constantine, see especially Peirce 1989 and Elsner 2000a, with more recent comments in Elsner 2006 and Johnson 2006.

[134] *Pan. lat.* 7.2.2; cf. Syme 1974. Again, although this link may have been an orator's invention, it seems unlikely that it would have survived any displeasure on Constantine's part.

allowing him to be presented both as a traditional 'good' emperor in the mould of a Trajan or a Hadrian and as the latest scion of a worthy and legitimate imperial dynasty. Constantine based his position not exclusively on his outstanding virtue, important though that was, but also on some versions of the hereditary principle. He seems to have recognised no contradiction between his allegiance to the Roman past and his personal stance on matters such as the promotion of Christianity.

Nor could Eusebius entirely omit Constantine's imperial ancestry – not only because it was valuable to show that Constantine had become emperor in legitimate fashion, but also because the emperor's sons, the addressees of the work, relied significantly on their hereditary claim to power. It is in this light that Eusebius' portrayal of Constantine's father, Constantius I, should be understood. Constantius receives more attention than any other Roman emperor, and yet he does not function as an exemplar of virtue to be surpassed, as would (for example) Trajan or Hadrian. He was far from being a conventional rhetorical model: indeed he was so obscure that by the time he came to write the *Life of Constantine* Eusebius found it necessary to revive his memory: although significantly, he chooses to give 'a brief account' of Constantius' life and character only 'where it touches upon the merit of his son'.[135] An emperor who could count among his forebears Trajan or Hadrian, or even Claudius Gothicus, was claiming a place in a long and familiar roll-call of imperial honour. Constantius I mattered only as Constantine's father.

Thus the presence of Constantius was intended above all to show that Constantine was a legitimate ruler: that 'the throne of Empire [had descended] from his father to him'.[136] Even this, however, might seem to link the first Christian emperor too closely to the pagan empire before him. As a result, the one aspect of Constantius' character that Eusebius chose to stress was his distance from the tetrarchs among whom he served: and in particular, his refusal to conform to their religious programme. Constantius was said to have taken no part in the persecutions organised by the other tetrarchs, although of course he could do little to prevent them.[137]

---

[135] *VC* 1.12.3. [136] *VC* 1.9.2; cf. 1.21.2. [137] *VC* 1.13.2.

52

He pursued 'an independent policy' on the question of religion: a generous one too, prizing loyalty to any faith above the tenets of any one in particular.[138] It was vital, of course, that Constantine should not be linked to the Christian persecutions, but Eusebius seems tempted at times to go further. Constantius, he claims, was a devotee of 'the one God of the Universe' – which he apparently considered a form of pagan monotheism, although his God was later discovered by Constantine to be the God of the Christians.[139] It is clear that Constantine's father was himself no ordinary Roman emperor, but Eusebius stops short of allowing him to have been a Christian emperor in his own right. Leaving his true allegiance aside, Constantius could not be allowed to usurp Constantine's status in this matter. The father of the first Christian emperor may have been 'on friendly terms with the God over all', but he was no match for the talent and originality of his son.[140]

In this way Eusebius balanced the competing demands of heredity and Christianity: the need to prove Constantine the rightful heir to the empire, and the need to prove that his ascent showed the miraculous power of the Christian faith. Moreover, he managed to limit Constantine's imperial ancestry to a single figure, who was himself barely implicated in the un-Christian attitudes of the Roman past. Constantius was a pious but ineffectual emperor; but the rest of the tetrarchs could be dismissed as nothing more than 'godless'.[141] Eusebius seems only to engage with the history of the Roman empire in order to paint it as the opposite of his prime concern: it seems he wishes to rule it out entirely, as it simply does not figure in Christian time. His approach in the *Life of Constantine* is therefore more radical than the one he took in his earlier *Ecclesiastical History*: the latter work featured the pre-Constantinian empire, if only as a vague, pagan backdrop from which Christianity could emerge in triumph; in the *Life of Constantine*, the empire was not granted any relevance whatsoever.[142]

Indeed, for Eusebius, Constantine's conversion had effectively converted the world. In the *Life*, he sought to redescribe the fourth century as a comprehensively biblical time: most clearly in providing it with a past no longer Roman-imperial but Judaeo-Christian.

[138] *VC* 1.13–16.   [139] *VC* 1.17; cf. 1.27–32.   [140] *VC* 1.13.1.   [141] *VC* 1.10.2, 1.12.2.
[142] For Eusebius' approach in the *HE*, see Drake 2000: 360.

This attempt at a kind of literary Christianisation can even be detected in Eusebius' initial statement of intent, as he sought to distinguish his *Life* from conventional Roman panegyric:

The greatest, the imperial parts of the history of the Thriceblessed, his encounters and battles in war, his valiant deeds and victories and routing of enemies, and how many triumphs he won, his peacetime decrees for the welfare of the state and the benefit of the individual, and the legal enactments which he imposed for the improvement of the life of his subjects, and most of his other acts as Emperor, and those which everybody remembers, I intend to omit. My purpose in this present work is to put into words and write down what relates to the life which is dear to God.[143]

Eusebius did not in fact avoid these themes entirely: his *Life of Constantine* was hardly lacking in battles or legal enactments. Yet, on closer inspection, his meaning becomes clear. Few of the incidents he narrated were to be understood as purely secular in their meanings. Whether they established him as a favourite of God, or as a figure for Moses or Christ, Eusebius tended to bring out the Christian significance in the most mundane of events.[144] At first glance his world may have resembled the later Roman empire, just as the *Life* itself may initially resemble a traditional panegyric: but Eusebius was writing in a biblical tradition, and his world was the world of the Bible.

The obtrusive presence of Moses and Christ, and the absence of imperial exempla, therefore point towards the same interpretation. Eusebius' portrayal of Constantine took the emperor out of a conventional Roman imperial context and reinserted him in an exclusively Christian tradition. In this polemical rereading of the past and the present, Roman imperial history was wholly effaced. Constantine's reign followed on instead directly from the days of the Old and the New Testament. In this light it should therefore come as no surprise that the speech of Constantine 'to the assembly of the saints' should have envisioned Constantine and Moses united by their presence in Memphis, and should have presented the emperor as an eye-witness of the desolation of Egypt at the hands of the Israelites.[145] What was ancient history even in late antiquity, and a matter of marginal interest at best for those Romans more

---

[143] *VC* I.II.I.   [144] Cameron and Hall 1999: 191.   [145] *OC* 16.

familiar with the classical tradition, was suddenly revealed as a matter of immediate importance to the empire, and to the emperor himself. Whatever audience the emperor had in mind when he made the original speech, it was now available to anyone who read the *Life of Constantine*; and in adding it to his biography, Eusebius had created an entirely new context for the speech. This was no longer an emperor reminiscing, or showing off his mastery of the appropriate rhetoric for a Christian audience. As an addendum to Eusebius, it was proof that the emperor was perfectly at home in a new biblical world.

Writing typology

Making Constantine the heir of Moses and Christ thus put forward Constantine's reign as further proof of the intervention of God in the world. As the similarities between the lives of the three figures demonstrated, the emperor betokened a new biblical age. Constantine was shown to have re-enacted in his own time the accomplishments of his predecessors in Scripture; and Eusebius managed and constructed his *Life of Constantine* in order to emphasise this. The intention was not to detract in any way from the importance or the uniqueness of Christ, but to present Constantine as the latest guarantor of God's covenant with mankind:

This is what ancient oracles of prophets, transmitted in Scripture, predict; this is what lives of Godbeloved men in ancient times illustrious with every kind of virtue attest when they are recounted to the new generation; this is what our own age also has proved to be true, when Constantine . . . became a friend of the all-sovereign God.[146]

Sacred history had not ended with the end of the biblical era: God's plan continued to unfold. And it did so through the agency of Constantine. His rule, as narrated by Eusebius, would reveal the detailed alignment of contemporary history with world set out in Scripture.

Thus Constantine's exploits were intended not only to be reminiscent of the biblical lives of Moses and Christ, but to be

---

[146] *VC* I.3.4.

understood as a precise re-enactment of the events in Scripture, so that they constituted 'virtually a recurrence of past history'.[147] For this to succeed, it was vital that Eusebius be seen to be a transparent recorder of events, since any hint that he was arranging the narrative for his own ends would have invalidated the claim that he was uncovering a genuine historical pattern – one decided and disposed by forces beyond the author's control. Of course, the *Life of Constantine*, like any historical account, necessarily imposed a literary structure on its raw material. Yet Eusebius took great care to emphasise the truthfulness of his own narrative, both by advertising his close relationship with the emperor and, as in the *Ecclesiastical History*, through the inclusion of original documents at every opportunity. Indeed, his determination to prove his accuracy in factual matters has led some to consider him as a founder of the modern discipline of history.[148] It certainly seems to have been unusually important for Eusebius to establish his *bona fides* – and to minimise his own role in constructing his story.

An explanation for this may be found in the apparently typological relationship he proposed between Moses, Christ and Constantine. For typological re-enactment differs from mere imitation in that it requires life to imitate life. It entails 'something real and historical which announces something else that is real and historical'.[149] And it requires the author who recognises these real correspondences to pose as nothing more than an objective observer. It was vital for Eusebius to establish in the *Life of Constantine* that the emperor was genuinely recapitulating the historical actions of Moses and Christ – that these figures were all to be regarded as equally real. Having told the story of Moses near the beginning of the *Life of Constantine*, he therefore made this point himself by going out of his way to concede the apparent unreliability of Scripture:

This ancient report, which most people regard as a kind of myth, was previously in everybody's ears, but now the same God has vouchsafed to us also to be eyewitnesses of public scenes, more certain than any myth because recently seen, of wonders greater than those in any story.[150]

---

[147] Hollerich 1990: 320. [148] Momigliano 1963: 88. [149] Auerbach 1959: 29.
[150] *VC* 1.12.2.

The story of Moses was previously regarded 'as a kind of myth', claims Eusebius – and yet the wonders seen in the present day, in all the ways in which Constantine re-enacted Moses, now served to validate it. It is surely permissible to suspect that the same relationship may have been working in reverse: that the story of Moses, which every Christian believed, would by the same token prove the reliability of the *Life of Constantine*. The correspondences between the two figures made the biblical world more real, but they also made the modern world – and the work of Eusebius – more like the Bible.

The apparently incompatible worlds of Scripture and late antiquity could thereby be brought together as elements in a unified sacred history. Moreover, the life and achievements of Constantine could represent a continuation of biblical history in another, stronger sense. For Constantine's life, and Eusebius' text, did not just follow on from the Bible but sought a place in the same authoritative tradition. The claim, in effect, was that Constantine belonged in the pages of the scriptures and not among the Roman annals; and by extension this placed the *Life of Constantine* as an authorised record on a par with the Bible. In establishing the reign of Constantine as the latest episode in an ongoing 'grand Christian narrative', Eusebius was asserting not only a genuine historical continuity between the contemporary world and the world of the scriptures, but also his own claim to be considered among the authoritative recorders and interpreters of God's purposes in the world. The *Life of Constantine* was to be understood as a new, official testament to God's presence and purpose in the world. It was a privileged account, and it constructed for the emperor and the world he ruled a definitive, authorised life.

2

GREGORY AND BASIL: A DOUBLE LIFE

. . . but misery still delights to trace
its semblance in another's case.
(William Cowper, 'The Castaway', written 20 March 1799.
First published in William Hayley, *The Life and Posthumous
Writings of William Cowper*, 3 vols. Chichester, 1803–4)

In life and literature, the reign of the Emperor Constantine could be seen to have inaugurated a new era of biblical history. For Eusebius, Constantine was the defining figure of the age – an age which had demonstrated the resumption of God's active intervention in human history. But the implications of this understanding of the new Christian empire of Constantine and his successors can be traced far beyond the works of Eusebius, so that they emerge as a consistent theme in Christian representations of the contemporary world – and in Christian biography above all. Importantly, however, this manner of interpretation did not focus exclusively, or even predominantly, on emperors. Although Eusebius has been identified as the source of a late-antique political model of 'caesaropapism', in fact the status of the emperor receives remarkably little attention in Christian engagements with contemporary history.[1] A 'Eusebian' interpretation of the later Roman empire as part of an ongoing grand Christian narrative is frequently expressed in biographical accounts of figures rather lower on the social scale. In a world understood as a new biblical era, it is not only the position and role of the emperor that must be reconsidered but – as the 'royal metaphor' might suggest – that of every member of society. The opportunity thus arose for a reinterpretation of the context

---

[1] For an authoritative account of the so-called 'caesaropapism' of the Byzantine emperors – beginning with Constantine and his treatment by Eusebius – see now Dagron 2003.

and meaning of the lives of more ordinary figures such as Eusebius himself: Christian bishops, and perhaps also Christian biographers. The intricacies to be found in portrayals such as these can be effectively explored by focusing on one of the best-documented Christian groupings of the fourth century: the close alliance of family and friends to be found among the Cappadocian fathers.[2] Based in the province of Cappadocia in Asia Minor and active throughout the decades after 360, this group included two of the greatest churchmen and theologians of the age in Gregory of Nazianzus and Basil of Caesarea, and one of the most significant of late-antique Christian biographers in Basil's brother, Gregory of Nyssa.[3] Gregory presented his and Basil's sister as a paragon of feminine virtue in the *Life of Macrina*, but the texts on which I intend to concentrate are two rather less straightforwardly biographical works: his speech on the anniversary of his brother's death known as the *Praise of Basil*, and his interpretative treatise on the *Life of Moses*.[4] As with Eusebius' *Life of Constantine*, then, it is important to recognise the close connections between biographical writing and other genres such as panegyric and eulogy, without losing sight of the way in which a work such as the *Praise of Basil* is offered as a comprehensive account of its subject's life and times; and in the case of the *Life of Moses*, it is possible also to appreciate the presence of the contemporary historical world even in what is ostensibly a commentary on the biblical past. Thus although the *Life of Moses* has been identified as an allegorical and mystical work, it also reveals an interest in typological and historical themes: and it is

---

[2] Fourth-century Cappadocia and the Cappadocian fathers are at the heart of three recent, connected works by Raymond Van Dam: Van Dam 2002 focuses on Roman rule in the province, Van Dam 2003a on Christianisation, especially in the generation before the Cappadocian fathers, and Van Dam 2003b on relations among the Cappadocian fathers themselves. A briefer account of relations among the Cappadocian fathers may be found at Meredith 1995.

[3] Van Dam's works, and especially Van Dam 2003b, tend to focus on the more public and political Basil of Caesarea and Gregory of Nazianzus at the expense of Gregory of Nyssa; recent accounts of the three as individuals may be found, for Basil in Rousseau 1994, for Gregory of Nyssa in Meredith 1999, and for Gregory of Nazianzus in Ruether 1969 and McGuckin 2001, now supplemented by the papers in Børtnes and Hägg 2006.

[4] The 1990 edition of the *In Basilium fratrem* by Lendle includes no paragraph numbers, and so citations here will follow the paragraphing established in the edition of Stein (1928), with references to the *Patrologia Graeca* [PG] edition in square brackets. My translations are based on those of Stein (1928). For the *Vita Moysis*, my translations are based on those of Malherbe and Ferguson (1978).

united with the *Praise of Basil* precisely by a shared concern with the extent to which Basil can be established as re-enacting the life and achievements of Moses.[5]

This, then, is the justification for pairing these two texts, and for offering them as an example of the close relationship between Christian biography and Scripture. Taken together, they emphasise the congruence of the biblical and contemporary late-antique worlds, in much the same way as did the parallel between Constantine and Moses in the *Life of Constantine*. In the works of Gregory of Nyssa, however, the transformation of the contemporary world is explored through its effects on less-elevated figures: the re-enactment of Scripture was not to be considered the preserve of emperors alone, but could be extended to comparatively minor figures, even to those of merely local importance. Gregory's reconsideration of Basil allotted to the Bishop of Caesarea, in the small eastern province of Cappadocia, a role in the ongoing development of sacred history from its origins in the Bible down to the present day. Basil took his place in this biblical tradition, authored and authorised by God. And so too did those friends and family who supported him, just as Aaron and Miriam had supported Moses. The interpretation of late antiquity as a biblical world meant that everyone could find themselves a place: even a brother – even a biographer.

Past and present

Gregory's *Life of Moses* originated precisely in the desire to relate the exemplary figures of Scripture to the practical matter of living in the contemporary world. As Bishop of Nyssa, but more probably as a prominent theologian and biographer, Gregory had been asked by an acquaintance for guidance on how the perfect

---

[5] A connection between Basil and Moses has been recognised before, and is discussed at length in Harl 1984, Sterk 1998 and Rapp 1998 – with the latter arguments expanded in Sterk 2004 and Rapp 2005. Note, however, that these works are primarily interested in Basil and Moses as abstractions of the bishop and the patriarch in general, offering idealised images of monastic or episcopal authority, and do not suggest (as here) a possible historical or typological relationship between the two figures.

Christian life ought to be lived.[6] In response, Gregory chose not to offer detailed instructions, arguing in the preface to the *Life of Moses* that perfection in virtue is impossible to attain, since virtue has no definite end-point and is a matter of constant striving towards the good.[7] The only possible guidance, therefore, came in the example of others who had succeeded in living a virtuous life: that is, in an account of an exemplary Christian life. Gregory's correspondent, the otherwise unknown Caesarius, was thus encouraged to turn to the examples set out in the scriptures: for example, to the lives of Abraham and Sarah.[8] Indeed, Gregory suggested,

it may be for this very reason that the daily life of these sublime individuals is recorded in detail, that by imitating these earlier examples of right action those who follow them may conduct their lives to the good.[9]

As a more substantial and considered example, Gregory offered his treatise on the *Life of Moses*, which he divided into two books: a history of the life of Moses, and its interpretation as a guide to the life of virtue in the modern world.

The epistolary frame of the work, of course, is a conventional attribute of works of philosophical and especially moral instruction, and was already a familiar feature of Christian biography.[10] The address to Caesarius should not blind us to the fact that Gregory's treatise would be read by a much wider audience, many of whom might feel that the imitation of such a spectacular and virtuous life as that of Moses to be beyond them. Gregory acknowledged this objection in his preface, voicing a potential fear that later Roman life was so different from that of the Bible that any attempt to draw a parallel would inevitably be defeated:

---

[6] The date of the *Life of Moses* is unclear, but it is usually placed in the early 390s, towards the end of Gregory's life. For arguments in favour of this date, see Malherbe and Ferguson 1978: 1–2, based ultimately on Daniélou 1955a: 351–3 and on Jaeger 1965: 118–19, 132–42. But Harl (1984: 71) and Meredith (1995: 68) remain unconvinced, and provide no specific date.

[7] See *VMoys.* 4–10 for the argument, along with the excellent discussion in MacLeod 1982.

[8] *VMoys.* 11–13. 'Caesarius' is named in the conclusion of some of the manuscripts of this work, and in the title of two others (one of which labels him a monk); alternative recipients are suggested in some manuscripts, but Caesarius seems to be the most common. He is not believed to be the same Caesarius who was brother to Gregory of Nazianzus. See Malherbe and Ferguson 1978: 2 for details.

[9] *VMoys.* 13. [10] As noted by Wilson 1988: 125–6.

Someone will say, 'How shall I imitate them, since I am not a Chaldaean as I remember Abraham was, nor was I nourished by the daughter of the Egyptian as Scripture teaches about Moses, and in general I do not have in these matters anything in my life corresponding to anyone of the ancients? How shall I place myself in the same rank with one of them, when I do not know how to imitate anyone so far removed from me by the circumstances of his life?'[11]

There was an immediate and obvious answer to this question: the particular objections made here focus on matters irrelevant to the aim of the exercise, since 'we do not consider being a Chaldaean a virtue or a vice'.[12] Yet Gregory goes on to admit that there is a more profound difficulty in the idea of imitating the example of the Bible, and that there is a need for 'some subtlety of understanding and keenness of vision to discern from the history how . . . we shall embark on the blessed life'.[13] His solution to this problem can be understood by considering the ways in which Gregory relates the world of Scripture to the contemporary world not only in the *Life of Moses*, but also in his *Praise of Basil*.

The two-part structure of the *Life of Moses* emphasises the need to provide alongside the biblical example a guide to its proper interpretation. The work is divided into a 'historical' narrative and a commentary setting out the meaning: *historia* is thus followed by *theoria*, providing a set of instructions for adapting this biblical life to the later Roman world. The use of this structure has led to suggestions that Gregory was directly influenced by an earlier *Life of Moses*, by the first-century Jewish scholar Philo of Alexandria – a work which also falls into two parts, which can be made to correspond to 'historical' and 'allegorical' approaches.[14] As a result, much has been made of the 'allegorical' or 'mystical' aspects of Gregory's own treatise, focusing above all on the extent to which the account of the historical life of Moses can be seen to correspond to the development of the Christian soul.[15] This, however,

---

[11] *VMoys.* I.14. [12] *VMoys.* I.14. [13] *VMoys.* I.14.
[14] As suggested by (among others) Malherbe and Ferguson 1978: 13. For more detail on the precise relationship between the two lives, see especially Runia 1993: 256–61; a number of clear differences are set out in Harl 1966: 557 and expanded in Peri 1974. For an account of the uses of allegorical exegesis in late antiquity, see esp. Dawson 1992; for the city of Alexandria itself, see Haas 1997; and for Philo's Alexandria, see Sly 1996. A study of the later influence of Philo's exegesis may be found in Runia 1993.
[15] Studies of the *VMoys.* focusing on its allegorical and mystical aspects and on the parallel with Philo include Bebis 1967, Otis 1976 and Ferguson 1976. A similar line is taken in

is to ignore the possibility that a work which engages in allegory might also engage in other modes of interpretation. Philo himself was certainly capable of incorporating into his works more than a single exegetical approach – and this applies all the more to Gregory of Nyssa.[16]

Gregory's approach to exegesis was, in any case, far from straightforwardly Philonic. His theology can be seen to have owed rather more to the work of Origen, in many ways the Christian successor to Philo – and even Origen's approach was 'transformed' in the hands of Gregory.[17] In place of any strict division between the levels of meaning that might be derived from the study of Scripture, Gregory presented such meanings as 'overlapping', or as having a tendency to 'shade off into one another'.[18] In this light, then, it is vital not to ignore the importance of the historical narrative of the life of Moses in Gregory's scheme.[19] In addition to any allegorical or mystical features, it is possible to recognise in Gregory's *Life of Moses* a recognition of the value of historical and typological interpretations.[20] Indeed, the *Life of Moses*, as might have been evident from its origins as a response to the request of Caesarius, and from Gregory's prominent concern with the apparent distance of the world of the Bible from that of his readers, was a treatise which was founded in large part on the possibility of a contemporary re-enactment of Scripture.

It is important to recognise that this remained a possibility which was not necessarily imposed on readers of the *Life of Moses*. As Gregory admitted in the preface, he himself had been unable 'to

the introductions to the editions of Daniélou 1955a and Malherbe and Ferguson 1978. The most recent discussions of Gregory's theology, however, see it as developing further Philo's allegorical approach under the influence of his Christian successor, Origen: see, for example, Louth 1981: 80–97 and Coakley 2002, esp. 136–41. Burrus (2000: 123–30) adopts a different approach to the *VMoys.* as an example of the gendering of knowledge, but continues to consider the work as 'explicitly allegorical' (123).

[16] For the various nature of Philo's exegesis, see Runia 1993: 257–8, and especially his n.113 there; more generally, Clark (1999: 70–3) argues that the exegetical 'schools' of Antioch and Alexandria were in fact less distinct than is often supposed: both used a variety of forms of 'nonliteral' exegesis, and did so in no particularly consistent fashion.

[17] Louth 1981: 81, and 80–97 on Gregory's adaptations of Origen's approach.

[18] Louth 1981: 82, 86.

[19] Typical is Malherbe and Ferguson 1978: 5. 'Of more interest . . . [is book two]'.

[20] One clear example of conventional typological exegesis – in which Moses is explicitly presented as prefiguring the Incarnation – is recognised in Ferguson 1976: 312; cf. Bebis 1967: 369.

show in my life the insights of this treatise', and it seems likely that the perfect Christian life would be similarly difficult to live for the vast majority of his readers.[21] And yet there is no reason to think that Gregory believed his counsel of perfection to be impossible to follow. Elsewhere in his writings he had already recognised a modern re-enactment of Moses in his *Life of Gregory Thaumaturgus*, the third-century bishop adopted as a common ancestor by the fourth-century Cappadocian fathers.[22] It has been suggested that this *Life* as a whole was 'an oblique meditation on the career of Basil', and it certainly seems to be true that Gregory of Nyssa offered his brother as a truly contemporary model of the perfectly virtuous Christian life lived on the pattern of Moses.[23] His speech *In Praise of Basil* is constructed around a series of re-enactments of major biblical figures, culminating in the presentation of the Bishop of Caesarea as 'a new Moses' for the late-antique world.[24] Thus where the *Life of Moses* offered a theoretical account of how the events of the Bible could be made relevant to contemporary life, the *Praise of Basil* was able to prove the case by the force of a direct example. The two texts may therefore be understood as complementary, in such a way that the *Praise of Basil* emerges as a practical application of the appeals and the arguments of the *Life of Moses* – and in such a way that the re-enactment of Scripture could be established as an appropriate model for a modern Christian life.

Not everyone, perhaps, could hope to imitate Moses; and few could hope to live a life as exemplary as that attributed by Gregory to his brother. But the fact that Basil of Caesarea could be represented as reviving the spirit and the achievements of the biblical patriarchs required a reassessment of the world in which he lived – which was also the familiar world of Gregory's readers. The appearance in their midst of such an extraordinary figure, a modern fulfilment of the biblical model, rendered their own world

---

[21] *VMoys.* 1.3.

[22] For this understanding of Gregory Thaumaturgus and the *VGThaum.*, see Van Dam 1982: 278–9.

[23] Van Dam 2003b: 73.

[24] See especially the detailed discussion contained in Harl (1984), along with the brief comments on this text at Wilson 1988: 125; cf. also the characterisation of the structure of the work in Stein 1928: xxxviii–xli.

more like the Bible and the biblical world less distant.[25] Indeed, just as Basil could be understood as a modern Moses, it might be possible for Moses to now be understood as a man similar to Basil: for his biblical life, in effect, to be modelled on the conventions of late antiquity.[26] This was an effective response to the concern that Gregory had aired about the differences between then and now, between a world of Chaldaeans and a world of Cappadocians. In truth, Gregory would maintain, there was very little significant change: the people of today, he affirmed, were in no way inferior to the people described in the holy scriptures.[27] In the case of Basil and Moses this could be demonstrated, where for others it had to be taken on trust. But even readers who did not see themselves in heroic terms – who, like Gregory himself, could not live up to the example of Moses – could find a place in this understanding of their history. If they were not themselves patriarchs, then they at least lived in a world in which patriarchs still existed.

Friends and family

In his account of Basil's life as in his biography of his sister Macrina, Gregory of Nyssa was inevitably forced to deal with matters that touched on his own career and personality. Yet in contrast to Basil, and in contrast also to their friend Gregory of Nazianzus, very little is known about the life of Gregory of Nyssa. In his writings in general, there is a surprising lack of emphasis on his personal achievements or upbringing, and even when such matters are mentioned they are largely limited to the background he shared with Basil.[28] Information can be gleaned in similar fashion from his *Life of Macrina*, and from the letters of both Basil and Gregory of Nazianzus, so that it is possible to construct at least an

[25] Harl 1984: 78, 'une nouvelle réalisation du modèle'.
[26] As suggested by Wilson 1988: 126.
[27] Harl 1984: 103, citing *In Bas.* 2 [*PG* 46: 789C–792A].
[28] A similar charge can be levelled at his letters, which are poor ground for biographical details: see the comments of Maraval 1990. The lack of direct biographical information means that Gregory can be discussed only briefly in, for example, Van Dam 2003b: 59–74, and even there he is explicitly counted among the 'forgotten brothers' of Basil and Macrina.

outline account of Gregory's life.[29] There is, however, no possibility of extricating Gregory from his involvement with these relations and friends, who have come to dominate our modern idea of late-antique Christian Cappadocia. Gregory must be seen as one of the Cappadocian fathers, or else he is not to be seen at all.

It can be established, then, that Gregory of Nyssa came from a large family, Christian for at least two generations and perhaps involved in Christianity for longer.[30] He had three or four brothers and five sisters, not all of whose names are known.[31] The family was able to claim a Christian heritage reaching back at least as far as Gregory's grandmother, another Macrina, who was said to have been a disciple of 'the great Gregory Thaumaturgus himself'.[32] They certainly represented, in any case, one of the more prominent upper-class families in the region.[33] Basil and Gregory's father was a rhetor, and Basil as the eldest of the brothers would receive a university education in Athens and perhaps in Constantinople.[34] In contrast Gregory claimed to have no significant teachers other than Basil and seems for the most part to have been educated locally; nevertheless, he evidently had some training and a sincere interest in classical rhetoric.[35] In later years, of course, all involved sought to stress that none of this was necessarily opposed to a Christian way of life.[36] Gregory himself would later claim that Christian

---

[29] Gregory's *Vita Macrinae* was written soon after the deaths of both Macrina and Basil, around 379–80, and contains a large amount of biographical information. The fullest modern accounts of Gregory's life may be found in Meredith 1999: 1–15 and in Rousseau 1994: 3–11, both of which depend heavily on Daniélou 1965; Van Dam (2003b: 67–71) makes much of hints in the later works but is often speculative. The account in Maraval 1990: 15–27 depends on the acceptance of certain key dates, and is provisional at best: cf. Rousseau 1994: 360–3.

[30] The Christian history of the family, or at least its claims and traditions in that area, are discussed in detail at Van Dam 2003a: 72–81.

[31] Three brothers in Van Dam 2003b: 67–71; four in Meredith 1999: 2; some further discussion in Rousseau 1994: 1, 4, and Meredith 1999: 1, following Maraval 1990.

[32] Rousseau 1990: 48 – although Rousseau (1994: 4) suggests only that the elder Macrina 'had known disciples' of Gregory Thaumaturgus; alternative possibilities are explored in Van Dam 2003a: 77–8. The claim is ultimately derived from Basil, *Letter* 204.6.

[33] Meredith 1999: 2, citing *VMac.* 6.

[34] Basil's time in Constantinople (with Libanius) is discussed in Gregory of Nyssa, *Letter* 13.

[35] Gregory's education is discussed at Rousseau 1994: 4–5, citing *VMac.* 3, 6, 8 and 12; and in more detail at Van Dam 2003b: 67–71.

[36] See especially Gregory of Nazianzus, *Oration* 43 (on Basil).

piety had been instilled in him by his mother, and that at times he was unwilling to comply.[37] Basil, meanwhile, had spent much of his time at Athens in the company of Gregory of Nazianzus, and some time after their return the two of them embarked on a 'philosophic' or ascetic life.[38] Part of this time Basil spent on the family estates at Annesi, where Macrina and others in the family had apparently also adopted an ascetic regime.[39] A few years later, in 362, both Basil and Gregory of Nazianzus were ordained as priests; and ten years after he had returned from Athens, Basil took on a public role in the metropolitan bishopric of Caesarea.[40] He would be made the city's bishop in 370.[41] Throughout all of this, by contrast, Gregory of Nyssa seems to have remained at home following a secular career. A letter, written in 365 by his namesake Gregory of Nazianzus, confronts him with the accusation that 'you would rather be thought of as a rhetor than as a Christian'.[42] At some stage he even seems to have married, although little more is known about that.[43] He perhaps took some interest in local Christian affairs, but seems to have had little intention of embarking on an ecclesiastical career.

Yet in 372, Gregory was appointed by Basil as bishop of the new diocese of Nyssa.[44] This 'more or less forced consecration' appears to have been a result of Basil's desire to keep as much control as possible over his province of Cappadocia, by populating the ecclesiastical hierarchy of the region with his relatives and friends.[45] Basil, of course, was eager to dispute any charge of nepotism, but his decision to appoint Gregory as Bishop of Nyssa would appear

[37] Van Dam 2003b: 68, citing Gregory of Nyssa, *Encomium in XL martyres* 2 [*PG* 46: 784D–785A].

[38] See especially Rousseau 1994: 61–8 for the circumstances and difficulties of this decision.

[39] Although Rousseau (1994: 62–3) notes that this need not imply any common ascetic project. On the uncertain location of Annesi (or 'Annisa'), see Rousseau 1994: 62 n. 7.

[40] Rousseau 1994: 67, 133–4.

[41] Rousseau 1994: 136.

[42] Gregory of Nazianzus, *Letters* 11, quoted at Meredith 1999: 3; for more details see Daniélou 1965.

[43] The evidence – two stray references – is discussed in detail by Wilson 1990: 263 n. 28, and she and Meredith 1999: 2 both conclude that a marriage is the most likely explanation.

[44] Meredith 1999: 4. The see of Nyssa had been created after the partitioning of Cappadocia into two separate provinces by the Emperor Valens. The see of Sasima was created at the same time, and Basil appointed Gregory of Nazianzus as its bishop.

[45] Rousseau 1990: 48.

to have owed little to any confidence in his brother's abilities.[46] In a letter the previous year, Basil had accused his brother of being 'naïve'; even after appointing him bishop, Basil would continue to bemoan Gregory's 'simplicity' and general unsuitability for the position.[47] Later, Basil would be a little more conciliatory, preferring to excuse his brother on the grounds that he was 'quite inexperienced in ecclesiastical matters'.[48] The impression, right or wrong, is of a man entirely unsuited to the life of a bishop. It is hardly all that surprising (although it must have dismayed Gregory) to find that this opinion seems to have been widespread. The Bishop of Nyssa, in fact, was frequently regarded as little more than Basil's ambassador.[49]

As it happened, there was little for Gregory to do as Bishop of Nyssa – at least during Basil's lifetime. In 375, Gregory was replaced in his see by order of the Emperor Valens, and he would remain in exile until restored by a decree of 378.[50] Basil died soon after Gregory's return, and shortly afterwards their sister Macrina died too.[51] These deaths seem to have prompted the beginning of Gregory's career as a writer. The vast majority of his works can be dated to the years after 380, and among the earliest of them are the *Life of Macrina* and the oration *In Praise of Basil*.[52] Yet although these works were both written in response to a sibling's death, that might appear to be practically all that the two of them have in common. The *Life of Macrina* relates a remarkably domestic tale, with Gregory's sister firmly situated in the context of her familial responsibilities: it is only through her relations with her mother and with her brothers that she is portrayed as the 'guiding force' of the Cappadocians' ascetic project.[53] The *Praise of Basil*, by contrast,

---

[46] For Basil's denial of nepotism, see Rousseau 1994: 8.

[47] Basil, *Letters* 58, 100: see Daniélou 1965, Rousseau 1994: 6–7, and Van Dam 2003b: 70.

[48] Basil, *Letters* 215, quoted at Rousseau 1994: 7–8; cf. Sterk 1998: 231.

[49] This impression is given particularly strongly in Gregory of Nazianzus, *Oration* 11.

[50] These are the dates given in Meredith 1995; they are disputed by Maraval 1990, who places the return from exile earlier; but that view is discussed and finally rejected by Rousseau 1994: 360–3.

[51] These deaths are likely to have occurred in the years 379–80, although the exact dates are disputed.

[52] For the dating of Gregory's works, see esp. Daniélou 1955a and Daniélou 1955b.

[53] See Rousseau 1994: 9–10, quoting 10.

presents its hero in a more solitary guise, whether in public life as a bishop or in his private retreats. Gregory, indeed, explicitly disowns the conventional praises of family and fatherland.[54] As Arnaldo Momigliano defined the issue, in a characteristically acute comparison of the two biographies, 'Gregory speaks of his sister as his sister, but does not speak of his brother as his brother.'[55]

Gregory's decision to exclude from his discussion of Basil any mention of his family background, or indeed of Gregory's own family relationship with the man he was praising, is all the more noticeable when the *Praise of Basil* is compared with a similar speech, delivered by Gregory of Nazianzus.[56] In that speech, more remiscent of a traditional funeral oration, Gregory of Nazianzus spends a substantial amount of time describing in detail Basil's family, education and career.[57] Why, then, did Gregory of Nyssa not do the same? The explanation may be that the two orations were of different types, and intended for different occasions. Gregory of Nyssa may perhaps have previously delivered a funeral oration, and in that work there may have been all of the biographical information that is now missing.[58] Whether or not this is true, the speech that survives is by no means a traditional funeral oration or work of consolation. It is, as the modern title suggests, devoted to praising Basil; it certainly contains 'no allusions to a recent bereavement . . . no mention of his recent death, no expression of sorrow'.[59] It was therefore most likely delivered a good time after Basil's death: and its function was not to mourn his death but to commemorate his life.

Gregory of Nyssa's oration, in fact, appears to have been delivered on an anniversary of his brother's death. The time of year can be established with reasonable accuracy, as being 1 or 2

---

[54] *In Bas.* 24–5 [*PG* 46: 813B–816C]. [55] Momigliano 1985a: 449.
[56] For the comparison, see Meredith 1997; for the speech of Gregory of Nazianzus, see McLynn 2001.
[57] Gregory of Nazianzus, *Oration* 43 (on Basil) 3–59; cf. Meredith 1997: 164.
[58] Gregory of Nazianzus, in his *Oration* 43.2, certainly implies that there have been other speeches on Basil before his own; but of course this need not mean that there had been more than one – or indeed any at all – delivered by Gregory of Nyssa.
[59] Stein 1928: xxxii. Van Dam (2003b: 71–4) prefers to explain the distancing effect in psychological terms, as a result of a lack of close sympathy between the brothers – and this must of course remain a possibility.

January, but the year itself is open to much debate.[60] There seems to
have existed a tradition of sorts dedicated to the memory of Basil –
presumably in Caesarea and presumably in the early 380s.[61] It is
clear, however, that the speech given by Gregory of Nyssa was
aimed at establishing or continuing such a tradition. The *Praise of
Basil* began by noting its place in a series of celebrations, beginning
with Christmas and continuing with the feast-days assigned to the
saints Stephen, Peter, James, John and Paul.[62] Gregory's intention
appears to have been to add Basil himself to this list, offering him
a place among the biblical saints with a feast-day of his own at
the start of January. Basil would be added to the calendar, and so
re-imagined as a saint, or else as 'a distant biblical figure'.[63]

[60] A date at the start of January is suggested at the very start of the oration, as Gregory refers
to a series of festivals that have happened recently, following Christmas: see *In Bas.* 1
[*PG* 46: 788c–789c], and cf. Stein 1928: xxxi. This date is presumed to be the anniversary
of Basil's death, as little other reason can be found in the speech for commemorating
him at this particular time. Basil's death, which is presumed from other evidence to have
taken place in the winter of 378–9, is therefore usually placed on 1 January 379. This
date, however, has been challenged in particular by Maraval (1988) – later summarised
at Maraval 1990: 18–20 – based on the evidence of the *VMac.* and the known movements
of Gregory around that time. Maraval prefers a date in summer or early autumn 379. Note
also the refinement of Maraval's arguments in Moutsoulas 1997, who suggests an earlier
date. Maraval's view is also discussed in Rousseau (1994: 360–3): and Rousseau prefers
to place most confidence in the traditional date of 1 January 379. For convenience, then,
I shall assume that Basil's death in fact took place on that date, and that Gregory of
Nyssa's oration on his brother was delivered on a later anniversary.

[61] Such a tradition is suggested by Gregory of Nazianzus, *Oration* 43 (on Basil) 2, where he
excuses himself for speaking only 'so long after the occasion, and after so many others
have eulogised him in public and private'. From this it is argued that a series of orations
on Basil had been given already, and that they are likely to have included at least one
by his brother, Gregory of Nyssa. On the assumption that Gregory of Nyssa's oration
was delivered on the anniversary of the death of Basil, and that Basil died in 379 (see
previous note), Daniélou (1955a) argues that Gregory of Nyssa's oration was delivered in
January 381. The oration is assumed to have been delivered in Caesarea, and it is argued
that Gregory could not have been in the area on the first anniversary of Basil's death,
in 380. It is further assumed that Gregory of Nyssa would have delivered his oration
at the earliest opportunity. These dates are at best uncertain: there is no real reason to
believe that Gregory of Nazianzus' mention of previous speeches should necessarily
have included the *In Bas.*, which may well have been given at an even later date. For
my immediate purposes, in any case, it will not be necessary to establish the exact date
on which Gregory's oration was delivered. I shall for convenience, however, assume
Daniélou's preferred date to be correct, and place the *In Bas.* at the beginning of January
381.

[62] *In Bas.* 1 [*PG* 46: 788c–789c].

[63] Momigliano 1985a: 449. That Gregory hoped to establish a feast-day for Basil has been
suggested most recently by Meredith (1997: 163). If this was indeed part of Gregory's
aim, then he succeeded: Basil's feast-day is now placed by the Roman Catholic church
on 2 January; in the eastern churches it is celebrated on 1 January.

It might seem strange that Gregory, usually so 'full of family', should have chosen to portray his brother in such aloof, 'theologised' terms.[64] Yet the distancing effect of Gregory's *Praise of Basil* – and the extent of the contrast between it and the *Life of Macrina* – should not be overstated.[65] Gregory is as present in his speech about his brother as he is in his account of his sister: only in the latter does he feature as a character, but in both cases the narrative is his. It is reasonable to suppose that the audience for Gregory's oration would have recognised him as the brother of Basil, even despite his claims that these family connections were irrelevant.[66] In portraying Basil as a biblical figure, then, Gregory was unveiling a complex irony: for the man his oration reveals to have been a modern re-enactment of Moses was at the same time a familiar figure for both the speaker and his audience. Basil was surely known to the audience as their great contemporary; but rather than situate him in the late-antique world, Gregory chose to supply his brother with 'an alternative biblical genealogy' which represented him instead as 'the spiritual descendant of Abraham, Moses, Samuel, Elijah, John the Baptist, and the apostle Paul'.[67] In the process he brought that biblical world into the world of late antiquity. Moreover, Gregory himself marked the point at which these two worlds coincided. The scriptures could dimly be glimpsed, albeit at one remove, through the figure of Basil's brother and valedictorian.

Possible pasts

Gregory's speech *In Praise of Basil* thus offers a distinctive presentation of Christian time. It begins with a reference to the time of year, and to the cluster of religious festivals that have just been celebrated, beginning with the birth of Christ on Christmas Day. The precise order of the subsequent feast-days, beginning with St Stephen's on 26 December, is then claimed to accord with the

---

[64] Gregory is described as 'full of family' by Meredith 1995: 52; 'theologised' is Rousseau 1994: 89.

[65] Momigliano (1985a: 449) offers a strong contrast in (perhaps slightly misleading) generic terms: that 'while Macrina is brought near by a biography, Basil is made distant by a panegyric'.

[66] Momigliano 1985a: 449.   [67] Van Dam 2003b: 74.

teachings of Paul – 'for he says that the apostles and prophets were placed first and the pastors and teachers after them'.[68] The festivals just celebrated had honoured the apostles; Gregory identifies the occasion of his speech as the transitional moment at which the congregation turns instead to its pastors and teachers. Specifically, the people are being asked to remember that 'teacher and pastor next after the apostles', Basil of Caesarea.[69]

That Basil should be considered to be 'next after the apostles' is itself a grand enough claim. But Gregory goes further still, insisting that the priority of the apostles exists purely in temporal terms, and that this is by no means a sign of their superiority. Even the biblical past, he argues, was no more intrinsically virtuous a time than is the present day of the later Roman empire: indeed, for Gregory 'the nature of time with reference to virtue and vice is alike in the past and in the future, being neither the one nor the other'.[70] Time, that is, has no relevance to virtue at all. Basil can be considered as virtuous as any of the prophets or apostles. The place of each in the divine plan means that such figures might appear at different times, but they are all directly comparable:

For if Paul has priority in time, and Basil has been raised up many generations later, then you are recounting the works of the divine dispensation on behalf of men, and not a demonstration of inferior virtue; because even Moses was born many ages after Abraham, and Samuel the same with regard to Moses, and then Elijah after him, and then the great John [the Baptist], and after John came Paul, and after him Basil.[71]

Basil is not intended to stand out from such company. Had he been alive at the time, Gregory notes, then he would surely have taken part in the ministry of Paul and Timothy.[72] It was only the passage of time that separated the Bible from late antiquity.

Gregory's ostensibly spontaneous listing of prominent biblical figures would provide the structural foundation for the remainder of the *Praise of Basil*. The oration proceeds with a brief account of biblical history, focusing on the successive contributions of Abraham, Moses, Samuel, Elijah, John and Paul.[73] These six figures are

[68] *In Bas.* 1 [*PG* 46: 788C–789A]. [69] *In Bas.* 1 [*PG* 46: 789B].
[70] *In Bas.* 2 [*PG* 46: 792A]. [71] *In Bas.* 2 [*PG* 46: 792A].
[72] *In Bas.* 2 [*PG* 46: 789D]. [73] *In Bas.* 4–7 [*PG* 46: 792B–794D].

each shown to have fulfilled a virtually identical function in their own particular era, reconciling and restoring their people to the true path and the proper worship of God. The implicit comparison between them is offered, not in terms of their individual virtues, but as a result of their common performance of 'one and the same function, that of doctor of humanity for their own generation'.[74] In effect, they re-enact one another in the role of God's physician. A typological chain is established, so that from Abraham to Paul, the Bible is seen to repeat a familiar story. God sends to every age its own salvific figure, a leader to triumph over his people's enemies.[75] And even the most recent of these biblical saviours, as Gregory was keen to repeat, was yet 'in no respect inferior in the commandments of the Lord to those who had preceded him in the exercise of virtue'.[76]

Basil of Caesarea is then assigned his rightful place in this tradition. He too was to be seen as a doctor to the church, a modern-day prophet or apostle. His particular challenge, and his inevitable triumph, is set out at length by Gregory as the latest chapter in the history of the Christian faith carried down from the Old and New Testaments.[77] Basil's mission is shown to have been to rid the world of the Arian heresy, which had indeed been a major preoccupation for him and for all the Cappadocian fathers.[78] In this case, Gregory presented the argument in particularly revealing terms. He seized upon the 'Arian' belief that Christ was not a begotten son of God, but was rather a created being, and represented this as a subtle form of idolatry.[79] Just as the Israelites had worshipped a golden calf, so the Arians deified a mere creature that they (blasphemously) called

---

[74] Harl 1984: 77, 'une seule et même fonction, celle de "médecin" de l'humanité pour une génération'; cf. *In Bas.* 3 [*PG* 46: 792B] for the medical metaphor (ὁ ἰατρός).

[75] Harl 1984: 72. Note that Christ is preserved as superior to each of these other biblical figures; all the same, of course, each can be seen in some sense as a figure for Christ.

[76] *In Bas.* 6 [*PG* 46: 793C]; and cf. esp. *In Bas.* 8 [*PG* 46: 793D–796A].

[77] *In Bas.* 8–10 [*PG* 46: 793D–797B]; see also Meredith 1997: 165 and Harl 1984: 97.

[78] It was perhaps still a live issue: Arianism (in this case primarily the 'neo-Arianism' associated with Eunomius) was definitively condemned in the summer of 381 at the Council of Constantinople, but the debate certainly continued in the following years: see Hanson 1988: 676–737. That Gregory makes no reference to this has been offered as evidence that his oration was given in January 381 or before; of course, it is also possible to argue that Gregory's triumphalist language presupposes a victory already achieved, and in fact places the oration *after* 381.

[79] See especially *In Bas.* 9 [*PG* 46: 796B–C].

Christic.[80] This presentation of the issue at stake was perhaps not unjustified, but was certainly polemical. It gave a spurious biblical pedigree to Arian beliefs – and therefore to Basil's role in opposing them.

Basil's triumphant opposition to Arianism, 'when almost all men had come under its sway', thus placed him in the same tradition as those biblical heroes who in Scripture had wrested the people of God from their error.[81] Gregory notes that Basil, like Elijah, stood alone against the idolatry of the Israelites; so too had Moses when confronted with the golden calf.[82] These in their turn had re-enacted Abraham, whose example had overcome 'the deceit of his fathers' and the impiety of their race.[83] Basil's struggle with Arianism was thereby inflated to biblical proportions. Nor was this a distant, unfamiliar contest: Gregory, of course, had taken his own part in the struggle he described.[84] There were doubtless some in the audience who also knew that the battle was a recent one. Late antiquity itself was thus implicitly elevated to the status of Scripture; the Arian heresy was just another manifestation of the familiar biblical tendency of God's people to drift away from the true faith. In such circumstances, Gregory's question was perhaps a reasonable one:

Why then should [Basil's] passage through life, coming after the other saints, thus diminish his glory before God, so that the celebrations for him should be deemed inferior to the festivals that the other saints receive?[85]

That Basil merely happened to live later on in history than the biblical saints, argued Gregory, no more disqualified him from being considered their equal than did the fact of his having a day to himself in the church's festal calendar. The challenges he had faced had been just as serious, and his contribution just as important, as anything in Scripture. For Gregory it was fortunate indeed that God had provided the Christians of late antiquity with a leader of

[80] *In Bas.* 10 [*PG* 46: 796c].   [81] *In Bas.* 10 [*PG* 46: 796d].
[82] *In Bas.* 10 [*PG* 46: 796d].   [83] *In Bas.* 4 [*PG* 46: 792c].
[84] Gregory relates that Basil had no 'fear of exile', perhaps recalling his own exile from Nyssa at the instigation of the Arian Emperor Valens: *In Bas.* 10 [*PG* 46: 797a–b]. He had also written (perhaps by 381) a defence of Basil's arguments against Eunomius, who is also mentioned as an Arian and an enemy at *In Bas.* 10 [*PG* 46: 796c].
[85] *In Bas.* 11 [*PG* 46: 797b–c].

Basil's calibre, and so had favoured them all with the same divine grace as in former times.[86] Having set out to portray Basil's struggle with Arianism as a thoroughly biblical task, Gregory continued on to the second part of his oration – indeed, the second part of what was a broadly chiastic structure.[87] For after describing in turn the contributions to biblical history of Abraham, Moses, Samuel, Elijah, John the Baptist and Paul, and placing Basil squarely in the same tradition, Gregory sought to reaffirm his brother's biblical credentials through a detailed comparison with each of these figures. Beginning with Paul and proceeding in reverse order, Gregory's oration demonstrates how Basil's familiar fourth-century life can be understood as an imitation, and perhaps a typological re-enactment, of his biblical predecessors. The effect is not only to make Basil seem a biblical figure, but is often to render the world of the Bible in remarkably familiar, contemporary terms. For if Basil was just like the prophets and apostles, they too might seem very much like Basil.

Basil, in fact, is immediately presented as both an apostle and a prophet. The apostle Paul is first examined, and his love for God is declared unsurpassed. Yet Basil's love for God is placed alongside that of Paul, and is rapidly revealed to be its equal: as Gregory concludes, 'there is one measure of love in both'.[88] Basil's teaching is also reminiscent of Paul, although in this case it perhaps even surpasses it – for whereas Paul preached the gospel throughout the Holy Land and 'from Jerusalem to Illyricum', Basil's preaching 'embraced almost the whole world, and was desired by everyone just as were the discourses of Paul'.[89] This broader scale on which Basil seemed to act even allowed him to out-perform John the Baptist as a prophet. For in acting the role of the prophet at court, as John had done when confronting King Herod, Basil's success was all the greater because his challenge was issued to a far grander figure in the Emperor Valens. After all:

---

[86] Harl 1984: 73, 'une grâce égale aux précédentes'.
[87] As recognised by Meredith 1997 and Sterk 1998.
[88] *In Bas.* 11 [*PG* 46: 800A–B].   [89] *In Bas.* 12 [*PG* 46: 801A].

The one was appointed by a vote of the Romans to the government of a part of Palestine; and the boundary line of the other's rule was almost the entire course of the sun, extending from the borders of Persia to the Britons and the edges of the oceans.[90]

Basil's object in challenging Valens, furthermore, was more profitable and high minded – for while Herod was being dissuaded from an unwise and unlawful sexual adventure, Valens was arraigned for the threat he was posing to the fabric of the Christian faith.[91] Basil was warding off heresy, that is, and not merely moral incontinence. In the end, too, he suffered the less for it, Basil's greater authority allowing him to be sentenced only to exile, whereas John had been sentenced to death. Even this exile was eventually rescinded, as Gregory was eager to remind his audience, and by a personal decree of the Emperor Valens himself. Basil, meanwhile, had 'in no way . . . weakened his opposition on account of the punishment'.[92]

Basil's time in exile also allowed Gregory to portray him as a type of biblical prophet in the wilderness. This aspect is central to the initial comparison of Basil to John the Baptist, in which the bishop's asceticism is extolled as by no means inferior to that of John:

Who does not know that [Basil] considered an effeminate and luxurious mode of life inimical, in everything seeking fortitude and manliness instead of pleasure, enduring heat from the sun, exposing himself to the cold, disciplining his body with fasts and acts of self-control, living in cities as in deserts (with his virtue in no way harmed by social contact), and making the deserts into cities?[93]

The echo of the phrase from the *Life of Antony*, concerning 'making the desert a city', might also suggest the importance of Elijah, that other biblical paradigm of the ascetic life. Indeed, the image of Elijah that appears in the *Praise of Basil* seems remarkably modern: rather more like the figure inherited from the contemporary monastic tradition than the biblical prophet.[94] To begin with,

---

[90] *In Bas.* 14 [*PG* 46: 804A].   [91] *In Bas.* 14 [*PG* 46: 804B]; cf. Mark 6:18, Luke 3:19.

[92] *In Bas.* 14 [*PG* 46: 804B]. Basil's interactions with Valens are discussed at Rousseau 1994: 283–4; the religious policies of the emperor may be seen from a more sympathetic perspective than Gregory's in Lenski 2002: 234–63.

[93] *In Bas.* 13 [*PG* 46: 801B].

[94] *VA* 14; the effect of the phrase in linking Basil to the world of monasticism is recognised by Harl 1984: 94.

Elijah's miraculous forty-day fast is compared, not to any particular incident in the life of Basil, but to the bishop's notably abstemious life in general.[95] As with the desert ascetics, re-enacting Elijah's sojourn in the wilderness, Basil had adopted the Bible's example of abstinence as a pattern for the whole of his life.[96]

There were also some individual correspondences, of course. Elijah had secured food and water for a widow in the midst of a famine; and Basil (as Gregory's audience were sure to remember) had guided the people of his city of Caesarea through famine in rather more recent times.[97] The re-enactment was admittedly not exact in every detail, as Gregory was willing to recognise; but, he added, 'it makes no difference whether the divine plan is fulfilled through a flask or through some other means'.[98] Basil's actions – again on a more impressive scale than their counterparts in Scripture – were certainly carried out in the same spirit as those of Elijah. For the most part, however, Gregory would seem to have identified his brother's re-enactment of Elijah as a more comprehensive phenomenon. Their common concern with the care of the needy merely indicated a fundamental connection between the two of them.

Thus Gregory, on first taking up his comparison with Elijah, designated the attributes that the prophet shared with Basil:

Zeal in faith; enmity against those who break their word; a love for God; desire for that which truly is, that turns aside to nothing of material things; a life in all things circumspect, a manner of living austere; a countenance attuned to the tone of the soul; unaffected dignity; a silence more effective than speech; a concern for the things that are hoped for, a disdain for the things that are seen; an equal consideration for anything that appears before him, whether someone high in dignity should come, or whether someone despised and lowly.[99]

What is remarkable here is the distance of this image of Elijah from the scriptural model. It is of course entirely possible that the historical Elijah was exactly like this; yet his actions are all that the biblical tradition records. Gregory's vivid description is founded on a picture of Basil and not of Elijah. This Basil, stripped of

---

[95] *In Bas.* 16 [*PG* 46: 805A–B]. [96] See Sterk 1998: 233.
[97] See Sterk 1998: 233; the Elijah story is told at 1 Kings 17:8–16 [AV]; for the famine in Caesarea, see Rousseau 1994: 136–44.
[98] *In Bas.* 18 [*PG* 46: 808A]. [99] *In Bas.* 16 [*PG* 46: 805A].

his immediate concerns as an individual late-antique bishop, can very easily be imagined in an Old Testament context. At the same time, however, Gregory's depiction of Basil has a similar, complementary effect. By assigning these familiar features to the images of both Basil and Elijah, the passage renders Elijah himself as a notably modern character. Elijah is presented, not in terms of his miracles, but through a description of his personality and attitude, all of which seem to fit comfortably into the late fourth century AD. Far from making Basil, in his role as a modern-day biblical figure, seem unattainably distant from his audience, Gregory instead succeeds in bringing the Bible into the world of late antiquity.

Basil remains, then, firmly grounded in the same reality as Gregory and his audience. This can be seen in Gregory's repeated insistence that the biblical aspect of Basil's life is not to be found in his performance of any miracles. Basil's equivalent of the 'wonders' of Elijah is the remarkable level of his faith, and no more; his excellence is achieved from the confines of his 'human nature'.[100] This is not to say that Basil can offer no equivalent for the miracles of Elijah; and for Gregory, even the prophet's ascension into heaven in a chariot of fire has a parallel.[101] Gregory's interpretation might be labelled 'spiritual': Elijah's ascent is compared with 'that other form of motion upwards . . . [just as] whenever anyone through sublime living is removed from earth to heaven'.[102] Although the comparison is expressed in general terms, however, Gregory is quick to reinforce its application to the particular case of Basil – and his listeners are expected to recognise its suitability for themselves. As Gregory says, 'that this very thing was accomplished by our teacher, everyone, who examines his acts accordingly, will conclude'.[103] Even an apparently allegorical interpretation is thus returned to the realm of familiar late-antique experience.

Basil's re-enactment of Elijah, then, was as complete as could reasonably be hoped, although it was inevitably limited by his insuperable human nature. Yet while Basil remains a plausible (and non-miraculous) late-antique figure, Elijah himself was not necessarily made so distant by the miracles he performed. Gregory's

---

[100] *In Bas.* 16 [*PG* 46: 805A] ('wonders'); cf. *In Bas.* 15 [*PG* 46: 804D] ('human nature').
[101] Sterk 1998: 233; for the story, see 2 Kings 11 [AV].
[102] *In Bas.* 18 [*PG* 46: 808B].   [103] *In Bas.* 18 [*PG* 46: 808B].

original re-telling of the story of Elijah's ascension into heaven in the *Praise of Basil*, a few pages before Basil's repetition of the feat, was remarkable for its concern with the plausibility of the event. For just as Basil could not have hoped to survive very long in a flaming chariot, Gregory insists that not even Elijah, if he remained 'within the confines of nature', could have endured such a fire.[104] He suggests that the prophet had instead been transformed into some sort of spiritual being.[105]

Very little might seem to be gained by thus converting one miracle into another – for if God could arrange for Elijah to be transformed into a spiritual being, he might just as easily have fire-proofed the prophet's flesh. Yet Gregory's aim was to make clear that some kind of change must have taken place before Elijah's ascension. Divine assistance had been required for him to perform that miracle, and it had been required for him to perform his many others. Except on those rare occasions when God had intervened directly, however, Gregory's claim was that Elijah was only a man. He was as human as Gregory and his audience and, crucially, he was just as human as Basil. Gregory, then, took a rather sceptical approach to the miraculous events of the Bible. He did not deny, in the *Praise of Basil*, that miracles took place from time to time; yet he preferred an historical account wherever possible. The effect was to make the heroes of Scripture seem more familiar to a late-antique audience. It thus appeared perfectly plausible that Basil could be the latest figure in this biblical tradition.

Moreover, and although Gregory could point to few modern miracles as spectacular as the ascension of Elijah into heaven, the *Praise of Basil* made it clear that miracles at least comparable to those in the Bible did occur in the contemporary world. One such miracle is described in Gregory's account of Samuel, the fourth of his biblical exemplars, and a figure whose very birth he represents as 'a gift from God'.[106] This wondrous achievement is one that Basil could match in the present day: 'for just as the mother gave birth to the one as a result of a petition to God, so too was the other

---

[104] *In Bas.* 15 [*PG* 46: 804B–C].
[105] *In Bas.* 15 [*PG* 46: 804C]: 'whatever was heavy and earthly' was first transformed into 'the buoyant and light'.
[106] *In Bas.* 19 [*PG* 46: 808B].

conceived as a result of the father's petition to God'.[107] Although such miracles were not to be expected at every turn, even in the life of someone as impressive as Basil, they did continue to occur in late antiquity. Basil was a biblical figure, even down to the miracles that marked his life. Whether loosely re-enacted as in the case of Elijah, or repeated precisely as in the case of Samuel, Basil's actions situated him fully in the biblical tradition.

The other thing Basil and Samuel shared, for Gregory, was the possession of a divine mission. Basil's defeat of the Arian heresy was once again recognised as his allotted task, its magnitude guaranteeing the 'biblical proportions' with which Gregory consistently portrayed his brother.[108] Thus both Basil and Samuel endured sacrifices in the cause of defeating God's enemies: 'the one for the sake of the dissolution of heresies; the other for the expulsion of the Philistines'.[109] These actions were shown to be directly comparable, the latter a re-enactment of the former. They each took their place in the list of similar triumphs throughout the course of biblical history, and so established Basil as 'the man of God for his own generation'.[110] Basil had been appointed by God to continue the tradition of Samuel, which was similarly the tradition of Elijah, of John the Baptist and of Paul.

This sense of congruity between the Bible and the present day was essential if it were to be demonstrated that the same divine power acted in both. Thus Basil, it might be said, was never taken bodily up to heaven as Paul had been, at least according to his own account in 2 Corinthians.[111] But as in the case of Elijah, Gregory is unwilling to allow that miracles set the biblical world apart. Paul, he suggests, was more like Basil, a human being interpreting his religious experience. His bodily journey to heaven need not be believed to have taken place:

Clearly not even [Paul] received such a grace in this flesh of ours. For he does not conceal his doubt when he says 'Whether in the body, I know not, or out of the body, I know not: only God knows'. And somebody, becoming bold about it,

[107] *In Bas.* 19 [*PG* 46: 808B–C].   [108] Momigliano 1985a: 449.
[109] *In Bas.* 19 [*PG* 46: 808C–D].
[110] Harl 1984: 97, 'l'homme de Dieu de la génération actuelle'.
[111] *In Bas.* 12 [*PG* 46: 800D]; 2 Corinthians 12:1–13.

might say that not in the body did he see a thing of this kind, but . . . through the unembodied vision of the intellect.[112]

In such circumstances, Basil's re-enactment of Paul could easily be complete: for in his mind Basil had surely also had a glimpse of heaven. This 'de-mystification' of the scriptures suggests that the image of Basil in the oration was by no means 'theologised', but instead that he remained Gregory's brother throughout.[113] As in his *Life of Macrina*, Gregory continued to respect 'the convention' by which 'saints . . . must remain firmly in everyday life'.[114] Into that everyday life, however, he imported the world of the Bible. Scripture was accordingly 'de-mystified'. In effect, it was brought up to date.

The biblical Basil

The hagiographical literature of the fourth century AD 'abounds with comparisons between holy men and Moses', and the writings of Gregory of Nyssa were no exception.[115] Gregory had made use of Moses in previous works: thus, in his *Life of Gregory Thaumaturgus*, he had adopted the now familiar technique of comparing his namesake to a variety of biblical figures, and above all to the Jewish lawgiver himself. In fact, the elder Gregory is revealed to have imitated Moses in almost every aspect of his life, from his acquisition of 'Egyptian' wisdom and his subsequent retreat into solitude, to his return as a wonder-worker and as the undisputed leader of his people.[116] The identification was so close that ultimately 'the analogy vanished', and Gregory acknowledged that this third-century bishop 'became in our parts another Moses'.[117] Basil of Caesarea himself had also adopted this image, portraying Gregory Thaumaturgus as a Moses for his times.[118] Of course,

---

[112] *In Bas.* 12 [*PG* 46: 800D–801A]; quoting 2 Corinthians 12:3.
[113] Rousseau 1994: 89; cf. n. 65 above.   [114] Momigliano 1985a: 452–3.
[115] Rapp 2005: 126. The use of Moses as a model of leadership for bishops in general is discussed at Rapp 2005: 125–36, which builds on much of the material in Rapp 1998.
[116] *VGThaum.* [*PG* 46: 901C–D, 913B, 925D, 949A]; see Van Dam 1982: 278–9 and Sterk 1998: 236.
[117] *VGThaum.* [*PG* 46: 908C] (tr. Slusser); cf. Van Dam 1982: 279.
[118] Basil of Caesarea, *De spiritu sancto* 74; see Van Dam 1982: 284 and 304.

the two brothers claimed a family connection with Gregory Thaumaturgus. Yet if the elder Gregory was an important figure for the Cappadocian fathers, it is clear that Moses was no less significant. That significance is fully confirmed in the *Praise of Basil*.

The chiastic structure of Gregory's oration, which began with Abraham, should have meant that Gregory ended with him too. In fact, after his initial mention, Abraham would be ignored for the remainder of the speech. Gregory's last and longest comparison of Basil with his biblical predecessors would be focused instead on 'the great Moses . . . a common example for all those who look to virtue'.[119] By thus concluding with Moses and not with Abraham, Gregory seems to make clear that Moses is the most important link in his typological chain. It is the figure of Moses that lies behind all his other examples; his life is the origin and the culmination of the biblical life he describes. Basil is seen to have re-enacted Samuel, Elijah, John and Paul; and like them, he re-enacts Moses in his own fashion. The scriptural pattern of prefiguration and re-enactment, which ties together all of these figures, thus extends even outside the Bible. First Gregory Thaumaturgus, and then Basil, would become what Gregory hailed as 'a lawgiver for our own times', a modern Moses.[120]

That Moses could be imitated successfully by both Basil and the elder Gregory, along with his presentation in the *Praise of Basil* as the 'common example' of virtue, might suggest that Moses was considered a model available to be copied by all contemporary Christians. A more restrictive view, and perhaps a more warranted one, is to see Moses as a model for only the most spiritually expert. In particular, it has been proposed that Gregory's image of Moses established him as the paradigm of the late-antique bishop, or at least of the more ascetically inclined brand of bishop to be found in fourth-century Cappadocia.[121] Basil is taken to be the ideal contemporary model of Cappadocian bishop, and his proximity to the biblical image of Moses thus promotes a kind of 'episcopal

---

[119] *In Bas.* 20 [*PG* 46: 808D].   [120] Harl 1984: 78, quoting *In Bas.* 21 [*PG* 46: 809C].

[121] As noted, this (general) argument is the focus of Sterk 1998, strongly influenced by Harl 1984; a similar case is made in Sterk 2004 and Rapp 2005: 125–52.

ideology'.[122] Certainly there was a conventional model of episcopal authority, which the Cappadocian fathers themselves played
a prominent role in promoting; and Gregory of Nyssa's image of
Basil can be placed in this tradition.[123] Yet this is to ignore the
extent of Gregory's focus on Basil as an individual, and on the
many achievements and qualities that were specific to Basil himself. At no point in the *Praise of Basil* is the comparison extended
to any other contemporary churchman; nor is Moses put forward
in defence of the abstract requirements of the episcopate. In this
work at least, the correspondence with Moses is applied personally
to Basil of Caesarea.[124]

Together with the use of Moses in the *Life of Gregory Thaumaturgus*, the *Praise of Basil* in fact suggests a consistent understanding of Scripture with regard to specific historical figures.
Gregory seems to propose that re-enactments of Moses are constantly succeeding one another through time. This can be seen in
the succession of scriptural figures already set out in the *Praise of
Basil*, and elsewhere in the presentation of Gregory Thaumaturgus as the Moses of the third century. Basil, in turn, is compared
with Moses for the remainder of his brother's speech, and in a
manner quite distinct from the comparisons with biblical figures
earlier in the work. Where Basil's re-enactment of his biblical predecessors had previously been partial, and often with respect to
isolated events, with Moses, Gregory sets out 'to portray Basil as
in all points like him'.[125] Fittingly, there is even a change in the
kind of language used. There is no longer any suggestion that Basil
was merely 'comparable' to Moses, but instead that he specifically
're-enacted the lawgiver through his own life'.[126]

---

[122] Harl 1984: 71, 'il exprime une idéologie de l'épiscopat'; while for Sterk 1998: 234, the
In Bas. expresses 'a comprehensive view of episcopal leadership'.
[123] The biblical element here is brought out especially well in Rapp 2005: 125–36, with
reference to both the living examples of late-antique bishops such as Basil, and the more
theoretical approach of the Cappadocian fathers and other writers.
[124] It may incidentally have helped to justify the new phenomenon of the Cappadocian
'monk-bishop', as suggested at Sterk 1998: 234, but this requires a level of abstraction
not found in Gregory's work.
[125] Meredith 1997: 166.
[126] Harl 1984: 78; *In Bas.* 20: [PG 46: 808D: τὸν νομοθέτην ἐπὶ τοῦ βίου μιμούμενον].
Harl (1984: 78–9) goes on to discuss the meaning of the Greek term μίμησις, which in
Gregory's discussion of Basil and Moses replaces ὅμοιος – which was used in the earlier

What ensues is a full account of Basil's career, in which Gregory seeks to establish that the lives of Moses and Basil each possessed the same general outline. The connection is made clear from the very beginning of Gregory's account of Moses, who was brought up by his Egyptian foster mother (although his real mother was also present as a wet-nurse).[127] This is then associated with Basil's combination of Christian and secular education, 'for although nourished by pagan learning, he always clung to the bosom of the Church, strengthening and maturing his soul with its teachings'.[128] The Egyptian foster mother stands, perhaps allegorically, for pagan philosophy; at the same time, of course, she might represent the actual Egyptian learning with which the historical Moses was credited. In either case, Basil precisely re-enacts the historical example of Moses in the attitude he takes.

Like Moses, too, Basil would later be ashamed of this 'Egyptian' or pagan education, or so Gregory insists. This claim provides the excuse for the second major aspect in which his life re-enacts that of Moses. Gregory compares Basil's 'struggle against Egyptian learning' to Moses' murder of an Egyptian who had struck a Hebrew slave.[129] The subsequent exile from Egypt that Moses endured also has its counterpart, in Basil's adoption of an ascetic life on the family estate at Annesi:

Leaving Egypt after the death of the Egyptian, Moses spent much time living by himself in exile. In the same way, this one [Basil] left the turmoil of the city and the affairs of the world, and spent his time in the most secluded regions learning his philosophy with God.[130]

This period of exile is characteristic of comparisons with Moses, and in fact forms the second of 'les trois quarantaines' of the life of Moses, as it was understood in late antiquity.[131] The third of these

---

comparisons: see, for example, the start of *In Bas.* 15 [*PG* 46: 804B]. Her conclusion is that μίμησις or μῑμήσθαι are not equivalent to the French verb 'imiter', but are better translated as '"reproduire" – c'est à dire être une nouvelle réalisation du modèle' (78). I will follow Harl's example by translating μίμησις and its cognates with the English term 're-enactment'.

[127] *In Bas.* 20 [*PG* 46: 808D–809A]; cf. Exodus 2:1–10.   [128] *In Bas.* 20 [*PG* 46: 809A].
[129] *In Bas.* 20 [*PG* 46: 809A–B]; cf. Exodus 2:11–12.   [130] *In Bas.* 21 [*PG* 46: 809B–C].
[131] See Harl 1967 for an account of the familiar late-antique image of Moses; Rapp (2005: 132–6) gives an account of the conventional tripartite division of Moses' life in late antiquity, and identifies a number of literary uses of the model; the importance of the

three phases was, of course, his return as the leader and lawgiver of the Jewish people. In this respect, too, Gregory was able to portray his brother re-enacting the example of Moses: for just as Moses delivered his people from the Egyptian tyrant, so through his priesthood Basil ensured that his people 'were restored to the promise of God'.[132]

Gregory's broad account of the life of Moses, with its pattern of a foreign upbringing, a repudiation of that past and a retreat into exile, before a return as a charismatic and effective leader, thus provides a framework in which to situate a number of more specific correlations. Gregory therefore tells how:

what was invisible to others was made visible to him through his initiation into the mysteries of the spirit, so that he seemed to be inside the dark cloud within which the knowledge of God was to be found. Many times he arrayed himself against the Amalekites, using only prayer as his shield. And when he raised his hands, the true Jesus conquered his enemies. He put an end to the witchcraft of the many sorcerers of Balaam.[133]

By this stage, the respective lives of Moses and Basil no longer appear very distinct. Gregory is able to describe Basil almost entirely in terms re-appropriated from Moses, so that the actions he relates could as easily be thought to apply to one as to the other.[134] The mention of Jesus and the hint of personal experience suggest that the primary subject here was not Moses but Basil. Yet Gregory is no longer explicit about the modern-day equivalents of Balaam or the Amalekites: everything is re-enacted precisely, with no allowances made for the passage of time. Just as in the *Life of Gregory Thaumaturgus*, any element of analogy has vanished. Basil is presented unconditionally as the new Moses for his generation.

Indeed, although he announces that there are many other individual correspondences between the life of Moses and the life of Basil, Gregory repeatedly resolves to pass over them so as not to exhaust the patience of his audience.[135] As he explains,

element of exile in any comparison with Moses was earlier underlined at Rapp 1998: 289, noting that Athanasius identified with him during his own wanderings in the desert.
[132] *In Bas.* 21 [*PG* 46: 809C]; cf. Sterk 1998: 233.   [133] *In Bas.* 22 [*PG* 46: 812C].
[134] Cf. Harl 1984: 78, 'Grégoire substitue l'attribution à Basile des actes du modèle'.
[135] *In Bas.* 20, 22 [*PG* 46: 809B, 812D].

Why should we mention every individual incident, how many he too led through the water; to how many by his preaching he brought that pillar of fire, how many he saved by the cloud of the spirit; how many he fed with heavenly nourishment; how he imitated the rock, where once with a rod a spring of water was opened . . . [and] how he gave that water to the thirsty to drink?[136]

Much of this interpretation is borrowed from 1 Corinthians, in which Paul's contemporary Christian church is identified with the Israelites in the desert under the command of Moses.[137] Gregory takes this interpretation and re-applies it to Basil, making his brother a re-enactment not only of Moses, but also of the leaders of the early church. Basil, again, is portrayed as the latest in a long line of biblical figures – and, indeed, as a continuation of that divine patterning which tied together the Old and New Testaments.

For this passage of Paul's letters was much cited in late antiquity as a justification for the figural interpretation of Scripture.[138] In addition to arguing for the continued relevance of the events of the Old Testament to his modern church, Paul also provided an example of the manner in which the life of Moses anticipated Christ. Moses had struck a rock in the desert, and the rock had brought forth water. According to Paul, his followers 'all drank from the supernatural rock that accompanied their travels – and that rock was Christ'.[139] Basil, in turn, not only re-enacted Moses, but also imitated the rock itself, and 'gave that water to the thirsty to drink'.[140] In effect, through his connection with the story of Moses, Basil also re-enacted Christ. It was a continuing connection that can perhaps be seen in the respective deaths of the three figures. Christ's assumption into heaven was frequently seen to have been anticipated in the mysterious disappearance of Moses at his death.[141] For Gregory, Basil's death was remarkably similar:

[136] *In Bas.* 21 [*PG* 46: 809C–D].

[137] 1 Corinthians 10:1–22; the connection is noted by Harl 1984: 88.

[138] In particular 1 Corinthians 10:11: 'All these things that happened to them were symbolic, and were recorded for our benefit as a warning' [NEB]; cf. the account of figural exegesis in Clark 1999: 85–6.

[139] 1 Corinthians 10:4 [NEB].

[140] *In Bas.* 21 [*PG* 46: 809D]. The water may be a reference to Basil's administering of the sacrament of baptism, or else to his powers of oratory: cf. the suggestions of Harl 1984: 88.

[141] The references to Moses in Jude 9 seem to imply such a tradition, and other references exist to a lost parabiblical document on the *Assumption of Moses* – although it should not

for just as 'a tomb of Moses is not to be found, nor was [Basil] buried with any material lavishness'.[142]

The modern Moses

Gregory's *Praise of Basil* thus made use of Moses in particular as a way to present his brother as a modern-day biblical figure. But the portrayal of Basil as identical to Moses might also imply the reverse: that Moses can best be seen as a Basil-like figure who simply happened to inhabit the world of the Bible. For just as Gregory's *Praise of Basil* offers little to anchor his brother firmly in late antiquity, so his depiction of Moses in the same work is often free from any details that might bind him to Scripture. The ambiguity works both ways. Gregory's careful selection of those character traits that Moses and Basil can be shown to have shared provided his audience not only with a biblical Basil, but also with a remarkably late-antique Moses. Like Basil, then, this Moses is a powerful and charismatic leader of God's people, occupying a public role while combining it with both philosophical and spiritual wisdom.[143] Such a combination of authority and asceticism is a fundamental attribute of the idealised late-antique bishop: it was certainly on display in the likes of Basil of Caesarea.

Such a modern, 'episcopal' image of Moses was common to much Christian writing in late antiquity. The example of Moses could easily be raised in connection with any of the contemporary figures who seemed 'not only distinguished by their exemplary lives of piety, but who also occup[ied] positions of responsibility'.[144] That in effect meant bishops, and it was bishops who were most frequently identified as 'our Moses' or 'a new Moses'.[145]

---

be confused with an extant *Testament of Moses* which sometimes has it as an alternative title: for details, see Nickelsburg 1973.

[142] *In Bas.* 23 [*PG* 46: 812D–813A]; cf. the comparison of Moses and Antony at *VA* 92.2 (above, p. xx).

[143] As characterised by Harl 1984: 100; cf. Rapp 2005: 20, where Moses is 'the divinely appointed leader who proved himself worthy through his deeds to hold pragmatic authority over the people of Israel'.

[144] Rapp 2005: 127.

[145] Rapp 2005: 127–9, citing the examples of Ulfilas, Gregory Thaumaturgus, Jacob of Nisibis and Pope Sixtus; although she also notes exceptions that were made for emperors

Some late-antique bishops were also prepared to associate themselves with Moses, not least when the issue arose of the proper balance between religious and worldly power.[146] The constantly vexing issue of secular learning, too, made Moses an appropriate ancestor for many prominent bishops, and particularly for those in the Greek east who might hope to justify an apparently 'pagan' education.[147] It is unsurprising, then, that Moses should appear as a scriptural champion of the peculiar episcopal practices of many bishops in late-antique Cappadocia.[148] Yet Gregory of Nyssa seems to go beyond even this. He not only cites Moses in support of his portrayal of Basil in the *Praise of Basil*; he offers a full-length discussion of Moses' life which makes him into a suspiciously fourth-century figure.

At first sight, it might seem that the *Life of Moses* has very little in common with the *Praise of Basil*. Whereas, in the *Praise of Basil*, Moses is used as an historical example, in the *Life of Moses* he is conventionally seen as the figure of the spiritual man striving towards the vision of God.[149] The same image of Moses representing 'progress in perfection' or 'a pattern of accomplished virtue' has conventionally been seen as the guiding principle behind Gregory's use of Scripture in that work.[150] In effect, it is implied that the *Life of Moses* is a theological treatise disguised as a life. Yet the foundation of the work in the life of Moses is not merely a sustaining metaphor; it is not merely a device to help collect together Gregory's conclusions concerning abstract virtue. His *theoria* is grounded in history, and the *historia* set out in the first book is to be understood as 'absolutely reliable and trustworthy'.[151] The *Life of Moses* was intended to examine the lessons to be learned from

such as Constantine and (in the seventh century) Heraclius: Rapp 2005: 129–30, with Rapp 1998: 291.
[146] This tactic was used in the fifth century by Theophilus of Alexandria, but both John Chrysostom and Athanasius had also proved willing to associate themselves with Moses: see Rapp 2005: 127–9.
[147] Jaeger 1965: 134.
[148] The comparison was in fact a particular favourite of Gregory Nazianzus, who applied the example of Moses to Athanasius, to Basil and to his own father, Gregory the Elder. See Rapp 2005: 126–7.
[149] Harl 1984: 100, 'la type du spiritual "tendu" en avant vers la vision de Dieu'.
[150] Ferguson 1976; Jaeger 1965: 132.
[151] Bebis 1967: 374, characterising Gregory's own view of the *VMoys*.

actual scriptural events; and so, in addition to being a portrait of virtue, it was necessarily a portrait of Moses. Gregory's image of Moses' biblical life is thus everywhere on display.

This image, as might be expected, owed much to the conventions and commonplaces of late-antique spirituality. In some contrast to his portrayal in the Bible, Moses is made into a surprisingly deliberate figure, who takes a conspicuously active role in the direction of his fate.[152] A constant self-improver, Gregory's Moses has less in common with most biblical prophets – 'mere instruments possessed by the divine' – than he has with many late-antique holy men, those 'self-possessed arbiters, mediators who attempted to span the gap between God and his creatures'.[153] Similarly, his approach to intercessory prayer, and its evident effectiveness, is also much more the mark of a late-antique saint than it is of a biblical figure.[154] Even in the 'uninterpreted' first book of Gregory's *Life of Moses*, then, his image of the patriarch owes a great deal to contemporary incarnations of the holy. Like the Moses of the *Praise of Basil*, and indeed like Basil himself, the hero of the *Life of Moses* 'has been transformed into a fine expression of early Byzantine piety'.[155]

Gregory clearly conceived of Moses as a remarkably modern figure; and it is perhaps not unreasonable to suggest that he had a particular modern figure in mind. This indeed was a technique he had used before, in writing his early treatise *On Virginity*, in which an ideal life of asceticism is presented in the final chapter in ostensibly impersonal terms.[156] In the prefatory letter that he provided for the work, however, Gregory makes clear that he was

---

[152] Compare, for example, Gregory's account of Moses' voluntary choice of exile at *VMoys.* 1.19 – 'he made this rejection the occasion for a greater philosophy' – with the laconic account of the same event at Exodus 2:15 – 'Moses fled from the face of Pharaoh, and dwelt in the land of Midian' [AV]. Such a view of Moses, of course, might fit very well with the idea of 'perpetual progress' at *VMoys.* 4–10.

[153] Satran 1995: 102 – although his contrast is perhaps somewhat overplayed.

[154] Compare the way God responds to a direct prayer in *VMoys.* 1.29 with his unsolicited intervention at Exodus 14:13–16; Satran (1995: 103) notes that formal intercession was characteristic of miracles in the later Roman empire (although without explicitly discussing Gregory's work).

[155] Satran 1995: 96. Satran is referring primarily to the story of Daniel and Nebuchadnezzar, as told in the Byzantine compilation of the *Lives of the Prophets* 4.4–13; but his point here may be understood as having a general application.

[156] Gregory of Nyssa, *De virginitate* 23.

intending to describe an actual person – his brother Basil.[157] The life of the 'historical' Moses fulfils a similar exemplary function in Gregory's *Life of Moses*, representing the model of the virtuous life, and it is at least possible that there too he had Basil in mind. Gregory offers his readers a vision of Moses 'as he surely never was', shaping and perhaps distorting the image with his 'narrative simplifications and theoretical expansions', and much of the interest in the work is in analysing the Moses who remains.[158] But as a result of this reshaping, the *Life of Moses* turns out to share much with the earlier image of Moses in the *Praise of Basil*, which was explicitly structured according to Gregory's perception of his brother. Admittedly Basil, when he appears at all in the *Life of Moses*, only appears at one remove; but it is possible to see his influence in Gregory's selection of events and interpretations. The same parallels as were found in the *Praise of Basil* are returned to in the *Life of Moses*; and other events in the two lives are united by their sharing in a single meaning.

Hence, in the *Life of Moses*, the shape of Moses' life is characterised by the same three conventional phases: his Egyptian education, his flight into the wilderness and his return as a leader and lawgiver.[159] Gregory sets out distinctly what he regards as the key events within this story, each of which also had a prominent place in the speech on his brother: the birth and upbringing of Moses; his murder of an Egyptian overseer and his subsequent flight; and the appearance of God in the form of a burning bush.[160] The long and complex process of negotiating freedom for the Israelites is then dealt with in the *Life of Moses* in a notably brief account – expanded, although not to any significant effect, from the unadorned statement in the oration that Moses 'saved his people, delivering them from tyranny'.[161] Moses' later role as the leader of his people in the wilderness then receives rather more attention, and again the most prominent episodes in this section can be found in the earlier speech on Basil: the two pillars of cloud and fire; the

[157] Gregory of Nyssa, *De virginitate* pref.; see also Jaeger 1965: 133.
[158] Burrus 2000: 123–4, with subsequent analysis of Gregory's image of Moses.
[159] Rapp 2005: 132–3; see Harl 1967 for the application of this idea throughout the *VMoys*.
[160] *VMoys*. 1.16–21; *In Bas*. 20–1 [*PG* 46: 809B–C].
[161] *VMoys*. 1.22–9, taking in the appearance of Aaron, the plagues of Egypt and the Passover; the parallel quoted here is from *In Bas*. 21 [*PG* 46: 809C].

provision of manna from heaven; the war with the Amalekites, in which victory was assured through Moses raising up his hands; and his victory over the sorcery of Balaam.[162] Finally, Gregory ends his *historia* of Moses soon after with his death and burial, and with his lack of a monument, just where he had previously ended the comparison with Basil.[163]

The account in the *Life of Moses* thus provides a picture of the patriarch's life which meshes in all its essential details with that in Gregory's speech on his brother. In the *Life of Moses* these events are dealt with at greater length, as is only to be expected given the title and the nature of the work. Indeed, in the speech he repeatedly pleaded a lack of time, and left a number of things 'to the more diligent to apply in a figurative sense to our teacher' – and the *Life of Moses* itself can perhaps be considered an instance of this more expanded discussion.[164] In any case, Gregory is able to go into more detail on issues that he has dealt with elsewhere in relation to Basil, and in many cases his interpretation only confirms that the parallel is a relevant and significant one. Thus when he returns to his understanding of the Egyptian foster mother of Moses as a figure for secular education, he notes again that she was 'barren' and therefore in modern terms is 'rightly perceived as profane philosophy'.[165] As before, the 'natural mother' is understood as the church, and so Gregory concludes that 'if we should be involved with profane teachings during our education, we should not separate ourselves from the nourishment of the Church's milk'.[166] This was precisely the lesson encapsulated in Gregory's application of the passage to the life of Basil, who 'though nourished by pagan learning . . . always clung to the bosom of the Church'.[167]

Similarly, in the *Praise of Basil* Gregory had explained how his brother's training in such matters could even add to the riches of the church. The construction of the ark of the covenant is there seen to have been re-enacted by Basil in the form of his sermons to his congregation: for 'by his preaching he made the soul of each a

---

[162] *VMoys.* 1.30–5; 1.36–8; 1.39–40; 1.73–4; cf. *In Bas.* 21, 22 [PG 46: 812B–C].
[163] *VMoys.* 1.75; cf. *In Bas.* 23 [PG 46: 812D–813A].
[164] *In Bas.* 22 [PG 46: 812C]. 'Figurative' is Stein's translation of τροπικήν; perhaps 'tropological' would be closer, but that term has acquired a technical meaning that would be distracting here.
[165] *VMoys.* 2.10.   [166] *VMoys.* 2.12.   [167] *In Bas.* 20 [PG 46: 809A]; cf. n. 127, above.

true tabernacle to be inhabited by God'.[168] The same comparison is further extended as Gregory suggests that the gold and the jewels with which Moses adorned his tabernacle should be understood as referring to the particular brilliance of Basil's wisdom and oratory. In the *Life of Moses*, again, he expands on this interpretation, noting that the gold and jewels had been plundered from Egypt, and that they were brought to Moses as gifts from the people to be re-used for good effect on the ark. The association of Egypt with secular education seems to bring Basil to mind again, for as Gregory says:

It is possible to see this happening even now. For many bring to the Church their profane learning as a kind of gift. Such a man was the great Basil, who acquired the Egyptian wealth in every respect during his youth and dedicated this wealth to God for the adornment of the Church, the true tabernacle.[169]

Here Gregory interprets the historical events of the life of Moses in allegorical fashion – with the Egyptian gold standing in for secular learning – but does so in order to identify a parallel historical example from the present day. The lesson of the *Life of Moses* is made relevant to the contemporary world of the later Roman empire not through a philosophical image of the Christian soul, but through the identification of a modern Moses in the form of Basil. This is the answer to the perplexing question of how one might imitate a biblical patriarch: one must seek not to imitate Moses directly, but to learn to recognise his modern equivalent.

The evident affinity between Moses and Basil binds the two of them into a common history which exhibits a common range of meanings. Again in the *Life of Moses*, the passage of the Israelites through the Red Sea is understood as a figure for baptism, just as in the *Praise of Basil* it had been invoked as the precedent for those baptised by Basil, those whom he had personally 'led through the water'.[170] The connection between the parting of the Red Sea and the sacrament of baptism is a familiar and conventional one; but its importance here is that the Old Testament event does not merely refer to baptism in general but to a particular historical example of baptism. In effect, Gregory links two historical events by reference to a broader meaning that they both share, so that a

---

[168] *In Bas.* 21 [*PG* 46: 809D–812A]. [169] *VMoys.* 2.116.
[170] *In Bas.* 21 [*PG* 46: 809D]; cf. *VMoys.* 125.

spiritual or allegorical implication is not an end in itself, but the means by which to link the world of the Bible with the world of late antiquity. This manner of interpretation was of the same sort as used in Scripture itself, as when Paul in 1 Corinthians brought together the historical act of Moses striking the rock in the desert with the historical Incarnation of Christ.[171] Just as this claim served to emphasise the continuity of the biblical tradition across the Old and New Testaments, so too did Gregory's interpretations seek to incorporate the contemporary world into that tradition. The actions of Moses could be seen re-enacted by Christ in the gospels, and by Basil in the present day.

Thus it was important that events in the lives of Moses and Basil should be seen to share more than merely an accidental similarity; that instead they should reveal the same essential truth, and should testify to the continuing active intervention of God in the world. The incident of the burning bush, for example, is understood by Gregory as a miraculous light, appearing from nowhere as an 'ineffable and mysterious illumination'.[172] In the *Praise of Basil*, Gregory had related a superficially similar occasion:

When it was night there came upon him [Basil] praying in the house the glow of a light; and that light was something immaterial, illuminating his room by divine power, suspended from no material thing.[173]

For both Moses and Basil, this visitation was a real and historical event. The justification for linking them together, however, comes in Gregory's interpretation of this light in each case as representing 'knowledge of the truth', so that for Basil in particular it referred to the power he possessed of 'lighting up the secrets of the soul with his preaching'.[174] Basil, like Moses, was the recipient of this divine wisdom and authority; the shared significance of events in their lives helped establish them as not only similar but historically parallel figures.

Moses' later experience of the divine is, as Gregory points out, precisely the opposite of his first: for at Mount Sinai, God appeared to Moses shrouded in darkness.[175] This, too, is presented in

---

[171] *VMoys.* 136; cf. *In Bas.* 21 [*PG* 46: 809D] and 1 Corinthians 10:1–22.
[172] *VMoys.* 2.19.   [173] *In Bas.* 21 [*PG* 46: 809C].
[174] *VMoys.* 2.22; *In Bas.* 21 [*PG* 46: 812A].   [175] *VMoys.* 2.162; cf. Exodus 19:16–20.

allegorical terms in the second book of the *Life of Moses*, with darkness standing for the obscurity within which the greatest secrets of Christianity are hidden:

When, therefore, Moses grew in knowledge, he declared that he had seen God in the darkness, that is, that he had then come to know that what is divine is beyond all knowledge and comprehension.[176]

Yet this interpretation is hardly justified by the Old Testament account of the event; it was, by contrast, very popular among the Cappadocian fathers.[177] Gregory, indeed, had pictured the intellectual achievements of his elder brother through the use of the very same figure:

Many times we perceived that he also was in the dark cloud wherein was God. For what was invisible to others was made visible to him through his initiation into the mysteries of the spirit, so that he seemed to be inside the dark cloud within which the knowledge of God was to be found.[178]

Basil's 'dark cloud' was a metaphorical one, a poor imitation perhaps of Moses' theophany. But it might be best in this case to understand the relationship in reverse. Moses, for Gregory, was a thinker who had penetrated to the darkness at the heart of Christianity and had reached the same conclusions as the Cappadocians.

It is in this company that this 'theologised' and theologising Moses belongs: he was perhaps to be considered less as a model for Basil, and more as a projection of Basil and his concerns into the distant biblical past. The connection between the late-antique bishop and the biblical patriarch not only gave Basil an outstanding biblical pedigree: it also brought Moses into the modern world. The 'spiritual link' forged between Scripture and the world of late antiquity came to mean that biblical figures such as Moses were imagined in remarkably contemporary terms: so that the Moses that Gregory describes seems remarkably late antique in his ideas and attitudes.[179] Thus the dynamic of prefiguration and re-enactment was not simply limited to late-antique figures re-enacting a biblical model, but could be extended to include the recreation of a biblical

---

[176] *VMoys.* 2.164.
[177] For the popularity of this kind of theology, especially in Cappadocia, see e.g. Mortley 1986.
[178] *In Bas.* 22 [*PG* 46: 812C] .   [179] For further examples, see Satran 1995: 105.

model in terms appropriate to late-antique piety. The subject in this case was the life of Moses, but the model was provided by Basil: thus 'the roles reverse and the wheel comes full circle'.[180] The world of late antiquity had now become the basis for imagining the world of the Bible.

Beyond the Bible

In spite of Gregory of Nyssa's notorious fondness for allegorical techniques and 'mystical' theology, then, his work seems to recognise that one of the most common and even natural modes of scriptural interpretation was the use of typology. It seems clear that his twinned images of Moses and Basil make use of a broadly typological understanding of Scripture; or rather, that they imply the existence of a unified Christian history in both the biblical and the post-biblical world. In this sense, Gregory's interpretation of his own world in his biographical writings presents a picture compatible with that presented in Eusebius' *Life of Constantine*: in this case, one in which figures rather less grand than the emperor could also be understood as reviving the biblical past. Like that of Eusebius, Gregory's portrayal of contemporary events implied that the Christian God continued to be an active presence in the world; that matters in the modern world continued to follow the patterns and conventions that governed the world of the scriptures; and that lives in the later Roman empire could be recognised as belonging to an ongoing grand Christian narrative.

But interpretation of the world, and of texts which described the world, was not the sole province of bishops and theologians. An audience of Christians did not have always to be told how to interpret an oration or a biography; and at times, a reader's interpretation might outstrip the direct intentions of the author. The implications of a redescription of the world such as appears in Gregory's works, then, were perhaps not limited to the carefully cultivated parallel between Moses and Basil. For where an emperor – and Constantine in particular – was virtually by definition a special case, a man such as Basil had a congregation, a network of

[180] Wilson 1988: 126.

social relationships, friends and family. If he was to be recognised as a biblical figure who yet inhabited the contemporary world, then so too might anyone in late antiquity. The power of such an interpretation is that in reassessing Basil's relationship with his immediate context, it must necessarily force a new examination of the context in which he had lived. This was a portrayal which could rebound on the biographer. If Basil was a new Moses, then it was only natural to speculate on the status of Gregory himself.

The hint of such a concern can be seen in Gregory's portrayal in these biographical works of Moses' brother, Aaron. Aaron is never mentioned in the *Praise of Basil*, although in many similar contexts a typological discussion of Moses would often include him.[181] It is possible to see Gregory's reluctance to talk about Aaron as a parallel to his unwillingness to talk about Basil's family – perhaps the result of a wish to see each of these two central figures in stark relief, without distractions. There might indeed be other reasons: Aaron was, after all, a compromised example in much of the Bible: and he was almost irrevocably tainted by his prominent role in building and worshipping the golden calf.[182] Yet the exclusion of Gregory himself from his account of Basil, and Aaron from his account of Moses, are each prominent enough to perhaps warrant some other explanation. For it is certainly possible that in inviting a connection between Moses and Basil, Gregory ran the risk of having himself identified with Aaron. Moses' brother could be safely avoided in the brief account in the *Praise of Basil*, but necessarily had a role in the *Life of Moses*. In his brief appearance there, we can perhaps see an author resisting – or at least seeking to control – the application of typology to himself.

It is easy to imagine that an identification of Gregory with Aaron might have caused a genuine problem. In addition to his role in the worship of idols, at which Moses himself intervened to save his brother from the wrath of God, Aaron returned to ill-considered ways when he fell to envying Moses.[183] Once again Aaron was

---

[181] Aaron is placed alongside Moses in the funeral oration on Basil by Gregory of Nazianzus, and he is a central figure in much traditional typology: see Harl 1984: 82–4, and Rapp 2005: 131–2.

[182] See esp. Exodus 31; cf. Harl 1984: 83, who suggests this reason for his absence from the *In Bas.*

[183] Exodus 32: 30–5; Numbers 12; cf. *VMoys.* I.62.

saved only by the intercession of his brother, and in the *Life of Moses*, Gregory focuses his account of the incident on this magnanimity on Moses' part.[184] Yet this occasion might have possessed a deeper significance than Gregory here suggests. In the past he had used the same example of the enviousness of Aaron (and of Aaron's sister Miriam) in an account of his own 'personal difficulties'.[185] He was, then, aware that a potential parallel existed in the story of Moses and Aaron, and that it would not work entirely in his favour. If he were to insist on connecting Moses with Basil, then his most likely supporting role would be as Basil's frequently incompetent brother. This was a position Gregory had allotted himself already in his own *Life of Macrina*, as when he reports her affirmation that he was unworthy of his achievements and that 'you have little or no ability within yourself for such success'.[186] This kind of relationship would be all too easy for Gregory, or his audience, to map on to the biblical model of Moses and Aaron.

It is therefore notable that when Aaron is mentioned in the *Life of Moses* Gregory makes no attempt to gloss over his various misdeeds. Instead, he takes care to recount them, and in most cases to adopt a broadly positive interpretation. Thus, in describing the first meeting with Aaron in Exodus, he casts Moses' brother as an angel appointed by God to help him.[187] He is aware that this is an unusually optimistic view: '[f]or someone will say . . . that it is not right to see Aaron, who led the Israelites in the worship of idols, as a type of the angel'.[188] His immediate answer is that angels, like brothers, can be good or bad – although this seems a rather unsatisfactory explanation.[189] Some anxiety clearly remains, and Gregory promises to return to the problem at the next mention of Aaron.[190] This he does, and once again he emphasises the potentially ambiguous connotations of the word 'brother', so that 'in the one case the person killing the Egyptian tyrant is the brother; in another it is the one fashioning the idol for the Israelites'.[191] This is

[184] *VMoys.* 2.256–63.
[185] Gregory of Nyssa, *De castigatione* [PG 46: 316 A–C]; cf. Malherbe and Ferguson 1978: 189 n. 374.
[186] *VMac.* 21.   [187] *VMoys.* 2.42–6.   [188] *VMoys.* 2.51.   [189] *VMoys.* 2.53.
[190] *VMoys.* 2.54; 2.210.   [191] *VMoys.* 2.210.

no more a solution than before: not least because Aaron furnishes the example for both the good brother and the bad.

A more considered response, however, had already been given as part of Gregory's account of his exegetical approach; and indeed, it had been given specifically 'concerning the interpretation of Aaron'.[192] Instead of defending the actions of Aaron, Gregory allowed that they might seem unworthy. He hoped, however, that these less agreeable acts could be ignored. The rule is a simple one:

[If] someone should somehow discover something in the account which does not coincide with our understanding, he should not reject the whole enterprise. He should always keep in mind our discussion's goal . . . [For] we have already said in our prologue that the lives of honoured men would be set forth as a pattern of virtue for those who come after them.[193]

Gregory, in effect, is ruling out any interpretation that does not lead to virtue. The misdeeds of Aaron are not to be considered significant; or rather, if understood correctly they would no longer be recognised as misdeeds. Once again, Gregory is attempting to deal with the issue of imitation as it was raised in the preface to the *Life of Moses*, in which he acknowledges the gap between the incidental details of contemporary life and of the biblical world. The search for parallels cannot depend, for Gregory, on the mere accidental repetition of situations and circumstances. Basil is to be identified with Moses because their two lives tend towards the same meaning – towards a meaning which establishes the continuing presence of God. In the same way, the similarity in situation between Aaron and Gregory is no proof of a significant connection. If the pattern has no positive divine meaning, then it is not a pattern at all.

Thus it is the potential identification of himself with Aaron which repeatedly prompts Gregory to discuss and defend his exegetical approach. Whereas in the *Praise of Basil* he was willing to allow his audience to draw their own conclusions about the relevance of the life of Moses – leaving it 'to the more diligent to apply in a figurative sense to our teacher' – yet in the *Life of Moses* each mention of

[192] *VMoys.* 2.51.   [193] *VMoys.* 2.48.

Aaron is provided with a caveat.[194] Gregory seems to have been very aware of the possibility of an unwarranted typological reading, and indeed, it might be said, of the temptations of typology. He certainly seems to betray his anxiety at the ways in which his work might be read, and in particular a concern that his readers might apply the techniques he had demonstrated to persons and events beyond those he had chosen. But if such a lack of control over the meanings of one's work is a source of anxiety for an author, it is at the same time a testimony not only to the freedom of the reader but to the ideas contained in the text. Gregory had established in detail the possibility of understanding Basil and Moses as counterparts in the ongoing grand Christian narrative. It was perhaps inevitable that, once applied to Basil, the same process would be applied to others in the same world – and as part of that process, to Gregory himself. Despite the instruction to only apply typology to positive examples, the *Life of Moses* will certainly permit – indeed, it might be said to *invite* – such a reading.

In these circumstances it is reassuring, and presumably not accidental, that Gregory's last mention of Aaron provides something of a happy ending. The Israelites had revolted against the authority of Moses and Aaron, and had demanded proof that the priesthood was in the right hands.[195] The test that Moses devised was to demand a wooden rod from every man who considered himself a priest.

Moses placed the rods before the sanctuary, and by them he made God's choice concerning the priesthood clear to the people. Aaron's rod alone budded and produced ripe fruit from the wood – and the fruit was the almond.[196]

Even after his misadventures, Aaron's priesthood was justified directly from above. This at last is a positive example with which Gregory might be associated – and indeed, one which might be taken to be directly relevant to his own situation. With Aaron having gained God's approval he was no longer dependent on his brother's support for his position; he could step out of his shadow, and come to serve in late antiquity as the model of a capable priest.[197] In

[194] *In Bas.* 22 [*PG* 46: 812C]; cf. *VMoys.* 2.48–9, 2.210.
[195] Numbers 16:3; cf. *VMoys.* 1.69–71.   [196] *VMoys.* 1.70.
[197] Rapp 2005: 131–2, who notes that in the western empire Aaron in fact took over from Moses as the model for a bishop; cf. also the use of Aaron in Eusebius, *HE* 10.4.23.

the same way, it should not be forgotten that Aaron was initially appointed as an authentic and eloquent spokesman for his powerful brother.[198] If the re-enactment of Scripture was in the end to expand beyond the author's control, to become more than a rhetorical exercise and affect the late-antique understanding of the contemporary world, then Gregory had at least provided the materials for what might come to represent his own biblical life.

[198] Exodus 4: 14–16.

3

ANTONY AND JEROME: LIFE ON THE EDGE

If *monachoi*, why are they so many? And if so many, how can they be *monachoi*?
O multitude of monks, that makes a mock of monachism!

('Palladas', in the *Greek Anthology* 11.384)

The example of Moses in particular was, as we have seen, very useful for those authors who wished to portray an authentic and powerful Christian leader – whether in the person of an emperor such as Constantine, or a bishop such as Basil of Caesarea. The lives of these heroic individuals were evidence that the age of the patriarchs had been revived in the world of late antiquity, and that the heroes of Scripture had their parallels in certain prominent Christian figures in the modern world. In addition, these biographies showed that the same patterns of significant events could be recognised in the contemporary world as in the Old and New Testaments, and could be provided with a similar set of meanings. When Constantine was envisioned as watching over the world from his place in heaven, then, or when Basil was seen to have received the kind of divine illumination previously granted to Moses, the links between events and interpretations served to reaffirm the continuation of sacred history from its origins in Scripture down to the present day. Christian biographies of prominent figures thus united the contemporary world with the Bible in an ongoing grand Christian narrative, in which the divine presence could be recognised and understood just as it was in the lives of the prophets and apostles.

Yet the influence of this view of the world extended far beyond the central characters of these works and came to affect the supporting cast. A bishop such as Basil had family and friends, and allies and supporters, and was heavily involved in the difficulties and disputes that characterised late-antique religious and political life. It was therefore perhaps inevitable that a reassessment of Basil would require a similar reassessment of the roles of his closest companions – and that a typological relationship between Basil and Moses might further imply, for example, a connection between Aaron and Gregory of Nyssa. Despite the efforts of Gregory to exclude himself and his brothers and sisters from the scene in the *Praise of Basil*, and despite the intrinsic bias of a biography towards representing an individual life in isolation, it was scarcely possible to render a late-antique bishop apart from his context. The portrayal of Moses as a late-antique personality made the biblical world seem more familiar; in the same way, to make Basil a biblical figure was to make his world more like the Bible.

These portrayals of Constantine and Basil thus implied a broader, more biblical world of which they represented only a part. That world, however, was already being filled out by the time Gregory of Nyssa came to write his biographies: for since the *Life of Constantine*, and perhaps directly influenced by that work, there had been an explosion in the number of Christian biographies written, circulated and read in the Roman empire. In the tradition inaugurated by the *Life of Antony*, these lives were those of ordinary men and women more commonly than of significant political figures; they were lives which would have remained obscure had they not been transfigured by the parallels they presented with Scripture, and by the proofs they thereby presented of the continuing active presence of God in the world.[1] These lives often took place on the margins of society: in social terms, among the poor and dispossessed, or among those who deliberately abandoned a high social position; and often also literally, as so many of them began in, or

---

[1] There is a vast bibliography on questions of the lives and biographies of holy men, although these are not always maintained as separate concerns. Much of the modern work takes inspiration from Brown 1971, and the concerns raised in that paper can be traced throughout such later contributions as Brown 1981, 1983, 1989 and 1995; explicit reflections on that tradition may be found in Brown *et al.* 1997 and Brown 1998, and in the collection by Hayward and Howard-Johnstone 1999, all of which contain additional bibliography. Recent works engaging with texts and issues additional to those founded in Brown's approach to late antiquity include A. G. Elliott 1987, Heffernan 1988, Noble and Head 1995 and Wyschogrod 1999; and on Egyptian monasticism especially see Gould 1993, Rousseau 1999 and Goehring 1999. More general issues relating to asceticism in antiquity and beyond are investigated in Rousseau 1978 and in the essays at Wimbush and Valantasis 2002.

retreated to, the edges of the civilised world, to the deserts or the wilderness of Egypt and Syria.[2] The contemporary world was thus rapidly populated with these new, remarkably biblical figures.

At first these saints and ascetics perhaps represented an alternative to the mainstream of late-antique life; but very soon they came to exert an influence on the familiar everyday world. This was increasingly true in the stories told in the biographies themselves, in which these strangers no longer confined themselves to the deserts but began to interfere in villages, and soon larger towns and cities. And it was true also of the way in which these biographies must have come to affect understanding of the world – often an educated, urbanised world – shared by the author and the reader.[3] The interpretation of modern life in the light of the Bible could not be confined to the text: as with Gregory's portrayal of Basil and Moses, it could be extended to the author and beyond. Thus when the (supposed) author of the *Life of Antony* appears in his own text, or when Antony himself appears in subsequent lives, or when in the *Life of Hilarion* the hero visits Sicily and Epidaurus, and finally settles in Cyprus – in all of these cases the contemporary world of the reader is re-imagined. And for authors and readers alike, re-imagining the world meant having to reconsider one's own place in it.

Rejecting the world

The *Life of Antony*, then, offered a Christian hero who opposed his way of life to the world. But whereas in previous centuries such a figure was likely to end up a martyr – and although Antony, who

[2] The ideological power of this 'awesome antithesis' between the city and the marginal areas of wilderness and desert is brought out most strongly in the works of Peter Brown, with the fullest account at Brown 1989: 213–24, reiterated in Brown 2004: 173–4; Markus (1990: 181–98) prefers to focus instead on the blurring of these strict boundaries, a project taken up throughout Goehring 1999, especially with regard to those texts relating to Pachomian monasticism in Egypt.

[3] For a discussion of the audience for Christian biography, see esp. Coon (1997: 5–13), who notes that while hagiographies from the fifth century onwards were often aimed at lower class and even illiterate Christians, fourth-century works seem to have a more 'patrician' bias. The clearest example of a work 'addressed to a public of educated Christians' is perhaps that of Jerome's *Life of Paul*: thus Rebenich 2000a: 25.

is said to have lived through the Great Persecution, at times anticipates this fate for himself – in the new world of the fourth century
AD his power lies in his ability to live out his life in the manner he
chooses.[4] Thus the hero of the *Life of Antony* was not an emperor
or a bishop, but an ordinary Christian made extraordinary precisely
by his decision to reject the concerns of the contemporary world.
And yet one of the most interesting aspects of the *Life of Antony* is
its refusal to conform to what might seem to be the most 'natural'
model for such a life: where it might be expected to record a solitary
and independent life, untouched by imperial and ecclesiastical, and
focusing on the holy man's actions and events, instead it goes into
extraordinary detail concerning Antony's opinions and interventions in theological and political matters in Egypt and beyond. The
Life of Antony thus betrays a persistent interest in problems such as
the Arian heresy, or the survival of pagan practices in rural areas:
concerns which seem rather more characteristic of the agenda of
a metropolitan bishop.[5] In particular, it seems possible to relate
the *Life of Antony* closely to the positions and policies of the often
controversial bishop Athanasius of Alexandria.[6]

For the coming of a Christian empire had not put an end to bitter
disputes between the secular and ecclesiastical authorities: indeed,
to construct either an emperor or a bishop in the image of Moses,
for example, was often merely to add the weight of Scripture to
the claim of one or the other to primacy in religious affairs.[7] Disputes between a Christian bishop and a Christian emperor have
rarely been so charged and so vocal as in the years following the
death of Constantine and the accession of his son Constantius II,
when opposition to the new emperor was led by Athanasius – himself to be subsequently portrayed by the Cappadocians as a latter-
day Moses.[8] Athanasius clung to his title as Bishop of Alexandria

[4] *VA* 46. Translations of this text are taken from Vivian and Athanassakis 2003 except
where noted.
[5] The most obtrusive examples may be found at *VA* 69, 81, 80–91.
[6] The most important recent accounts of Athanasius may be found in Barnes 1993 and
Brakke 1995, supplemented by Pettersen 1995 and Anatolios 2004.
[7] Once again, these aspects of the relationship, from the point of view of the bishop in
particular, are discussed in Rapp 2005: 100–52.
[8] Gregory of Nazianzus, *Oration* 21; see the remarks at Norris 2000: 145–6, and at Rapp
2005: 126–7.

despite long periods of struggle and exile, and was a tireless pro-pagandist in his own cause. Indeed, he has been accused of being something of a fabulist, eager to create and recreate his image in the most romantic and flattering terms, and to represent – or mis-represent – as his allies the most powerful and prestigious figures of his time.[9] One of these, it would seem, was the Egyptian monk Antony, famous as the author of a series of pastoral letters but above all as the hero of a Greek *Life of Antony*, dating from soon after AD 357.[10] Within twenty years Athanasius was established as the author – and although that attribution has remained controversial, and it has been suggested that the Greek text is itself a translation or adaptation of a pre-existing Coptic account, it seems reasonable to accept that Athanasius is at the very least a realistic candidate for authorship of the life.[11]

Thus whether the *Life of Antony* was written or rewritten by Athanasius himself, or merely 'by someone with intimate knowl-edge of his concerns', it is important to recognise that it must often be treated as being 'more an expression of [the author's] own views than a thoroughly reliable souce for information about the real Antony'.[12] Certainly the text of the *Life of Antony* as we have it continually assigns a surprisingly important place in the narrative

---

[9] This is the central contention of Barnes 1993: esp. 1–3, thus 'Athanasius consistently misrepresented central facts about his ecclesiastical career'.

[10] For Antony's letters see Chitty 1975 and the new translation with commentary at Ruben-son 1995; their significance is assessed at Gould 1993. For the date of the Greek version of the *Life of Antony*, see Gregg 1980: 2.

[11] It is attributed to Athanasius in manuscripts of the Latin translation of 374 (by Evagrius of Antioch), and also by Gregory of Nazianzus in his oration of 380, and by Jerome, *De uir. ill.* in 392. The case for a Coptic original is made in its most developed form in Barnes 1986, and is disputed most strongly in Brakke 1994a and 1994b; the balanced discussion at Rousseau (2000: 100–6) refuses to rule it out completely. Although an earlier Coptic account would have obvious implications for the idea that the work was composed by the Greek-speaking Athanasius, it would still be possible to assign him a significant role in translating or adapting it into Greek: see Louth 1988. Ultimately the attribution depends on the fourth-century evidence; attempts to identify parallels with other Athanasian writings are found wanting by Rousseau (2000: 101–2), who prefers to remain sceptical. The majority position in favour of Athanasian authorship may be found expressed most clearly in Bartelink 1994 and Brakke 1995.

[12] Cameron 2000: 85; Brakke 1995: 201. This point is made into a general expression of caution in Brown 1995: 57–78, where part of the object is to correct a perceived failure in earlier work to see the holy man in his social and historical context – one in which the interests of the author of his biography might come to overshadow the social realities of a holy man's daily activities.

to Athanasius and the metropolitan clergy of Alexandria; and it has been argued that the *Life* can usefully be understood as serving less as the inspirational life of a desert ascetic than as a 'tool for achieving political unity within the Egyptian church'.[13] The heading given in the prefatory letter of the *Life* in Evagrius' translation – 'Bishop Athanasius to the monks abroad' – thus seems to make Alexandria the place of composition, although perhaps only on the basis of the reference in the text to the approaching end of the sailing season.[14] The emphasis, too, given to Antony's two visits to Alexandria, on the occasion of the death of Bishop Peter and during a dispute with the Arians, seems to imply a close connection to the Alexandrian church; and the narrator is here established as both an intimate of Antony and a partisan of the Athanasian faction by the use of the first person which, excluding the preface, appears only in these two passages.[15] Antony and Athanasius are hereby discovered to be on the same side in these vital matters: the unity and the authority of the Egyptian church is on display to the monks abroad, and to any other readers of the text.[16]

The unity of the two traditions of Athanasius and Antony appears clearest of all in a coy third-person reference in the account of Antony's death. The monk is found to have divided his few possessions between two local disciples – who receive his hair shirt – and between two bishops: Serapion of Thmuis, who receives a sheepskin, and Athanasius, who receives both a sheepskin and a 'worn cloak' which he had originally given to Antony.[17] At this point the narrator seems to be expressing his own delight at the gifts:

---

[13] This argument is made at Brakke 1995: 264, where it is placed in the context of a broader engagement with 'the politics of asceticism' on the part of Athanasius; a comparable approach to the text, although without considering Athanasius as the author, is advocated in Rousseau 2000: 100–6. A continued emphasis on the literary and rhetorical aspects of late-antique asceticism is also on display in Brakke 2006 and in the papers collected in Brakke, Satlow and Weitzmann 2005.

[14] *VA* pref 1, 5; the reference to the sailing season may also allow a place of composition further south: Rousseau 2000: 103–4.

[15] *VA* 46, and most notably at 69–71: ὅτε δὲ ἀπεδήμει, καὶ προεπέμπομεν αὐτόν. See Bartelink 1994: 319 n. 2, and Vivian and Athanassakis 2003: 211 n. 404. Peter of Alexandria died in 311; the second visit perhaps took place in 338: Brakke 1995: 205–6.

[16] For appropriate scepticism about the presence of the 'real' Antony in the *VA*, see Cameron 2000: 86, citing Brakke 1995: 201.

[17] *VA* 91.8–9.

Those who received the sheepskin coat from blessed Antony and the worn-out cloak from him keep them and treat them as great valuables. For even seeing these things is like laying eyes on Antony, and putting them on is like bearing his admonitions with joy.[18]

The implication is that this is said from personal experience. Of course, whether this is really Athanasius or someone impersonating Athanasius is perhaps impossible to establish: the important point is that the bishop and the monk are established as partaking of the same tradition. As Antony hands over his cloak and his sheepskin, he is also passing his legacy on to the Alexandrian church: he is, in effect, placing his *Life* in their hands.

Moreover, the development of this tradition achieves much of its effect from a couple of biblical reminiscences – not confined here to Antony, but drawing in the two bishops and, in the process, the author and his community. Back in the preface to the *Life of Antony*, the narrator had named as his source one 'who followed Antony no short time and poured water on his hands' – modern commentators have suggested Serapion for this role, although it is not entirely clear that the author is not instead referring in obscure fashion to himself.[19] Whether this disciple is intended to represent Serapion or Athanasius, the image is certainly indebted to the biblical portrait of the prophet Elisha, who in his time had followed his master Elijah and poured water on his hands; and in the end he took up Elijah's cloak to carry on his mission.[20] In the same way, Antony is not only being drawn into close contact with the Nicene faction which Athanasius and Serapion represented, but in returning his cloak to Athanasius he is passing on his mantle to the metropolitan clergy. Athanasius and Serapion are thus incorporated into Antony's re-enactment of Scripture: twin Elishas to Antony's Elijah.

This interrelation of Antony's life with Scripture was confirmed at the very beginning of the narrative of the Greek *Life*. He is

---

[18] *VA* 92.3.

[19] *VA* pref. 6. This is the translation of Brakke (1995: 206), who dismisses the alternative reading in the Latin manuscripts ('feci' for 'fecit') as 'a corruption in the text': Brakke 1995: 207 n. 17. Gregg 1980 and White 1998 follow Brakke; Bartelink (1994) prefers the alternative reading. See also Williams 1982: 41 n. 2, who is willing to keep both meanings in play. Serapion is directly named as an informant at *VA* 82.

[20] 2 Kings 3:11, 2:13; for the parallel, see Bartelink 1994: 51 and Brakke 1995: 206–7 (who prefers to restrict the Elisha parallel to Serapion in each case).

portrayed as a well-born young man brought up as a Christian and inclined to take seriously the precepts he heard read out in church.[21] After acquiring his adult independence following the deaths of his parents, Antony soon demonstrated the potential effect of this straightforward attitude to the Bible, when he apparently accepted at face value the advice of Christ recorded in Matthew's gospel: 'If you would be perfect, go, sell what you have and give to the poor, and you will have treasure in heaven; and come follow me.'[22] Antony had been thinking about the same passage, and he took this imperative as directed towards himself; he shared out his property, sold all his other possessions and retained some small portion for himself and his sister.[23] Subsequently he abandoned even this and determined upon a life of virginity in the village for his sister and a solitary working life in the desert for himself: and here again the inspiration came from the reading of Scripture, in the admonitions 'Do not be anxious about tomorrow,' and 'If any one will not work, let him not eat.'[24]

Antony's ascetic lifestyle would come to revolve around the scriptures, which the *Life* has him learning by heart as he begins his apprenticeship with other solitaries on the edge of society.[25] The memorising of the biblical texts is as much a sign of his isolation as is the physical withdrawal from his home, because it emphasises what the *Life* has already worked hard to establish: that Antony was not only illiterate but had refused to learn to read and write; and that by the same token he had refused to participate in 'the normal activities of children', and indeed 'his whole desire was ... to live at home, unaffected by the outside world'.[26] It is highly unlikely even on the *Life*'s own later evidence, that Antony was indeed illiterate to the extent this implies; and even if his description as 'unlettered' is taken to imply the absence of a traditional literary education, this too can be disputed on the basis of Antony's own letters.[27] But whether or not it corresponds to the historical Antony, or indeed to his portrait elsewhere in the *Life*, this early section is an instance of what will be 'the theme of the entire biography, [and] the

---

[21] *VA* 1.3.   [22] *VA* 2.3; Matthew 19:21 [RSV].   [23] *VA* 2.5.
[24] *VA* 3: Matthew 6.34; 2 Thessalonians 3:10 [RSV].   [25] *VA* 3.2–7.   [26] *VA* 1.2–3.
[27] Rubenson 1995: 98, 185, with additional discussion at Vivian and Athanassakis 2003: 215 n. 413.

essence of Antony's character': thus Antony was already isolated from conventional society and, in this case, the value it placed on social and intellectual education.[28] Antony is immediately seen to be remote from the contemporary world into which he was born: he is, says the *Life*, instead more reminiscent of Jacob: pious, simple and 'unformed'.[29] From the beginning, Antony is seen to have rejected the modern world in favour of the Bible.

The explicit parallel made with Jacob in the opening chapter of the *Life of Antony* was only the first of the associations between Antony's life and those of prominent biblical figures.[30] This engagement with Scripture is so obvious that it may come to seem inevitable; for modern readers, of course, the pattern is familiar from other Christian biographies, and it is possible that Athanasius was himself familiar with Eusebius' use of the Bible in the *Life of Constantine*.[31] Nevertheless, the particular form and function of these biblical references is worth investigating further. To begin with, for instance, there is a noticeable shift away from the parallel with Moses, so appropriate to the lives of the institutionally powerful: bishops and emperors. There remain hints of an association between Antony and Moses: the solitary life of Antony might perhaps recall the wanderings of Moses in the Egyptian wilderness; and Antony's old age, death and burial seem to recall some of the reverence and mystery which surround the end of Moses' life.[32] But the most relevant Old Testament figure in this portrait of a desert ascetic was one who offered a different kind of spiritual leadership, representing an alternative to those embroiled in the concerns of the secular world. The obvious parallel was instead

---

[28] Rubenson 2000: 115.

[29] *VA* 1.3, referring to Genesis 25.27; Rubenson (2000: 115) picks out in particular the LXX term ἄπλαστος

[30] More than two hundred scriptural citations and allusions are claimed by Bartelink (1994: 48–9), noting that the intertextuality frequently serves 'à souligner le fond biblique de l'idéal ascétique' (49); the number is expanded to 'some four hundred' in Vivian 2003: xxvi, where Antony is labelled '*homo biblicus*'.

[31] Cameron (2000: 74–5) lists these biblical parallels among the common features of the two lives, and she later suggests that the *VA* may be an 'answer' to the *VC*: Cameron 2000: 85.

[32] Bartelink (1994: 49–50) notes various possible parallels, especially as regards Antony's miraculous preservation in old age (*VA* 93:2; cf. Deuteronomy 34:7) and his burial in a secret location (*VA* 92.2; cf. Deuteronomy 34:6); broader parallels are suggested in Wilson 1988: 122–3.

with the biblical prophets, and with Elijah in particular: '[for] he used to say to himself: "It is necessary for the ascetic to learn from the way of life of the great Elijah always to examine his own life, as from a mirror."'[33] This identification with Elijah represents, perhaps, the culmination of Antony's rejection of the conventional social world of his contemporaries and his adoption instead of a world governed entirely by the active presence of God. The image of the prophet as a mirror for the ascetic's own contemporary life can, however, cut both ways. While the biography may show Antony modelling himself after Elijah, at the same time it recasts the prophet in terms more appropriate to Antony's particular brand of late-antique piety. Antony's use of the Bible is therefore not a matter of simple imitation, but of complex interpretation. Thus,

He would also recall the voice of the prophet Elijah who said, 'The Lord lives, the One before whom I stand today.' He observed that in saying 'today', he was not counting time that had passed but was always making a new beginning for himself, endeavouring each day to stand with God as though he were about to appear before God, pure in heart and prepared to obey the will of God, and the will of no other.[34]

This is to take Elijah as a model of ascetic discipline – to abstract from his life a monastic ideal – but the implications seem to go deeper. In presenting the relationship between Elijah and Antony in this way, the text allows Antony to remain as 'unformed' as he was from the beginning, starting over each day and taking no account of the passing of time. Indeed, this interpretation amounts to a denial that time passes, or perhaps only of the idea that it matters:

So he himself did not dwell on time that had passed, but each day, as though beginning his ascetic discipline anew, made progress by working harder, reflecting continually on what Paul said: 'We are forgetting what lies behind and straining forward to what lies ahead.'[35]

---

[33] VA 7.13. This reference to Elijah is absent from the Syriac version of the Life of Antony – and so perhaps from a potential Coptic original of the Life – where the explicit association is instead with the angels.

[34] VA 7.12, quoting and adapting a combination of 1 Kings 17:1 and 18:15.

[35] VA 7.11, quoting Philippians 3:13.

By 'forgetting what lies behind', Antony was able to ignore the claims of his immediate past, and therefore the claims of the contemporary historical world. Instead, he could live his life focusing entirely on his desire for God: looking forward to salvation, but in the meantime inhabiting a permanent biblical present. The world around him had vanished, to be replaced by the world of Scripture. Antony's reward was the gift of prophecy, as it had been for Elijah and others; and so his life continues to recall the Old Testament even when the parallels go unmentioned. The example of Elijah functions as a kind of counterpoint to Antony. His shadow can be seen, perhaps, in Antony's conversation with God on the banks of the River Nile; and the prophet is more clearly recalled as Antony withdraws to the Inner Mountain, while 'the Lord showed him things that were distant'.[36] Antony's subsequent visions from his mountain retreat place him directly in this prophetic tradition, alongside Elijah and Isaiah.[37] Antony lives his life as if he inhabited the Old Testament; and having lived as a prophet, he dies as a patriarch:

> When he had finished speaking, and they had embraced and kissed him, Antony lifted up his feet on to the bed. Looking on those who came to him as on friends . . . he left them (ἐξέλιπε) and went on to join the fathers.[38]

For those who might have missed the allusion, Antony had provided a pointer when he began his final speech: 'As for me, as it is written, I am going the way of the fathers.'[39] The reference seems not to be an exact quotation, although it closely parallels what was said about Jacob and David, and perhaps also Joshua; but it is another example of the *Life of Antony* engaging with the broad extent of the biblical tradition, and in the process enlisting Antony among the most authoritative figures of Scripture.[40]

---

[36] The Nile: *VA* 49; cf. 1 Kings 19:9, with Bartelink 1994: 51, de Vogüé 1989: xv. The mountain: *VA* 59; cf. 2 Kings 1:9 ('and behold, he sat on the top of a mountain'), with Bartelink 1994: 50–1.

[37] *VA* 60.1, 66.1 – the latter referring directly to the scriptural warrant for Antony's visions.

[38] *VA* 92.1; cf. the death of Jacob in Genesis 49.33 [LXX]: 'Jacob ceased giving charges to his sons; and having lifted up his feet on the bed, he died (ἐξέλιπε), and was gathered to his people'.

[39] *VA* 91.2.

[40] Vivian and Athanassakis (2003: 257 n. 14) identify the allusion as being to Jacob joining his fathers at Genesis 49:33, repeated of David in Acts 13:36; Bartelink offers instead

Yet in this serious and profound engagement with the Old Testament, Antony risked, as the Greek *Life* acknowledged, languishing unknown 'hidden on a mountain'.[41] He was far from the first Egyptian wanderer to be identified with Elijah: indeed, the comparison is likely to have been assigned to 'any individual who appeared prophetlike in third-century rural Egypt'.[42] These earlier figures, however, had rarely affected the world beyond the Egyptian desert, and that Antony did so provides us with a way of understanding the *Life of Antony* itself.

Antony's fame was perhaps prior to the writing of the *Life* – in its preface and in its closing chapters, the Greek version attests to knowledge of Antony in the world beyond Egypt – but the biography both cements his fame and, importantly, interprets it.[43] Antony had not been permitted to retreat entirely into his own Old Testament world on the margins of civilisation; instead he was offered to the contemporary Roman empire as evidence of the truth and power of the Christian faith. The Greek *Life* ends with explicit instructions:

Therefore, read what I have written to the other brothers so they may learn what kind of life monks ought to live and may believe that our Lord Jesus Christ glorifies those who give glory to him . . . If the need arises, read this also to the pagans so they too may know in the same way that not only is our Lord Jesus Christ God and the Son of God, but also that those who truly serve him and faithfully believe in him are repudiating the demons whom the pagans themselves believe to be gods.[44]

It is no surprise that the *Life* should have had an inspirational and apologetic purpose, but it is important to note that this could only be achieved by bringing Antony's Old Testament life into contact with contemporary society. A balance had to be maintained between Antony's rejection of the world and his explicit engagement with its people and problems.

In this respect, then, it matters very much that Antony should have been established as a firm Christian believer – even despite his

Joshua 23:14 and the same phrase re-used of David at 1 Kings 2:2. In none of these passages does it seem to me to imply the same level of continuity as in the *VA*.
[41] *VA* 93.5.
[42] Frankfurter 1993: 77, on the naming of a third-century prophetic text as the 'Apocalypse of Elijah'.
[43] *VA* pref. 2; *VA* 93.5.   [44] *VA* 95.1–2.

apparent preference for Old Testament models. His ascetic project, it may be remembered, was presented as a response to Christ's call to discipleship; and his success in his struggles against temptation or in the performance of healing miracles attributed explicitly to Christ acting through him.[45] Indeed, it is possible to recognise 'an extensive . . . debt' to the synoptic gospels in aspects of Antony's presentation in the *Life*, to the point of allowing Antony to be seen as a figure for Christ himself; although given the close typological relationship established in the gospels between Christ and the Old Testament prophets, it is difficult to see this as more than a secondary element.[46] Nevertheless, Antony throughout the Greek *Life* combines these two aspects of the Christian tradition, living a lifestyle inspired by the prophets while constantly announcing the names of Christ and Paul.[47] His withdrawal from the world had to be combined with the potentially contradictory task of changing it.

So Antony's life can at times seem an awkward combination of splendid isolation and active intervention. The Greek *Life* has him commenting on matters of contemporary controversy ranging from the martyrdoms in Alexandria under the Emperor Maximin to the Manichees and the Melitian schism.[48] He engages too with the persistence in Egypt of pagan burial practices, and triumphs in a set-piece debate with pagan philosophers in which he proves the superiority both of the Christian faith and of his own scriptural education.[49] The most consistent target of Antony's ire, however, was the Arian faction of the church: their activities prompted his second journey out of the desert to Alexandria, where he spoke firmly against them; and the Arian 'persecutions' were the pretext for Antony's evident role in the death of the military commander Valacius.[50] By this time Antony was already moving in exalted company indeed, with the *Life* having recorded his unimpressed

---

[45] For example, at *VA* 5, 7, 48, 58.
[46] The quotation is from de Vogüé 1989: xxii; a similar case for Antony as Christ is made at Wilson 1988: 122–3.
[47] The most obvious instances may be found in Antony's speech to his followers at *VA* 14–43, which focuses above all on the interpretation of passages from the New Testament; see also *VA* 30 and 45 for Antony's use of Paul in particular.
[48] *VA* 46–7, 68, 89.   [49] *VA* 90–1, 72–80.
[50] *VA* 68–71, 86; see also his repeated condemnation of the Arian heresy in his last words, at *VA* 89. For Valacius, *dux Aegypti* under Fl. Abinnaeus, see *PLRE* 1.929.

response to the frequent letters sent to him by the Emperor Constantine and his sons.[51] As one version of this story has the narrator comment, 'the most remarkable thing about this man was that he who lived in obscurity on the furthest edge of the world found favour with the emperors and was honoured by the whole imperial court'.[52]

All of this, then, seems consistent with Antony's choice of two prominent bishops to play Elisha to his Elijah: for Serapion and Athanasius were as engaged in the contemporary world as Antony had wished to be distant from it.[53] Whether or not the portrait in the Greek *Life* captures anything of the 'real' Antony, it certainly seems to reflect a need to reconcile the rejection of contemporary life, and abandonment to a life based solely on the scriptures, with the need to bring out the implications of that radical step for those who had remained behind. Yet despite the immediate popularity and the immense influence of the *Life of Antony*, it is possible to remain sceptical about its success on this particular score. The disjunction between Antony's contemplative isolation on the Inner Mountain and his activity as a public figure on the streets of Alexandria can seem too great and its resolution unconvincing: indeed, the problem is perhaps that Athanasius is simply not a very plausible Elisha. But Antony had other heirs, and so too did the *Life of Antony*. Subsequent Christian ascetics and their biographies engaged with the same set of problems, often directly engaging with the *Life of Antony* and even featuring Antony himself. When future ascetics abandoned the world of the Roman empire in favour of Scripture, they had to deal with the fact that Antony had been there before them.

New Antonys

The monastic pioneer Pachomius had been a contemporary of Antony, and would himself be the subject of a number of competing

---

[51] *VA* 81.
[52] *VA* 81, tr. White 1998. White's phrase is a loose translation of the Greek: ἔφθασε δὲ καὶ μέχρι βασιλέων ἡ περὶ ηντωνίου φήμη.
[53] Cameron (2000: 86) sees the *Life*'s image of Antony as 'a fine foil to Athanasius's sophistication'.

biographies in Greek and other languages.[54] In what is usually considered the first Greek *Life of Pachomius*, dating from the years after 387 (and so a good thirty years later than the Greek *Life of Antony*) the question is addressed at the very beginning of the monk's predecessors both in the Bible and in his own day – and also in the literary tradition:

The life of our most ascetic and truly virtuous father Antony was like that of the great Elijah, of Elisha, and of John the Baptist, as the most holy patriarch Athanasius attests in writing.[55]

The ascription to Athanasius, although it is no more certain evidence of his authorship than other contemporary references, at least reveals the extent to which this *Life* sought to position itself as a successor to the *Life of Antony* and part of a tradition of Greek Christian biography.[56] And yet Pachomius is a very different kind of ascetic hero from Antony.[57] In the early part of the *Life* he undertakes a similar kind of training as a solitary in the desert, and soon finds that he has the ability to 'tread underfoot serpents and scorpions openly, and to stand on crocodiles in the water, and to brave wild beasts fearlessly and daringly without being harmed by them'.[58] But where Antony's feats link him above all to Elijah, and

---

[54] The date of Pachomius' death is given by Rousseau (1999: 174) as AD 346. I shall be focusing on the first Greek *Life of Pachomius*: the *Vita Prima* (*VP*), which represents one of three main traditions in Pachomian biography. One of these traditions consists primarily of the Coptic *Lives* of Pachomius, which exist in both Sahidic and Bohairic forms of the language, and which seem to have links with other (apparently Coptic) versions which survive today in Arabic translations. The other two traditions are Greek: the *Vita Prima* (also known as G[1]) already referred to, dating from after 387; and a distinct Greek version – the *Vita Altera*, or G[2] – which provides the basis for a sixth-century Latin account by Dionysius Exiguus, of which I will also make some use. There are a number of other Greek *Lives* – G[3] through to G[10] – but they can for the most part be assigned to one of these two traditions. This account of the various *Lives* of Pachomius is based on that found in Rousseau 1999: 37–55, Goehring 1986: 3–23, and on the introduction to the 1980 translation by Veilleux; a more recent account may be found at Gould 1997. The most substantial recent work on Pachomius is Goehring 1999, with relevant bibliography discussed at 26–32 and 208–16.
[55] *VP* 2. Translations from the *VP* are based on those of Veilleux.
[56] The *VP*, like the other Greek and Coptic *Lives* of Pachomius, is anonymous and has (unusually) remained that way.
[57] As noted by Rousseau 1999: 47.
[58] *VP* 21; cf. Luke 10:19 [NEB]: 'I have given you the power to tread underfoot snakes and scorpions', and Psalms 90:13 [LXX]: 'Thou shalt tread on the asp and the basilisk, and thou shalt trample on the lion and the dragon.' Cf. Antony's power over venomous snakes and the wild creatures of the desert, at e.g. *VA* 12 and 52–3.

(for the author of the *Life of Pachomius* at least) to the prophet's successors and avatars in the Old and New Testaments, Pachomius follows a different kind of biblical path.

Pachomius' early exploits as a solitary ascetic are presented in the first Greek *Life* as merely a kind of preparation for his true task: like Moses, who could also perform miracles over nature during his time alone in the wilderness, 'he was being preserved by the Lord who intended to teach him later how to act'.[59] The true destiny awaiting Pachomius was not that of an individual hero but that of a creator and leader of an institution: he would become the founder and the legitimating force behind the common life of the first monastic communities. His spiritual authority would therefore depend on his interaction in social relationships, with his own monks and with the wider world. Despite his apparent links to Antony, therefore, the chosen models for this Pachomius would be those familiar biblical figures who had served as leaders of their people: Moses, Abraham, Christ and Paul. His re-enactments of Scripture would be expressed in teaching and in serving those around him.

Thus as a pioneer of coenobitic monasticism, Pachomius necessarily found himself at times taking on the role of the apostle Paul, whose letters in particular were concerned with the instruction of neophyte communities. There are a number of examples in the first Greek *Life of Pachomius* re-using Paul's actual words, as when instructing his monks over dinner:

[H]e who has his mind in heaven ought to practise a worthy abstinence, and not to have a desire for foods. For surely it is not a sin to eat, especially the cheap things; but it is good not to be dominated by anything, as the Apostle says.[60]

Elsewhere, Pachomius adopted instead Christ's method of teaching his disciples in parables, sometimes adapting specific examples from the gospels to his own situation and purpose:

For ground that has been cleared is ready to be planted with vines step by step, but fallow land can scarcely be planted with good seed until after it has been cleaned with great toil. But we know that even clean ground, if it is neglected,

[59] *VP* 21; the parallel, drawn explicitly in these terms in the text, is with Exodus 4:1–5.
[60] *VP* 55, quoting Colossians 3.2. and 1 Corinthians 6:12, respectively. The letters of Paul are also quoted at (for example) *VP* 21, 24, 49 and 62.

will become fallow, as it is written, even if it was planted with good seed. Just as with fallow land then, purity is attained by care and proper zeal.[61]

In this case, the parable of the sower has been adapted to refer not to the Christian message in general but specifically to the training of children in a monastic vocation. Pachomius goes on to recommend children as the most perfect members of a spiritual community, perhaps further recalling Christ's advice that in order to enter the kingdom of God one should become like a child.[62]

The engagement with the Bible displayed here by Pachomius, then, distinguishes his life from that of Antony: for while both retreat from the contemporary world and adopt a set of roles familiar from Scripture, Pachomius' concern for his disciples prevents him from withdrawing completely from modern life. Something of the contrast can be seen in his own characterisation of the monks' daily routine, in which devotion to God is wholly assimilated to service of the community:

After the [daily] prayers, they retire to rest and eat in an appropriate and quiet place, where I wait on them myself as Abraham waited on the Lord alone under the oak tree.[63]

It is in this respect that the association of Pachomius with Christ in the first Greek *Life* is most significant. The parallel is made clear throughout the text, most notably in a string of healing miracles which extend even to the healing of a woman who had expectantly touched the hem of Pachomius' garment.[64] But as with Christ, his most important role was as the leader of a community: a connection emphasised all the more strongly when Pachomius sets himself to wash the feet of his principal disciple Theodore.[65]

In emphasising these particular biblical parallels, the first Greek *Life of Pachomius* was able to propose that 'the "apostolic life", the Church of the Apostles [was] reviving . . . after several

---

[61] *VP* 49; cf. the parable of the sower at e.g. Matthew 13.1–9.
[62] *VP* 49; cf. Luke 18:15–17, expanding Matthew 19:13–15 and Mark 10:13–16.
[63] *VP* 40.
[64] *VP* 41; cf. the healing of the woman with 'issue of blood', told in Matthew 9:18–26, Mark 5:25–34 and Luke 8:43–8. Further healing miracles reminiscent of the gospels may be seen at e.g. *VP* 43–4.
[65] *VP* 64; cf. John 13:12.

centuries'.[66] The life that Pachomius led was no less a re-enactment of Scripture than was that of Antony; but the manner of his life and the accumulation and demands of his followers required him to confront more directly the world he had left behind. Pachomius did not retreat to the Inner Mountain, as Antony had; instead, he sited his monastery rather closer to civilisation, 'on cultivated land near the Nile'.[67] There he was forced into contact with the local villagers of Tabennesi: ordinary Christians and 'men of the world' who, the *Life of Pachomius* reports, were overjoyed when they 'saw a man of God in their midst, [and] were very eager to become Christians and faithful'.[68] This profound impact on the world around him makes the *Life of Pachomius* in some ways a development of the *Life of Antony*: and the interaction is acknowledged when, upon the death of Pachomius, Antony himself appears as a character in order to comment on his counterpart's legacy.

What ensues is, predictably enough, a round of mutual congratulations – but in what may be considered revealing terms. Apa Zacchaeus, one of Pachomius' followers, praises Antony as 'the light of all this world'.[69] Antony, however, demurs and excuses himself for having spent his life as a solitary ascetic, when Pachomius has demonstrated the possibility of a very different kind of biblical life: 'I tell you', he comments, 'it was a great ministry he received . . . and he walks the way of the apostles'.[70] The competitive edge here is no doubt good-natured, and the essential point is rather the consistency of the two lives and, notably, of the world they both create. The appearance of Antony in the *Life of Pachomius* is important for more than his voiced approval: in addition, it helps to establish the two ascetics as participants in the same project and, above all, as inhabitants of the same world. Both of them sought to revive a biblical way of life in the Egyptian desert: and this final collaboration makes clear that the world of Pachomius is the world of Antony. Indeed, the relationship has perhaps been anticipated in

[66] de Vogüé 1980: xiii.
[67] White 1998: xx. Goehring (1999: 91) gives Pachomius a prominent role in the development of 'village asceticism', in contrast to the model set up in the *VA*; for the ideological significance of the opposition of desert and civilisation, see esp. Brown 1989: 217, although Pachomian monasticism is seen in less extreme terms in Brown 1971: 83.
[68] VP 30.   [69] *VP* 120; Christ is called 'light of the world' in Matthew 5:14 [AV].
[70] *VP* 120.

the prior appearance in the *Life of Pachomius* of Athanasius, who belongs to both the textual world of Antony and the 'real' world of its readers.[71] There is no actual meeting between the bishop and the monastic leader – indeed, Pachomius is presented as hiding to avoid ordination – but some level of mutual awareness is clearly implied.[72] That Athanasius is limited to a cameo appearance no doubt reflects the inevitably awkward relationship between the established church and the independent ascetics; but the fact that Antony can appear without the same kind of concern serves to confirm Pachomius' place in the world of Egyptian Christianity, and in a tradition which stretched back through Antony all the way to the prophets and patriarchs of the Old Testament.

Nor was this the first time that Antony had been employed to add weight to the biography of another ascetic, and his popularity as a character is a testament to the immediate circulation of the *Life of Antony* among a Christian readership. By 374 it had been translated 'from the Greek of Athanasius' into Latin by Evagrius of Antioch, as attested both in the Latin translation itself and in Jerome's catalogue of Christian literature, the *Lives of Illustrious Men*.[73] Jerome knew Evagrius from their shared time in northern Italy and he subsequently stayed with him in Syria, and it seems that he became deeply interested both in the idea and the practice of desert asceticism and in the literary tradition it had spawned.[74] When he came to write a Christian biography of his own, it was natural that he should seek to engage with that context and background, dealing with both the history of the phenomenon and the writings of his contemporaries. His *Life of Paul of Thebes* was probably written in 377, only a few years after Evagrius' translation, and makes explicit reference to the accounts of Antony which existed in both Greek and Latin.[75] Jerome, it seems, is continuing the Latin side of the tradition: where Evagrius had translated Antony 'into our own

---

[71] Athanasius appears at *VP* 30.

[72] Goehring (1999: 171) notes the differing responses of the Greek and Coptic traditions – in the former, Pachomius marvels at Athanasius, in the latter, Athanasius at Pachomius. In neither do they meet.

[73] *De uir. ill.* 87, 125.

[74] Kelly 1975: 33, 38–9; for Jerome's circle in northern Italy, see also Humphries 1996: 141–3.

[75] Kelly 1975: 60–1; Rebenich 2000a: 14; *VPauli* 1. Much of the scholarship on Jerome's biographical writings has focused on the extent to which they are connected to traditional

language', Jerome would reassess and rewrite the *Life of Antony* itself.[76]

The *Life of Paul* – also known as the *Life of Paul the First Hermit* – thus begins with an account of its hero's pedigree:

It has often been a matter of discussion among many people as to which monk was the first to inhabit the desert. Some, going back further into the past, have ascribed the beginning to the blessed Elijah and to John [the Baptist].[77]

The parallels here with Elijah and John are familiar from the *Life of Pachomius*; Jerome goes on to rule them out as true ascetic pioneers, since 'Elijah seems to us to have been more than a monk, while John seems to have started to prophesy before he was born.'[78] These biblical figures belong in a different time and perhaps in a different world; and yet the connection is clearly acknowledged between their lives and those of Antony and Paul. Jerome prefers to give primacy to Paul as an 'originator of the practice, though not of the name, of the solitary life', but admits that Antony also has a claim: 'for it is not so much that he came before all the others but rather that he inspired everyone with a commitment to this way of life'.[79] The terms in which Jerome summarises this debate are significant, for they allow all four figures a real claim. Elijah and John founded and re-founded the ascetic lifestyle for the Old and New Testaments respectively; Paul and Antony have revived it in at least a similar form and have brought it to public attention. However their contributions are defined or assessed, these four figures are the core of the tradition: Elijah, John, Antony and Paul are all, so to speak, on the same page.

Yet despite Jerome's assertions of his importance, and that he was a 'more perfect' ascetic than Antony, Paul remains a secondary

---

secular forms, most commonly the romance: the most important works along these lines are Coleiro 1957, Kech 1977, Fuhrmann 1977, Hamblenne 1993, Bastiaensen 1994 and Rebenich 2000b. Similarly, A. G. Elliott 1987 argues for a connection between classical romance and medieval hagiography largely on the basis of the form of the *VPauli* and its imitators. A more radical reading of Jerome's biographies, and of the *VPauli* in particular, may be seen in Burrus 2003: 19–52.

[76] *De uir. ill.* 125. There appears to be no independent evidence for the existence of Jerome's Paul, although it is usually supposed that Jerome believed him to be a historical figure, Kelly 1975: 61.

[77] *VPauli* 1.   [78] *VPauli* 1.   [79] *VPauli* 1.

figure even in his own biography.[80] The real concern in the *Life of Paul* seems to be with the traditional portrayal of Antony – to which Paul represents an alternative.[81] Although like Antony he is established as an orphan who has inherited plenty from his parents, Paul is distinguished from him as 'highly educated in both Greek and Egyptian letters'.[82] He was also apparently instinctively sociable, and whereas Antony withdrew into the desert by choice, Paul is forced there by persecution and betrayal.[83] Once there, he approaches complete withdrawal by degrees, as Antony had; but Jerome takes care to establish a practical basis for Paul's solitary life in the desert, allotting him a cave with a clear spring and a palm tree which 'provided him with food and clothing'.[84] Indeed, Jerome takes great pains to emphasise that this life would be eminently liveable, and cites examples from his own time in the desert of monks who had lived on as little or less.[85] In some ways, then, Jerome presents the life of Paul as a more believable model of the ascetic life than was offered by Athanasius.[86] Paul is not sent out into a featureless desert, but into a world which maintains its links with reality, with the familiar world of its readers. Even Paul's cave has a pre-Christian history, a place in the familiar Roman past: it was, says Jerome, formerly a clandestine Egyptian mint dating from the days of Antony and Cleopatra.[87]

For all that, Jerome was scarcely engaged here in bringing down to earth the marvels and wonders of the ascetic tradition. Paul

[80] *VPauli* 7; the extent to which Paul is defined in relation to Antony is well brought out in Leclerc 1988.
[81] That Jerome's text and its hero are in competition with the Athanasian (or Evagrian) Antony is clear from the title alone; the complexities of this relationship are neatly portrayed at Burrus 2003: 22–3.
[82] *VPauli* 4.
[83] *VPauli* 4: he is betrayed by his sister's husband, during the persecutions under Decius and Valerian, but initially expects to return to society once the persecutions are over. Leclerc (1988: 260), followed by Burrus (2003: 173 n. 27), notes that the opposition can be read differently: Paul is refusing martyrdom in favour of asceticism, whereas Antony would have preferred to be a martyr. In either case, there is a clear distinction drawn between them.
[84] *VPauli* 5–6: the comparison is presumably with Antony, who in *VA* 12–14 spends twenty years in a deserted fort with regular supplies of bread but no apparent source of water.
[85] *VPauli* 6.
[86] Kech (1977: 35) notes the concern with realism here, although Burrus (2003: 174 n. 35) notes the limits of this reality.
[87] *VPauli* 5.

belongs to the world of the *Life of Antony* as much as to the world of Antony and Cleopatra. Indeed, after the perfunctory introduction to Paul, the focus of the narrative shifts to the Athanasian Antony, who serves as the protagonist for the rest of the story, and who in the *Life of Paul* is granted adventures more remarkable even than in his own biography. Thus having had Paul's existence revealed to him, and having been advised that he ought to make a visit, Antony sets out and encounters on his travels a bestiary straight out of ancient romance.[88] There is a 'hippocentaur', half man and half horse, who points Antony on his way; and then a satyr or faun, who claims to be no evil spirit (as the pagans believe) but a mortal creature and a Christian besides.[89] In each case, Jerome acknowledges the unbelievable nature of this turn of events: in discussing the centaur, he leaves the reader in doubt as to 'whether the devil himself took the shape of this creature . . . or whether the desert, notoriously capable of engendering monsters, also gave birth to this beast'; with the satyr, however, he insists that such creatures exist, and cites an occasion on which one was brought alive to Alexandria.[90]

The *Life of Paul* therefore combines the narration of fantastic events with a contempt for anyone who might disbelieve them. That these things sit oddly together is, I think, largely the point.[91] At one level there is perhaps a mordant irony at work: if Jerome's readers will believe in centaurs and fauns, they can surely be expected to believe in the less extravagant miracles attributed to the desert ascetics. The desert is a strange and liminal place, and these monsters only reaffirm the extent to which Antony and Paul have left civilisation behind.[92] But it is also surely that Jerome's story is one in which fantasy and history live side by side. Paul's pragmatism makes Antony more realistic just as Antony's adventures make Paul more remarkable. Antony himself represents the romantic

[88] For the sources and the implications of Jerome's image of the desert, see esp. Harvey 1998: 44–9, along with (on particular aspects) Cox Miller 1996 and Merrills 2004.
[89] *VPauli* 7–8.
[90] *VPauli* 7–8: the satyr brought to Alexandria is placed by Jerome in the reign of Constantius II – true or otherwise, Harvey (1998: 51–6) notes that such claims can be traced at least to Pliny the Elder.
[91] Burrus (2003: 28–30) notes that Jerome's 'casual' explanation does little to resolve the problem.
[92] Cox Miller 1996: 215–31; cf. Merrills 2004.

excess of the literary saint's life. This aspect is brought into the *Life of Paul* only to be yoked more securely to the everyday world of its author and readers. The message is that the world of Antony and Paul is both amazing *and* familiar: and that the whole of the contemporary world may be understood in the same way. Thus Antony and Paul are engaged in a common enterprise and partake of a common tradition. There is a real emphasis in the *Life of Paul* on their competitive virtue and on their ultimate equality; and they are brought together not only in the narrative but also by what connects them to Scripture and to the contemporary Roman world. The tone is set during the first meeting, after Antony has entreated Paul from outside his locked door: after a little light teasing, they greet each other by name and Paul refers to Antony as his 'brother' and his 'fellow servant'.[93] When they set about eating bread they dispute over which of them is to break it – a priestly and hierarchical privilege – and resolve the problem by pulling it apart together.[94] But the bread denotes more than equality: in keeping with the *Life of Antony*'s characterisation of its hero, the loaf had been delivered by a raven just as the same birds had once fed Elijah.[95] But it is Antony and not Paul who is surprised by this turn of events: for as Paul comments, the real miracle is that 'for the last sixty years I have always received [only] half a loaf'.[96]

If Antony was beginning to recognise in Paul a fellow traveller in his own revival of the biblical life, it was soon brought even more vividly before his eyes as Paul neared death. Paul sent Antony away so that he might die alone: and as he acceded to this request, 'it was as if he saw Christ in Paul'.[97] When Antony returned to report the meeting to his disciples, he further recognised Paul's successful re-enactment of Scripture: 'I have seen Elijah, I have seen John in the desert and now I have seen Paul in Paradise.'[98] If the latter might be taken as an allusion to the apostle Paul, it would soon become literally true, as at the moment of his death Antony

---

[93] *VPauli* 9–11. Antony's actions here recall the poetic figure of the spurned lover at the locked door, as noted by Leclerc (1988: 262–3); for the possible implications, see esp. the discussion of the *VPauli* at Burrus 2003: 24–33.
[94] *VPauli* 11.
[95] *VPauli* 10: the parallel with 1 Kings 17:6 is noted by (among others) Frankfurter 1993: 67.
[96] *VPauli* 10.   [97] *VPauli* 12.   [98] *VPauli* 13.

saw his companion 'among the host of angels, among the choir of prophets and apostles, shining with a dazzling whiteness and ascending on high'.[99] That was paradise, but perhaps the desert of Paul was too – just as it was, simultaneously, the wilderness of Elijah's Old Testament and the hinterland of the modern Egyptian church. Like the apostle Paul, the ascetic Antony could visit this spiritual and biblical Paradise and report back on what he had seen; thanks to Jerome, the late-antique desert had become an accessible biblical world.

This network of allusions at the centre of the *Life of Paul* soon came to revolve around a familiar device: Antony had been sent by Paul to retrieve the cloak he had been given by Athanasius.[100] In this version the mantle was not passed on to the bishop but was used as a shroud for Paul's burial, while Antony would adopt Paul's tunic: another Elisha for another Elijah.[101] For all that the versions are incompatible – and for all that Paul himself, let alone his tunic, may have been constructed by Jerome out of whole cloth – the engagement here with the issues of inheritance and succession tie together not only Paul and Antony, but the outside world as well. Paul is newly connected to Athanasius; Jerome, as narrator, goes on to express his desire to wear Paul's tunic in preference to the purple robes of kings.[102] All are participants in the re-enactment of Scripture as it was seen to take place not only in Christian biography but in the historical world of late antiquity. Paul, a new Antony, was also a new Elijah and a new Christ: both for Jerome's characters and also for his readers.

With this in mind, Jerome's portraits can tell us something about his ambitions for a contemporary revival of the biblical life. Paul is an alternative to Antony, and perhaps also a corrective, with his classical education and his initial reluctance to embark on the solitary life. Despite his sixty years in the desert, the few words

---

[99] *VPauli* 14; the allusion to the apostle would presumably be to the vision described in 2 Corinthians.

[100] *VPauli* 12.

[101] *VPauli* 12, 16: the familiar parallel with Elisha is drawn in e.g. Rubenson 2000: 121; White (1998: 211 n. 3) suggests that this is 'Jerome's witty means of insisting on Paul's priority over Antony', but it may perhaps also be seen as making Paul the true heir of Antony in place of Athanasius.

[102] *VPauli* 18.

Paul exchanges with Antony perpetuate this sense of the ascetic as concerned with the contemporary world, as on Antony's arrival he is pressed for information:

Tell me, I beg you, how the human race is getting on. Are new buildings rising up in the old cities? What government rules the world? Are there still some people alive who are in the grip of the demons' error?[103]

The slight absurdity of Paul asking the solitary Antony for information of this sort is obvious enough, but it offers an interesting suggestion as to Paul's character: he is apparently more isolated even than Antony, but at the same time has not abandoned all involvement with the world. That this may be a corrective to Antony's attitude is then implied by the one piece of advice he receives from his time with Paul, who tells him:

You ought not to seek your own benefit but that of others. It might be to your advantage to lay down the burden of the flesh and to follow the Lamb, but it is also beneficial for the other brothers to be instructed by your example.[104]

This is a recommendation which would fit the Pachomian model rather better than the *Life of Antony*, although in this story Antony does return to his disciples and is apparently based in a monastic community.[105] Yet if the *Life of Paul* has a message, this would seem to be it: that an ascetic should not entirely reject the world, but ought to engage with it and instruct it. A biblical life will have value only when it can connect with and redefine the ordinary world.

Back from the brink

It is tempting to read into this attitude Jerome's own experience in the Syrian desert, which occupied him in the few years prior to his writing of the *Life of Paul*.[106] From Antioch, where he was staying with Evagrius, he had finally taken the decision to join the ranks of the monks he had long admired. There can be little doubt about Jerome's enthusiasm, if his previous letter to the anchorite Theodosius is any guide:

[103] *VPauli* 10.   [104] *VPauli* 12.   [105] *VPauli* 13, 16.
[106] Following the dating in Kelly 1975: 46–61.

How I long to be a member of your company, and to embrace your admirable community with the greatest joy – though indeed, these poor eyes are not worthy to look upon it. Oh! that I could behold the desert, lovelier to me than any city! Oh! that I could see those lonely spots made into a paradise by the saints that throng them![107]

The terms in which he here praises the desert would return in the *Life of Paul*, but by then it would scarcely appear to reflect his revised opinion. Jerome was rapidly disillusioned about the monastic life and his own suitability for it. In part he seems to have blamed his problems on the sheer numbers of ascetics in the desert and their refusal to leave him alone: he was called upon daily, he would complain, to declare his position on the Melitian schism, and his exasperation with this intrusion of church politics reached the point where 'All they want is that I should go away.'[108] Jerome did indeed abandon his ascetic life within three years of beginning it, and from this it would seem that he had found the monks too involved in the world for his liking.

It is permissible, however, to be sceptical about Jerome's stated reasons for his rapid change of heart. Doctrinal controversy was not entirely unexpected in the desert, as the *Life of Antony* had already attested – and Jerome is hardly likely to have been rounded upon by a gang of well-connected ascetics. It was Jerome who was the intruder, and Jerome who had kept up his connections with the world of theological debate and ecclesiastical patronage. He received regular visits from Evagrius, and received letters and books from his friends; it seems he even had a staff of copyists available; and *in extremis* he wrote two of his letters of complaint (in vain) to Bishop Damasus in Rome.[109] Jerome had not entirely abandoned the world. Even to the extent that he had, he seems to have found it difficult to cope, recalling in a later letter 'the vast solitude which gives to hermits a savage dwelling-place', in which:

I used to sit alone because I was filled with bitterness. Sackcloth disfigured my unshapely limbs and my skin from long neglect had become as black as an

---

[107] Jerome, *Letter* 2; the next letter in the collection further expresses Jerome's admiration for his friend Rufinus, who had already taken a similar step.
[108] Jerome, *Letter* 17, building upon his complaints in *Letters* 15 and 16: see also Kelly 1975: 52–6 for a broader account of the issue.
[109] See Kelly 1975: 48–52, taking into consideration Jerome, *Letters* 5, 7, 15 and 16.

Ethiopian's. Tears and groans were every day my portion; and if drowsiness chanced to overcome my struggles against it, my bare bones, which hardly held together, clashed against the ground. Of my food and drink I say nothing: for, even in sickness, the solitaries have nothing but cold water, and to eat one's food cooked is looked upon as self-indulgence. . . In my fear of hell I had consigned myself to this prison, where I had no companions but scorpions and wild beasts.[110]

No doubt this was partly a boast, and Jerome can hardly have expected the ascetic life to be pleasant and calm. Nevertheless, the hardships he describes coupled with his relatively brief sojourn in the desert suggest that his retreat there may have seemed to be a failure. It may be true that what is revealed in all this is Jerome's 'intense dislike of being alone'.[111] It is in any case true that, having abandoned the world, he in turn abandoned the desert.

Thereafter, Jerome's attitude towards monks and ascetics can be seen to be rather more qualified. The *Life of Paul* was probably written soon after his return to the civilised life of Evagrius at Antioch, and its praise of the solitary life is counterbalanced by Paul's advice not to exile oneself completely. A similar recognition of the problem of withdrawal from the world and one's responsibilities to it would return in Jerome's *Life of Malchus* – a biography in praise of chastity in which the motor for the plot is Malchus' desire to return to his family after years as a monk.[112] He is discouraged in this ambition by the abbot of his monastery, whose fears are founded in Scripture and in a knowledge of the wiles of the devil, and which are soon proved well founded; and yet Malchus eventually triumphs in his chastity and is discovered at the end of his life living quietly and continently with his wife in a small peasant village.[113] Although he has apparently never returned to his life in the desert, he is made no less praiseworthy for that – and no less biblical, as the couple 'were so zealously pious and such constant frequenters of the church that they might have been taken for Elizabeth and Zacharias in the Gospel, but for the fact that John

[110] Jerome, *Letter* 22.7.   [111] Kelly 1975: 51.
[112] Kelly (1975: 170–1) dates it to 390–1. The *VMalchi* is translated at Rebenich 2000a: 85–92, followed here.
[113] *VMalchi* 2–3; it is to be noted that the story contains a contradiction as to the fate of Malchus' wife, who at *VMalchi* 2 is discovered in old age living with Malchus despite having been previously sent to join a community of virgins (*VMalchi* 10). Burrus (2003: 37–8) centres much of her reading on this potentially productive gap in the narrative.

was not with them'.[114] Evidently Jerome saw no need to confine the biblical life to the desert, even where the parallel he offered required a certain amount of revision to account for the absence of a child – John the Baptist, no less. In his description and praise of a chaste marriage, and in the exclusion of John, he is perhaps offering a complementary model of asceticism to be pursued in the world.

At about the same time, Jerome expressed the same kinds of concerns in a full-length biography of a monk in Palestine: the *Life of Hilarion*.[115] In the preface Jerome sets this new *Life* as a direct successor of the *Life of Paul*, and contrasts the two works in revealing terms:

> If they criticise Paul for his solitude, they will criticise Hilarion for his sociability, believing that because Paul always remained out of sight he did not exist and because Hilarion was seen by many he should be regarded as of no importance. Their ancestors, the Pharisees, did exactly the same in the past: they did not approve of John's fasting in the desert, nor of the Lord and Saviour eating and drinking among the crowds.[116]

It is impossible to know whether the *Life of Paul* was in fact criticised on these counts, but it is clear that Jerome is establishing Hilarion as a very different model of the ascetic life – and indeed the biblical life. Paul's solitude had scriptural precedent in John the Baptist as well as in Elijah and Elisha; Hilarion's life finds an alternative precedent in the adult ministry of Christ. But the difference is exaggerated on both sides, with regard to Jerome's characters and also to their precursors. John emerged from the desert and began to preach, engaging with the world around him as Paul recommended; and Christ, of course, spent his time in the wilderness, fulfilling the prophets and the prophecies of the Old Testament. Hilarion, in fact, would take on all of these roles, both retreating from the world and returning to it – and once again, 'the

---

[114] *VMalchi* 2; cf. Luke 1:5–6.
[115] The *VHil.* is dated to AD 391 by Kelly (1975: 172). Remarkably little has been written on the *VHil.* in particular: the main exception is the account of the *VHil.* as a novel in the tradition of Apuleius in Weingarten 2005: 83–105, and the valuable account of its relationship to the Roman context at 105–54. Other recent contributions are the brief discussion in Burrus 2003: 39–45, and the discussion focusing on the work's dedication in Harvey 2005.
[116] *VHil.* 1.

emaciated figure of Antony is the pivot around which the tale of a holy man turns'.[117]

As a new contribution to the tradition of Antony, Hilarion's chief importance lies in his 'sociability'. That Jerome distinguishes him in this might seem odd after a reading of the *Life*, in which the constant theme throughout is Hilarion's search for isolation, and which culminates in his achievement of that solitude in a mountainous region where 'no one – or only the occasional person – was able – or dared – to climb up to see him'.[118] Indeed, Hilarion repeatedly affirms his distaste for crowds and for involvement with the general public: he ended his early career as a companion and disciple of Antony, when he 'could no longer put up with the crowds of people who came running to Antony on account of all kinds of illnesses or demonic attacks'; not unreasonably, he wished to test his vocation before becoming an ascetic celebrity.[119] His self-imposed exile in the deserts of Palestine lasted twenty-two years, before he was reluctantly persuaded to leave his cell even to the extent of going to the nearby village under cover of darkness.[120] Yet this compromise would be far more indicative of Hilarion's career than his continual desire to be alone: for it was the occasion of a miracle, and of the beginning of a reputation which would come to rival that of Antony himself.

Thus when news of Hilarion's miraculous power spread, soon 'people came flocking to him eagerly from Syria and Egypt' and ultimately from even further afield.[121] He soon attracted to himself the same crowds that had once besieged Antony – so that as the founder of monasticism in Palestine he became in effect a new Antony for the eastern empire:

[For] if ever exhausted visitors came to Antony from the regions of Syria, he would say to them, 'Why did you put yourself to the trouble of such a long journey when you have my son Hilarion near you?'[122]

The connection between the two of them was close, and that Hilarion possessed a similar prophetic power is clear when he

[117] Burrus 2003: 40.
[118] *VHil.* 43: 'aut nullus, aut rarus ad se uel posset, uel auderet ascendere'.
[119] *VHil.* 3.   [120] *VHil.* 14.   [121] *VHil.* 14, 22 (a visitor from western Europe).
[122] *VHil.* 24.

apprehends Antony's death despite the distance between them.[123] Still, however, Hilarion refuses to take on a public role: returning to Egypt, he takes the opportunity to visit Antony's retreat on the Inner Mountain, and in particular the cells 'in which Antony used to stay when he wished to escape the crowds of visitors and the company of his disciples'.[124] Hilarion makes another attempt to live in solitude just as Antony had; but before long his reputation catches up with him, and his desire to continue Antony's isolated life is thwarted once again.[125]

This same pattern comes to be repeated almost to the point of absurdity in the *Life of Hilarion*. The hero seeks solitude, but the miracles he performs cannot help drawing attention to him. This same thing happens successively at the Great Oasis in Egypt, in Sicily and Epidaurus – where Hilarion destroys a serpent and arrests a tidal wave in full flight – and at Paphos in his final resting place of Cyprus:

> Before twenty days had passed, all those throughout the island who were pos-sessed by unclean spirits began to cry out that Hilarion, the servant of Christ, had arrived, and that they must hurry to him. . . Within thirty days or not much more, two hundred people, men as well as women, came flocking to him. When he saw them he was upset that they would not leave him in peace.[126]

The constant tension between isolation and engagement is evident, and of course Hilarion did not refuse to help any who came to him; but despite his final withdrawal from the world into the mountains in the centre of Cyprus, the balance throughout the *Life* of Hilar-ion seems to weigh in favour of the 'sociability' that Jerome had promised. The *Life* is remarkable for its miracles, but above all for the dealings they forced Hilarion to have with the social world of both the desert and the city.[127]

As founder of the monastic life in Palestine, Hilarion inevitably found himself functioning as the spiritual counsellor to many new monks.[128] Following Paul's advice to Antony, and the example

---

[123] *VHil.* 29.   [124] *VHil.* 30–1.   [125] *VHil.* 32–3.

[126] *VHil.* 42; the tidal wave at Epidaurus was caused by the (apparently historical) tsunami in the reign of the Emperor Jovian: for other sources recording this event, see Kelly 2004.

[127] Burrus 2003: 42, 'the saint is at the mercy of his gift: . . . he finds himself besieged by the crowds he ostensibly seeks to avoid'.

[128] *VHil.* 15, 24, 29.

of Pachomius, Hilarion seems to have taken this responsibility seriously: far from isolating himself as a distant figure, he would tour the cells of his monks on a regular basis and was ready to manage any conflict or dishonesty or backsliding.[129] Yet even before this, according to Jerome, Hilarion had become heavily involved in the affairs of the villages and cities of Palestine – those he visited, such as the pagan outpost of Elusa, and those whose chief citizens came to him for help and advice.[130] Particularly unexpected is his intervention in a chariot race at Gaza, in which a public official named Italicus asked Hilarion for help in winning a race in the circus. Although the request is first dismissed as 'foolish' and 'trivial', Hilarion eventually accedes and opposes his Christian 'magic' to that of Italicus' rivals.[131] The story is a rare example of a holy man intervening in secular affairs and entertainments: it is hardly the act of an ascetic who has firmly rejected the world. As Jerome notes, however, this miracle was effective, and 'was the cause of many believing in Christ'.[132]

The inability, or unwillingness, of Hilarion to withdraw completely from the world around him seems then to be presented in the *Life* as a virtue. It makes him less like Elijah or the Old Testament prophets than it does Jesus Christ, who is himself portrayed in Scripture as a popular preacher who would have preferred a less spectacular progress.[133] The constant pestering of the crowds recalls in particular the miracle of the feeding of the five thousand, in which Christ is forced to escape to the centre of the Sea of Galilee; nor is the association an idle one, given the miraculous feeding of three thousand monks credited to Hilarion in the *Life*.[134] Hilarion's other exploits can also be seen as re-enactments of miracles in the gospels. At times the connection is pointed out, as when Hilarion himself compares his exorcism of a camel to the incident of the Gadarene swine; or when, faced by a women who had been blind for ten years, Hilarion 'spat on her eyes, and at

[129] *VHil.* 25–8: cf. the model of the late-antique holy man as sketched especially in Brown 1995.
[130] *VHil.* 25 (Elusa), 15–22 (prominent and wealthy visitors).   [131] *VHil.* 20.
[132] *VHil.* 20; see now the reading of this episode in Weingarten 2005: 126–35.
[133] For example, at Mark 1:37–8, 44; Cameron (1991: 184) also points out that the emphasis in the *Life* on miracles brings Hilarion particularly close to Christ.
[134] Mark 3:7–9; *VHil.* 27.

once the same miracle of healing occurred as when the Saviour did this'.[135] At others the style or the circumstances are clearly reminiscent of the New Testament, as with the various exorcisms of individuals and in particular with the healing of a paralysed man brought to Hilarion by his workmates.[136] Hilarion is less a prophet than a miracle-worker: his effect on the world is profound because he fails or refuses to oppose himself to it completely.

Indeed, it is possible to say that Hilarion, as a new Antony, actually re-imagines the role of the holy man: that the *Life of Hilarion* joins Jerome's other biographies in modifying the image of the ascetic to promote more engagement with the world. Moreoever, this is perhaps to develop the ascetic tradition in a direction consistent with the development of Scripture. The relationship between Antony and Hilarion had begun in the traditional way, with Hilarion receiving the gift of Antony's tunic at the very beginning of his ascetic career – once again a recollection of the relationship of Elijah and Elisha, and a reminder of the common tradition and the ascetic and biblical world they shared.[137] And yet although this tradition that binds them together is vital and continues to be emphasised, Hilarion's later career departs substantially from Antony's practice. Ultimately his imitation of Antony is rather less detailed than his imitation of Christ: no longer a prophet crying in the wilderness, but a bringer of truth to the world. Without replacing or dismissing Antony as a predecessor, or denying what they had in common, Hilarion has perhaps fulfilled his promise just as Christ fulfilled that of Elijah, and just as the New Testament fulfilled the Old. Jerome's model of the biblical life matched more closely the exile and return of Christ or John the Baptist than it did the permanent exile of the prophets.

There is therefore surely some irony in the fact that Hilarion's quest for solitude brought him to settle in the Mediterranean, the very centre of the Roman world; and in the fact that his reputation spread as far as St Peter's in Rome.[138] But it is to this

---

[135] *VHil.* 23, with Mark 5:9 and Luke 8:30; *VHil.* 15, with Mark 8:23.
[136] *VHil.* 16, 18, 19 (paralysed man); cf. Mark 2:1–12, plus Matthew 9:2–8 and Luke 5:17–26.
[137] *VHil.* 4.
[138] *VHil.* 37; Jerome's loyalty to (and identification with) the church at Rome is clear from his *Letters* 15 and 16.

familiar world, as well as to those of the Bible and of the desert, that Jerome had sought to connect his characters: within the *Lives*, with their references to Jerome's own experiences and to contemporary people and events, and through the network of sources and dedicatees who appear in the prefaces – Evagrius of Antioch as his source for the *Life of Antony*, Epiphanius of Salamis for the *Life of Hilarion*.[139] These bishops, like Athanasius, had their place both in the *Lives* and outside them; and there were other ways in which Jerome was able to continue his stories beyond the confines of the text. For example, the first recipient of the *Life of Paul* was an aged ascetic, also named Paul, at Concordia: a figure who in thus establishing himself in the monastic life in Italy exemplified his namesake's advice to Antony not to withdraw from the world entirely.[140] By bringing together in his dedicatory letter the two Pauls, of Thebes and Concordia, Jerome was helping to bridge the gap between Egypt and the rest of the Roman empire – between 'the desert' and 'civilisation'. His letter is a supplement to the *Life*, and a reminder of the world it seems to exclude. Indeed, it is a reminder of the whole purpose of the *Life*: as revealed in the final paragraphs, in which Jerome explicitly contrasts Paul's poverty with the empty possessions of the idle rich.[141] The aim was not to leave Paul stranded in the desert, but to promote his commitment and his values among the ordinary people of the empire.

The model of engaged asceticism which may be recognised in Jerome's biographical writings, then, can be seen as part of a broader commitment to the promotion of asceticism in the secular world. Jerome is likely to have encountered Paul of Concordia during his own time at Aquileia, where he belonged to a circle of dedicated Christians which he would later characterise as a 'community of the blessed'.[142] Rufinus, later Bishop of Aquileia, would in turn describe it as a monastery – but if so, it was a loosely organised one and close to the centre of worldly affairs.[143] Nevertheless, Jerome had an example before him of how a spiritual commitment might reach out beyond the desert at the edges of the world and take

---

[139] *VMalchi* 2; *VHil.* 1. [140] Jerome, *Letter* 10. [141] *VPauli* 17–18.
[142] Jerome, *Chronicle*, AD 374; for this group, see Kelly 1975: 32–3, and for its wider context see Humphries 1996: esp. 141–3.
[143] Rufinus, *Apologia contra Hieronymum* 1.4.

hold of the centre; and if he was not the first to bring asceticism to the cultivated regions of Italy and the West, he was a powerful propagandist in favour of that move not only in his *Lives* but also in his letters.[144] For although Jerome had initially sought his ascetic vocation in the deserts of Syria, and although his *Lives* showed the contemporary re-enactment of Scripture in the lives of the desert ascetics, his letters were already relocating this biblical life to less distant and less hostile surroundings. Even before he entered the desert, Jerome wrote to Rufinus in praise of a mutual friend: Bonosus was pursuing the life of an ascetic not in Egypt or Syria, but on an all but deserted island in the Adriatic.[145]

Jerome's vision in this letter of Bonosus' lifestyle amounts to a biographical sketch, a kind of miniature hagiography. The language is typically allusive, and at times can seem glib and superficial – Bonosus is compared to Jonah, 'shut up in the fish's belly in the middle of the sea', or is said to be climbing Jacob's ladder, or preparing for a vision like that granted to John of Patmos – but it is surely significant that Jerome is prepared to see a real continuity between Bonosus and the more familiar model of desert asceticism.[146] The contrast is explicitly noted between the desert and Bonosus' island, but the hopes and ambitions of Bonosus are no different, as 'alone upon the island . . . he seeks the glory of God which the apostles themselves saw only in the desert'.[147] In Jerome's account his real surroundings soon become immaterial, as Bonosus battles with demons in familiar fashion, and in language borrowed from the gospels and the letters of Paul.[148] Bonosus is imitating Christ, or the apostles; more explicitly still, 'after the example of Moses, he is lifting up the serpent in the desert'.[149]

---

[144] Ambrose of Milan, *Letters* 63, 66 and 71, credits Eusebius of Vercelli with first encouraging clergy in Italy to adopt a communal and ascetic lifestyle; Kelly (1975: 32 n. 35) suggests that this took place after his return from exile in 363, approximately ten years before Jerome's stay in Aquileia.

[145] Jerome, *Letter* 3; Rufinus was on a pilgrimage to the holy men of Egypt: see Kelly 1975: 45.

[146] Jerome, *Letter* 3.4–5; cf. Jonah 1:17, 2:1, and Genesis 28:12.

[147] Jerome, *Letter* 3.4.

[148] Jerome, *Letter* 3.4; thus Labourt identifies allusions here to John 19:34 and Ephesians 6:11–17.

[149] Jerome, *Letter* 3.4: 'et sacramento Moysi . . .'. The Latin here may support a stronger sense than 'example': two other translators give 'mystère' (Labourt) or 'type' (Parker).

Bonosus, for Jerome, is living out a biblical life on his island in the Adriatic. He has found himself a desert in the middle of civilisation, or he has created his own desert. Most importantly, he has managed to bring the re-enactment of Scripture out of hagiography and into Jerome's own world.

This movement from text to life – or at least, from biography to personal letter – can be seen to be promoted in a letter by Jerome about another of his friends, in this case a friend made during his time in Rome in the 380s. Jerome had found himself closely involved in a community of upper-class women enthusiastic about Christian asceticism: among them were Paula, who would subsequently accompany him to Jerusalem, and Marcella, perhaps their pioneer.[150] Certainly for Jerome, writing in 413, the year after Marcella's death, she had been the first 'lady of rank' who 'had made a profession of the monastic life'.[151] Indeed, according to his account, she had been inspired by a visit of Athanasius to Rome, from whom 'she heard of the life of the blessed Antony, then still alive, and of the monasteries in the Thebaid founded by Pachomius'.[152] Marcella would have been a young girl when Athanasius was in Rome, but the precise truth of the matter is perhaps unimportant: the effect was to place her in the tradition of Antony, following on from him just like the heroes of Jerome's *Lives*, but at the heart of the Roman empire.[153] Into her home on the fashionable Aventine she brought the asceticism of the desert and the spirituality of Scripture. Far from the holy land, Marcella was reviving the biblical life of Mary Magdalene, or the prophetess Anna; so that if she was not in fact Anna's superior, still 'as both have one task, so both have one reward'.[154]

Jerome's letters attest to his ongoing commitment to the ideal of the ascetic life, but above all to a consistent desire to combine the biblical life with the secular world. His *Lives* of Paul, Malchus and Hilarion offer advice on how to achieve such a balance or offer models of how such a life might be lived. Yet those *Lives*

---

[150] For more detail on these women and their circumstances, see Kelly 1975: 91ff.
[151] Jerome, *Letter* 127.5; Kelly 1975: 92.   [152] Jerome, *Letter* 127.5.
[153] Kelly (1975: 92 n. 9) remarks that Marcella would only have been ten or twelve years old at the time of Athanasius' visit, and that any inspiration was not immediate enough to prevent her from marrying.
[154] Jerome, *Letter* 127.2, 127.5; cf. Luke 2:36.

do more than simply offer supplements to Antony: they engage directly with the Antony tradition, actively modifying his character and criticising his methods. At the same time, Jerome's obtrusive presence in his biographies – pointing morals or citing his own experiences, or using the prefaces to acknowledge his friends and debate with his enemies – works to connect the lives of these desert ascetics with the world of patronage and politics, the world Jerome and his readers share. There is no uncrossable line between Paul of Thebes and Paul of Concordia, between Hilarion in the Mediterranean and Bonosus in the Adriatic, or between the chaste life of Malchus and that of Marcella. In the *Lives* written by Jerome the desert ascetics are in some ways domesticated. Like the fauns and the centaurs who assisted Antony on his way to visit Paul of Thebes, their wildness is pressed into the service of civilisation.

A strange land

Jerome's praise of Marcella at her death, then, is a reminiscence of his own 'contribution to the dissemination of asceticism of the Oriental type at Rome'.[155] He may not have been the first to inspire or encourage these ascetic men and women, but he offered firm and consistent support and, notably too, 'a firm biblical foundation'.[156] But his enthusiasm for this project must have been tempered by the memory of his personal rejection by the church authorities at Rome, when in 385 he had been forced to leave in controversial circumstances.[157] As he left the city for good he would condemn himself for his folly as one 'who wished to sing the Lord's song in a strange land'.[158] He had come to portray the city as Babylon – and himself as an exile reclaiming the biblical life as he re-enacted Scripture, an exile returning to Jerusalem from the tyranny of Nebuchadnezzar.[159] Just as he had found the life of a desert ascetic

---

[155] Kelly 1975: 94.   [156] Kelly 1975: 94.
[157] Some possible explanations are put forward at Kelly 1975: 110–15.
[158] Jerome, *Letter* 45.6; Psalms 137.4 [AV].
[159] Jerome, *Letter* 45.6: his reference here seems to be to Haggai 1:1, with Nebuchadnezzar imported from Daniel.

unsustainable, he had recognised that the life of a monk in the world could be equally prone to disillusion.[160]

Instead Jerome set out with Paula to settle at Bethlehem, where they would found a set of monastic communities similar to that already present in Jerusalem under Jerome's old companion Rufinus.[161] In these communities, set apart from the world but still able to play a full part in ecclesiastical and scholarly matters, and situated neither in the desert nor in the metropolis but in a small town of unignorable Christian significance, Jerome perhaps found the compromise he had sought between the holy life and the life of the world. Not the least virtue of a monastic community, as Jerome would later note, was that it could combine both inspiration and correction.[162] Between the abbot and the other monks a novice had not one but many masters: 'From one of them you may learn humility, from another patience; this one will teach you silence, that one meekness.'[163] A monastic vocation could therefore provide a kind of halfway-house for a would-be ascetic.

But there were other advantages to establishing a monastery in the Holy Land in particular. It was, after all, those living on the edge of the desert who were confronted most of all with the lives of the ascetics in Egypt and Syria. In one sense, then, the accessibility of the desert allowed Christians in the Holy Land to live, as it were, within one enormous monastic community. Those monks who might already belong to a monastery in Jerusalem or Bethlehem, could make the relatively short journey into the desert and find a whole range of different practices from which to learn – as did one party who set out around 394 from the monastery of Rufinus on the Mount of Olives.[164] Their journey was recorded in Greek in what is now generally known as the *History of the Monks in Egypt*, and was later translated into Latin and in part

---

[160] Jerome had already begun to rail against false monks and virgins in Rome while he was there, as in *Letter* 22 (to Eustochium); years later he would return to the theme in *Letter* 125 (to Rusticus). For his complaints, see esp. Curran 1997 and, for their satirical nature, Wiesen 1964.

[161] Kelly 1975: 129–35.   [162] Jerome, *Letter* 125.9, 125.13.

[163] Jerome, *Letter* 125.15.

[164] Translations from the *HM* are taken from that of Russell 1981, based on the Greek text established by Festugière. The date is furnished by the references to imperial affairs in (especially) *HM* 1.64.

rewritten apparently by Rufinus himself.[165] Without losing contact with civilisation, the monks on their pilgrimage to the desert were offered the endless variety of contemporary ascetics and their gifts and their lessons: 'some in their speech, some in their manner of life, and others in the wonders and signs which they performed'.[166]

Continuing the tradition of the *Life of Antony* and the biographies it had inspired, the *History of the Monks in Egypt* provided a series of brief portraits of Egyptian ascetics, their practice, their advice and the stories they told. It can be thought of as a series of biographies, and a recent English translation has labelled it the *Lives of the Desert Fathers*.[167] As before, these new lives were not intended to supplant those of earlier ascetics, and Antony himself is acknowledged in this collection as the master or companion of some of the living ascetics.[168] Instead, these additional lives supplemented the example of Antony, giving a new perspective on his lifestyle and sometimes revealing his limitations – as when, for example, his disciple Paul the Simple is said to have been able to exorcise demons where even Antony himself had failed. These new desert fathers ultimately helped to present readers with 'the widest possible range of ascetic ideals and models'.[169] At the same time, these Christian biographies all share a common underlying theme, and the commonality is perhaps especially obvious in the case of a 'collective biography' such as this one. Thus the various accounts can be said to represent merely aspects of a single 'angelic life'; and that life, in turn, is specifically presented as part of the 'imitation of our divine Saviour'.[170]

The pilgrims therefore depicted themselves as moving from the familiar world of the Roman empire into 'a place where the distant past – in this case the biblical past – [was] restored among the monks'.[171] This is not to say that the monks they encountered were intended to take the place of the spiritual figures found in

---

[165] The Latin text is found in *PL* 21:387–462; for Rufinus as the author, see Ward 1981: 6–8, with his changes compiled at 139–55.

[166] *HM* 5.7.   [167] The translation is that of Russell 1981.

[168] As for example in the accounts of Pityrion (*HM* 15) and, especially, of Paul the Simple (*HM* 24).

[169] Elm 1994: 313; cf. Anderson 1994: 202.   [170] Cox Miller 2000: 231–2; *HM* prol. 5.

[171] Frank 2000: 54.

Scripture, as the travellers are immediately reminded in their first meeting, with John of Lycopolis.[172] The encounter with John may represent a transition from the civilised world to the desert: he is introduced with a series of references to prophecies made for and concerning the Emperor Theodosius I and other Roman generals and officials, and he takes his leave of the narrators in the same way, with unsolicited predictions of the deaths of the usurper Eugenius and of Theodosius himself.[173] And yet even John draws attention to explicit parallels between the monks and the likes of David and Job.[174] In this, the first and longest section of the work, it is possible already to recognise the interaction of the secular world and the biblical life.

Certainly examples of the latter seem to have been easy to identify. Indeed, some of the ascetics encountered on the journey are identified by little more than a reference to the scriptures: the strict anchorite Elias, whose name could only reinforce the popular impression 'that the spirit of the prophet Elijah rested on him'; and John of Diolcos, the final ascetic in the work, whose primary distinguishing feature was that 'he looked like Abraham and had a beard like Aaron's'.[175] But the revival of the biblical world in the desert is best captured in the travellers' account of Apollo, whose home of Hermopolis is introduced as the place 'where the Saviour went with Mary and Joseph in fulfilment of the prophecy of Isaiah', and where they personally saw 'the temple where all the idols fell on their faces on the ground at the entrance of the Saviour into the city'.[176]

Apollo's preaching and miracles are described in great detail, but his significance is shown most clearly in his dealing with a famine that had struck the Thebaid. Having persuaded his own community to share what they had with the local villagers, the point was reached when only three baskets of bread remained. Bringing them out, Apollo invoked the scriptures, saying:

[172] *HM* 1.20.   [173] *HM* 1.1–10, 1.64.   [174] *HM* 1.31, 1.33.   [175] *HM* 7.1; 26.1.
[176] *HM* 8.1; cf. the Gospel of Pseudo-Matthew 22–3, tr. Elliott 1993: 84–99, with Sozomen, *Historia ecclesiastica* 5.21. For a similar example of a speculative biblical topography, see *HM* 18.3, where the Greek narrator reports having seen the granaries built by Joseph (identified by Ward as the pyramids at Giza).

Is the hand of the Lord not strong enough to multiply these loaves? For the Holy Spirit says, 'The bread from these baskets shall not be consumed until we have all been satisfied with new wheat.'[177]

Immediately it was found that the baskets of bread were now sufficient for four months' food, and the same miracle was performed with the reserves of oil and wheat.[178] The story ends in remarkably familiar fashion, as 'those who brought in the bread placed full baskets on the tables of the brethren, and after five hundred brothers had eaten their fill took them away still full'.[179]

Apollo's feeding of five hundred monks is said to have caught the attention of Satan, who appeared to Apollo in person to ask: 'Are you not Elijah, or one of the other prophets or apostles, that you have the confidence to do these things?'[180] The fact that the comparison is given such an unreliable source is perhaps a reason to be sceptical about it, but even the 'sarcastic exaltation of hermits as Elijah' reflects the possibility of a real comparison – and one not unusual in Christian biography.[181] In any case, Apollo accepts the charge, and replies with a declaration of faith in Scripture and history:

Were not the holy prophets and apostles, who have handed on to us the power to do such things, men themselves? Or was God present then, but is now away on a journey? God can always do these things, for with him nothing is impossible.[182]

Such confidence in God's continued active presence in the world seems entirely appropriate for Apollo, who as an adolescent had already received a personal revelation from the Lord:

Apollo, Apollo, through you I will destroy the wisdom of the wise men of Egypt, and I will bring to nothing the understanding of the prudent pagans. And together with these you will also destroy the wise men of Babylon for me, and you will banish all worship of demons. And now make your way to the inhabited region, for you will bear me 'a peculiar people, zealous of good works'.[183]

---

[177] HM 8.45.   [178] HM 8.46.   [179] HM 8.47.   [180] HM 8.47.
[181] See Frankfurter 1993: 72–3 for such a sceptical reading of this incident.
[182] HM 8.47; it may be possible to recognise here a reminiscence of 1 Kings 18:27, where Elijah mocks the priests of Baal for the silence of their god with the suggestion that he may be away on a journey.
[183] HM 8.3, quoting Titus 2:14; cf. for the first sentence Isaiah 29.14.

The revelation places Apollo firmly in the tradition of the Old Testament prophets, Elijah and Isaiah in particular; he is thus revealed to be what the narrator calls him, 'a new prophet and apostle raised up for our generation'.[184]

But it is worth noting, perhaps, that to fulfil his mission Apollo will be required to seek out the inhabited regions: that his exercise of divine authority and power requires an audience beyond the solitude of the desert. Whether or not he achieved that in his own life, the travellers from Jerusalem were able to bring him into contact with the inhabited world simply by including him in their collection. For the pilgrims who set out from the Mount of Olives, and who returned to write the *History of the Monks in Egypt*, were not intending to provide a comprehensive account of the varieties of desert asceticism.[185] It is important to remember that the work is above all an account of a journey. It may represent an actual pilgrimage, and it is certainly one for which a plausible itinerary can be reconstructed.[186] Nevertheless, it is a report and not a guidebook: it is a narrative – and as with so much travel writing, the primary interest lies in the narrators' observations and responses.[187]

One effect, then, is to focus attention not on the ascetics encountered in the desert, but on the travellers themselves – and on the experience of making a pilgrimage.[188] Details of the journey are largely confined to the epilogue, but the visiting monks are a constant and often intrusive presence: they provide opportunities for the ascetics to display their powers, as when one of the party falls asleep and is miraculously awoken; and are witnesses to many other miracles, so that it can be asked, 'what need is there to speak of any of the works of this saint other than those which we

[184] *HM* 8.8.   [185] Frank 2000: 29; see also Goehring 1993: 291–3.
[186] As in Ward 1981: 4–6, following on from the work of Dom Cuthbert Butler. For a more detailed discussion of a parallel account of a pilgrimage, see Elsner 2000b; Christian pilgrimage in general is considered in similar terms at Coleman and Elsner 1995: 78–99.
[187] Thus Frank approaches these accounts of visits to holy places and holy people 'more as literary creations than as historical chronicles' (2000: 5), and focuses on the interaction of the audience with the narrators as well as with holy men themselves. Her ch. 2 reads the *HM* and similar texts in these terms as primarily travelogues; and notes the distancing effect which allows the desert to become a site of the re-enactment of Scripture: on this see esp. Frank 2000: 49–61. My engagement with these ideas should be clear in what follows.
[188] See esp. Goehring 1993 for accounts of pilgrimages replacing actual travel, and Elsner 2005 for the question of the audience for such texts.

perceived with our own eyes?'[189] Their accounts, then, are more than just stories: they could offer their readers eye-witness testimony.[190] Thus for those readers who were unable to travel to the desert and see for themselves the re-enactment of Scripture, such an account was the next best thing: a travelogue such as this allowed them still 'to *engage* the biblical world'.[191] Through the text, readers 'witnessed not only the world of monasticism but the world of the Bible itself'.[192] And whether in reality or simply in the imagination, it was a world that one could go and visit.

Like the *Life of Antony* and its imitators, the *History of the Monks in Egypt* told 'biblical stories of exemplary saints', and situated them firmly in the contemporary world.[193] The sheer number of ascetics in the desert – so many that 'a countless host' went undescribed – provided Christians in the Roman empire with 'a pictorial world thickly populated by holy people'.[194] Christian biography was a supplement to Scripture, perhaps even an extension of a reader's biblical studies; and those who read or only heard about the lives of the ascetics would nevertheless be aware of the continuities.[195] Antony was indeed a new Elijah, and a new John the Baptist; and his imitators were also their imitators. They each served as a link in the chain that connected the modern world with the Bible. Thus it was only to be expected that an author should begin his work 'with the coming of our Saviour Jesus Christ' with the intention of showing 'that even in these times the Saviour performs through [ascetics] what He performed through the prophets and apostles'.[196] Surrounded by scriptural figures, by saints re-enacting the scriptures, readers of Christian biography could understand themselves to be living inside the Bible.[197]

This too was something Jerome had experienced for himself. Before even entering the Syrian desert, he had written to Rufinus enthusiastically imagining the details of the latter's Egyptian pilgrimage: 'I hear you are penetrating the secret recesses of Egypt,

---

[189] *HM* 10.23; *HM* 1.13; see also e.g. *HM* 8.48, 10.26.
[190] See esp. Frank 2000: 50–2 for the importance of autopsy in these accounts; note too the connection with typology, as discussed at Krueger 1997: 415–16, and now in Krueger 2004: 15–32.
[191] Frank 2000: 29–30.   [192] Frank 2000: 172.   [193] Brakke 1995: 217.
[194] *HM* 18.3; Cameron 1991: 151.   [195] Frank 2000: 11.   [196] *HM* prol. 4; prol. 13.
[197] As suggested by Blowers 1997: 231.

visiting the companies of monasteries and paying a round of visits to the heavenly family on earth.'[198] Subsequently, as he began his exile from Rome to Bethlehem, Jerome would make a similar journey with Paula, taking in the holy places of Palestine and Egypt. They would visit both living monks and the historical sites familiar from the words of Scripture; and after the death of Paula in 404, Jerome would write an account of the journey – or rather, journeys – in a letter to her daughter Eustochium.[199] The centrepiece of the letter is a travelogue, deliberately focused on 'such places as are mentioned in the sacred books'.[200] But Jerome's account is rather more than an itinerary: it is a record of the 'wonder and awe felt by Christians as they came face to face with the actual spots, as they believed them to be, at which the signal events of sacred history had been enacted'.[201]

Jerome's description of the journey is exhaustive, and takes in a whole range of familiar people and places. He and Paula visited 'the sands of Tyre on which Paul had once knelt', and 'Elijah's town on the shore at Zarephath'.[202] The tour also took in Jericho and the Jordan, and 'every conceivable spot with Old or New Testament associations'; but the most significant aspect throughout was the effect that these sites had on the lives of the pilgrims themselves.[203] This was no mere tourist jaunt, but an event of considerable emotional force. The most remarkable impression was made by places associated with the life of Christ – above all, the crucifixion and the nativity – and Paula's response in each case is suggestive. At the first, 'before the cross she threw herself down in adoration as though she beheld the Lord hanging upon it'.[204] The power of the site was enough to revive a 'tableau vivant' in which Paula took her place, re-enacting Scripture as it played out before her.[205] More dramatic still was her experience at Christ's birthplace in Bethlehem:

---

[198] Jerome, *Letter* 3.1 (tr. Frank).

[199] Burrus 2003: 63, noting that Paula's journey is ongoing and that 'her search for the incarnate Lord knows no end'.

[200] Jerome, *Letter* 108.8; for Paula as a pilgrim, see Elsner 2005: 412, placing this letter in the context of other pilgrimage narratives, Pullan 2005: 403–7 and Burrus 2003: 62–3.

[201] Kelly 1975: 120.   [202] Jerome, *Letter* 108.8.   [203] Kelly 1975: 118.

[204] Jerome, *Letter* 108.9: 'prostrataque ante crucem, quasi pendentem Dominum cerneret, adorabat.'

[205] Frank 2000: 61.

When she looked upon these things . . . she protested in my hearing that she could behold with the eyes of faith the infant Lord wrapped in swaddling clothes and crying in the manger, the wise men worshipping Him, the star shining overhead, the virgin mother, the attentive foster-father, the shepherds coming by night . . . She declared that she could see the slaughtered innocents, the raging Herod, Joseph and Mary fleeing into Egypt.[206]

Such visions of the supernatural were only to be expected at sites with such a powerful past. For Paula and Jerome, and for other pilgrims and those who merely read about their travels, the holy land had become 'a stage for biblical spectacles', a place in which the world of the Bible had not only once been but was present again.[207]

Paula's transformative experiences in the Holy Land are brought together by Jerome with her visits to the monks in Egypt, where 'in each of the saints she believed she saw Christ himself'.[208] And it is here that the special character of the Holy Land becomes clear: for in both the Holy Land and in the desert Christian pilgrims – and those who read or heard about their exploits at second hand – were confronted with the biblical past as it had survived into the present, and for someone such as Paula, 'to gaze at holy people or holy places was to gaze at the scriptures'.[209] Whether discovered by a pilgrimage to the ascetics of Egypt or by a reading of Christian biography, it was clear that the biblical life was alive and well and being lived in the Roman empire. The juxtaposition of the modern empire and these manifestations of the biblical world not only made the Bible more real and more accessible but also, at the same time, 'biblicised the present'.[210]

The way of the fathers

These various *Lives* of desert ascetics, then, depended for much of their effect on the difficult task of rendering the world they described as simultaneously exotic and familiar.[211] That this was a concern from the start is evident even in the Greek *Life of Antony*, which alternates between the image of Antony as a wild and

[206] Jerome, *Letter* 108.10.   [207] Frank 2000: 2.   [208] Jerome, *Letter* 108.14.
[209] Frank 2000: 11.   [210] Frank 2000: 172.   [211] As noted at Frank 2000: 72.

unlettered ascetic performing feats of endurance and clairvoyance in the Inner Mountain, and the image of the would-be martyr who engages with imperial and ecclesiastical politics at Alexandria, and whose legacy is taken up by the bishops Serapion and Athanasius.[212] Moreover, with the inclusion of Athanasius – certainly the presumed author if not the actual author – the involvement of Antony with the world breaks out into the 'historical' world of authors and readers: just as Antony is not to be confined to Upper Egypt, his *Life* is not to be consigned to the world of romance but insists on presenting itself as history. Verisimilitude is vital to these Christian biographies: the miraculous world they record is to be associated directly with the readers' own.

The same dynamic can be identified in the *Lives* of Pachomius and of Paul the First Hermit. In both cases Antony appears, making clear the place of these heroes in what was a developing literary tradition; but there too is Antony's author Athanasius, albeit in a cameo appearance or recognised solely through his gift of a cloak.[213] In each case, however, more of an effort is made to emphasise the connection between the ascetic and the world around him: Pachomius founds his community close to the village of Tabennesi; Paul is connected to the world of Antony and Cleopatra, and retains his curiosity about public affairs despite his long years in the desert.[214] For Jerome the conceit is carried further in the *Life of Hilarion*, whose hero may pay lip-service to the idea of isolation exemplified (in the text and in the preface) by Antony and Paul, but is unable to prevent himself from drawing a crowd. Indeed, the strategy of the *Life of Hilarion* might best be summed up by his intervention on behalf of Italicus in the chariot-race at Gaza – a reclusive holy man exerting his powers at the most popular of public occasions.[215] Nevertheless, in Jerome's *Lives* this historicising impulse is balanced by the presence of the miraculous. The centaurs and fauns of the *Life of Paul* are matched, perhaps, by

[212] *VA* 93.
[213] *VP* 30 (Athanasius sailing down the Nile); *VPauli* 12: 'Antony was dumbfounded at hearing that Paul knew of Athanasius and his cloak.'
[214] This tension between involvement and withdrawal is suggested as a central component of desert asceticism in Goehring 1993; the specific examples here may be found *VPauli* 5, 10.
[215] *VHil.* 20.

the serpent destroyed at Epidaurus in the *Life of Hilarion*; and the tsunami which in the latter account establishes the saint's credentials as a historical figure also offers the opportunity for what must have been the most spectacular of his many miracles as he stopped the wave as it broke.[216]

But this difficult compromise between familiarity and exoticism is negotiated above all by means of the Bible. The Bible was a familiar text to Christians, but it might easily have seemed irrevocably tied to the past; in these biographies, however, it was brought back to life and brought into contact with the contemporary world. That Antony should have re-enacted the life of Elijah, or that Hilarion's miracles should have recalled those of Christ, is therefore more than a matter of idle pattern-making. It implied an understanding of the world which reimagined it as something other than merely the later Roman empire. It located a continuing biblical tradition on the margins of the everyday world; and it proceeded to bring it closer to the centre. The stories of these new biblical figures, and of their miracles, and their adherence to the way of life of the patriarchs, were increasingly located not in the desert but in civilised Egypt and Syria, and even in Greece and Italy and Gaul. Bridging the gap were authors such as Athanasius and Jerome, who presented themselves as moving with ease between the world of the metropolitan clergy and the world of the desert fathers. And Jerome in particular soon extended this 'precarious middle ground' to his friends and companions, and to his readers.[217] Thus Paula, Marcella and Melania graduated from upper-class, urban Christians who might devour a saint's life 'as if eating dessert', to pilgrims who could visit the biblical world for themselves – and who could be incorporated directly into it as their lives were written up in their turn.[218]

Thus late-antique Christian biography challenged its readers to accept the miraculous as a component of the everyday world. In the process, the prophets and apostles of the Bible became familiar contemporary figures; and the boundaries and underpinnings of the

---

[216] *VHil.* 42.   [217] Frank 2000: 51.
[218] *Vita Melaniae* 21, tr. Clark 1984: 44; for the absorption of these women into the biblical world, see e.g. Frank 2000: 107–8, quoting Jerome's anticipation of Marcella's visit in Jerome, *Letter* 46.13.

familiar world became proportionately more strange. The Bible now permeated the Roman world and could no longer be confined to the past, just as the first Greek *Life of Pachomius* had said:

> What we have heard and known and our fathers have told us should not be hidden from the next generation. For, as we have been taught, we know that these words of the psalm are about the signs and portents accomplished by God for Moses and those after him. And after the model of the benefit given by them, we have also recognised in the fathers of our time their children and imitators, so that to us and to the rising generation, until the end of the world, it might be known that Jesus Christ is the same yesterday, today and forever.[219]

The conventional comparisons of contemporary monks to biblical figures cannot therefore be taken for granted. The 'recent acts' of the saints attested to the continuity of sacred history, making their own contribution to that 'unified structure of narrative and imagery' which identified Scripture.[220] That strain of Christian biography which took its inspiration from the *Life of Antony* soon filled the Roman empire with re-enactments of Scripture, and allowed contemporary Christians to reconsider the presuppositions on which their lives were founded. This was a lesson that Jerome himself was eager to apply to the raising of Paula's eponymous granddaughter, advising her to take Scripture as her guide: for 'in our own time we see such things as seem to belong in the books of the prophets'.[221]

---

[219] *VP* 17, quoting Psalms 77:3 [LXX]; Psalms 70:18 [LXX]; and Hebrews 13:8.
[220] Frye 1982: xvii; Van Uytfanghe 1985: 609, 'la "geste récente" des saints atteste la continuité de l'histoire du salut dans l'Église'.
[221] Jerome, *Letter* 107.3: 'uidimus aliquid temporibus nostris de prophetalibus libris'.

4

AUGUSTINE: THE LIFE OF THE MIND

Laying aside the lighter burden – that is, blaming ourselves – we take up a heavier one: that is, doing ourselves justice.

(John the Dwarf, XXI, in the *Apophthegmata Patrum* (alphabetical collection))

There is some continuity, then, between the biographies of significant political figures such as Constantine and Basil, and between the accounts of ascetic heroes with which the late-antique world came to be populated. Emperors and bishops could be picked out and shown to recall the Bible in their personalities and their deeds; and this representation could come to imply the presence of a broader continuity with Scripture in the world they inhabited and perhaps dominated. Thus if Basil was a new Moses, it was possible to recognise a new Aaron in his brother Gregory. Moreover, the world in which Scripture was re-enacted was also the world of the author and the reader. This was true when it applied to men such as Constantine and Basil, with whom significant numbers of people were familiar; but it was no less true when applied to an obscure inhabitant of an Egyptian village. In either case, these figures inhabited both a recognisable contemporary environment and, at the same time, a biblical world which might otherwise have seemed to have vanished forever.

The heroes of Christian biography, therefore, along with their authors and readers, seemed to occupy a single reality: one which could incorporate the strange feats of the ascetic heroes, their encounters with monsters and demons, and their re-enactments of Scripture, into the familiar world of the later Roman empire. Indeed, the world of Scripture itself was both exotic and familiar to late-antique Christians; and in a sense, these *Lives* merely transferred the events from long, long ago to far, far away. The biblical past was no longer irrecoverable, but continued in a distant corner of the empire. It was brought closer by Athanasius and, above all, Jerome, who presented himself as combining the roles of author and ascetic hero; but also by pilgrims such as Melania, Paula and Marcella, who had graduated from the role of reader to that of participant in the 'biblicised' world of asceticism.[1] Thus the world of the Bible became – for a select few – a part of everyday experience.

That experience was related in *Lives* and pilgrim narratives to readers elsewhere in the empire: 'armchair pilgrims' who may never have encountered an ascetic outside of a contemporary Christian biography.[2] To understand the broader changes that these Christian biographies made, or encouraged, in later Roman culture and society, it will be useful to view the phenomenon from the perspective of one such reader.

Admittedly, Augustine of Hippo was scarcely in any sense an ordinary Christian. A professor of rhetoric at the imperial court, and with an abiding interest in metaphysics, he was by the time he encountered the *Life of Antony* already familiar with the Christianity and Manichaeanism of his native North Africa, and had schooled himself in academic philosophy. For all these reasons, he is far from the kind of unsophisticated reader at whom medieval 'hagiographical romances' were often aimed.[3] Augustine's response to the *Life of Antony* is important because it reminds us that Christian biographies could indeed be taken seriously; and that the effect of a saint's life was not always simple or easily characterised. These lives were intended for a wide reading public, and were appreciated at all levels of later Roman society, so that it may be argued that 'holy *vitae* were part of a universal Christian culture'.[4] In this light, Augustine's response is important too because it is by far the fullest account that survives of a contemporary reading of a late-antique Christian biography. It is not, as might be expected, an immediate or unconsidered response, but rather forms part of a sophisticated narrative. Writing in the last years of the fourth century AD, Augustine was describing the moment – in

---

[1] Frank 2000: 51–2. [2] Frank 2000: 4.

[3] Thus Coon (1997: 6) notes that 'Merovingian hagiographers themselves remark that they are aiming at illiterate audiences.'

[4] Coon 1997: 5.

Milan in 386 – when he felt himself to have been finally and permanently converted to the Christian belief in God. Thus the *Life of Antony* was reappropriated to play a vital part in Augustine's own Christian autobiography, the *Confessions*.[5]

This scene has been quoted and recounted at length in countless modern works, but remarkably the precise role of Antony seems to have received rather less attention than it deserves.[6] In part this must be because the scene constitutes an exception: for Antony is 'astonishingly invisible' elsewhere in the many and voluminous works of Augustine.[7] And yet here in Book 8 of the *Confessions*, Augustine insists not only on the importance of the life of Antony in his own personal development, but also on Antony's cultural importance in the wider Christian community. The story he tells seems to involve rather more than merely the disproportionate impact on a spiritually eager young man of 'a relatively obscure saint's life'.[8] On the contrary, it may reveal something of the impact on late-antique life of the new phenomenon of Christian biography.

Antony and Augustine

The introduction of Antony comes towards the middle of Book 8 of the *Confessions*, as Augustine finds himself living in a heightened state of anxiety, wishing to be converted to Christianity but unable himself to take that step.[9] It is at this point that Augustine receives an unexpected visit at home from 'a certain Ponticianus', a fellow-African but apparently otherwise a stranger.[10] Ponticianus held high office at the imperial court and was a baptised Christian. Presumably he knew Augustine by reputation, and was apparently

---

5 English translations of the *Confessions* here are those of Chadwick (1991), except where specified; since the exact meaning is so often at issue in my readings here, I have in most cases given the Latin in a footnote.

6 Thus Brown (2000: 107–9), for example, chooses not to describe the episode but instead to quote at length Augustine's own account. Antony is mentioned but rarely lingered over even in major works on Augustine: there are only brief comments in Courcelle 1973: 193; O'Meara 2001: 175–7, 189; Brown 2000: 113; and even in O'Donnell 1992: III.38, III.66. The most extended account remains that of Monceaux 1931, although he focuses for the most part on Augustine's monastic project; the best recent discussions of Antony's role are Olson 1995: 50–4 and Stock 1996: 98–109.

7 O'Donnell 1992: III.38.   8 Olson 1995: 50.   9 *Conf.* 8.6.13

10 *Conf.* 8.6.14: 'Ponticianus quidam'.

surprised to find the former Manichee reading the letters of the
apostle Paul.

When I had indicated to him that those scriptures were the subject of deep study
for me, a conversation began in which he told the story of Antony the Egyptian
monk, a name held in high honour among your servants, though up to that moment
Alypius and I had never heard of him. When he discovered this, he dwelt on the
story instilling in us who were ignorant an awareness of the man's greatness, and
expressing astonishment that we did not know of him. We were amazed as we
heard of your wonderful acts very well attested and occurring so recently, almost
in our own time, done in orthodox faith and the Catholic church. All of us were
in a state of surprise, we because of the greatness of the story, he because we had
not heard about it.[11]

Augustine's final line makes a number of complex points in the
grandly rhetorical image of the three interlocuters all marvelling at
one another.[12] Evidently the life of Antony must have been common knowledge among Ponticianus' circle, or his astonishment
would make no sense. Indeed, Ponticianus was surprised that even
men such as Augustine and Alypius, on the fringes of the Christian
community – for until he found them to be reading Paul he did not
imagine them to be Christians – should be unaware of Antony.
Augustine, in recalling this surprise, is surely sharing it; and he
records also the astonishment he felt at the time that such an extraordinary story should have passed him by. The substantial point here,
then, is that Augustine and Alypius were unusual, among educated
men with an interest in Christianity, in not knowing the story of
Antony. Although it was perhaps 'not . . . a canonical text' of the
order of Cicero or Virgil, the life of Antony was evidently part of
a common Christian culture in the Latin west by the 380s.[13] It is
not an example chosen by Augustine for its obscurity, but for its
significance among the Christians of his own time.

That significance can be seen in the next story Ponticianus tells.
After mentioning the communities of monks both in the deserts
of Africa and Syria and in more domestic contexts, even just outside Milan, Ponticianus returns to the importance of the life of

[11] *Conf.* 8.6.14. The 'wonderful acts' are those of God, to whom the *Confessions* is
addressed.
[12] 'omnes mirabamur, et nos, quia tam magna erant, et ille, quia inaudita nobis erant.'
[13] Olson 1995: 50.

Antony in the lives of his friends and contemporaries. He describes two of his friends from the imperial service – *agentes in rebus* in the court at Trier – who when walking in the gardens by the city walls had encountered what seems to have been a small Christian community.[14]

> In their wanderings they happened upon a certain house where there lived some of your servants, poor in spirit: 'of such is the kingdom of heaven'. They found there a book in which was written the *Life of Antony*. One of them began to read it. He was amazed and set on fire, and during his reading began to think of taking up this way of life and of leaving his secular post in the civil service to be your servant . . . He read on and experienced a conversion inwardly where you alone could see and, as was soon evident, his mind rid itself of the world. Indeed, as he read and turned over and over in the turbulent hesitations of his heart, there were some moments when he was angry with himself. But then he perceived the choice to be made and took a decision to follow the better course.[15]

The man thus affected chose to stay in the community by the walls of Trier, and immediately persuaded his companion to join him, while Ponticianus and a fourth member of the group decided to continue their secular careers.[16] The story was therefore not inevitably one which would have an effect on its hearer, as Ponticianus at least had remained unchanged by it; but nevertheless, it is this story which immediately precedes, and seems to precipitate, 'the final crisis' in Augustine's account of his own conversion.[17] Even while Ponticianus was speaking, says Augustine, his thoughts had turned to his own spiritual state.[18] His immediate response was to cry out against his own hesitations and, followed by Alypius, to head out into his garden. The stories told by Ponticianus – and in particular the ones, emphasised in retrospect by Augustine, concerning the life of Antony – had had a catalytic effect.

The rest of the story is well known, but two of the most famous incidents in particular deserve to be quoted in this connection. They follow one from the other at the climax of the conversion scene, and indeed represent a return to narrative after Augustine

---

[14] *Conf.* 8.6.15. Augustine cannot recall the date of this incident; it must date from a time when the imperial court was at Trier, and could therefore be assigned to any year between 366 and 381.

[15] *Conf.* 8.6.15. The quotation is from Matthew 5:3.   [16] *Conf.* 8.6.15.

[17] O'Meara 2001: 189; cf. Monceaux 1931: 63.

[18] *Conf.* 8.7.16: 'tu . . . inter uerba eius retorquebas me ad me ipsum'.

has digressed on to an analysis of the workings of the will and the precise form of his own indecision.[19] In tears Augustine has left Alypius behind and sought refuge in another part of the garden: 'I threw myself down somehow under a certain fig tree.'[20] Then, in the midst of his subsequent self-accusations, a crucial series of events takes place:

Suddenly I heard a voice from the nearby house chanting as if it might be a boy or a girl (I do not know which), saying and repeating over and over again 'Pick up and read, pick up and read.' At once my countenance changed, and I began to think intently whether there might be some sort of children's game in which such a chant is used. But I could not remember having heard of one. I checked the flood of tears and stood up. I interpreted it solely as a divine command to me to open the book and read the first chapter I might find. For I had heard how Antony happened to be present at the gospel reading, and took it as an admonition addressed to himself when the words were read: 'Go, sell all you have, give to the poor, and you shall have treasure in heaven; and come, follow me.' By such an inspired utterance he was immediately 'converted to you'.[21]

Augustine then returned to his copy of Paul's letters and opened the codex at random, to find a passage (Romans 13:13–14) which he interpreted as fitting his own situation.[22] Immediately he felt himself to have been converted, and told the story to Alypius – who followed his example by finding his own passage in the letter and being converted on the spot.[23]

There is too much here to even contemplate offering a complete interpretation of the episode, but it is important to note that in these climactic events the life of Antony – which is to say, his example – plays a vital role. Not only was Augustine initially strongly affected by the story of Antony as retold by Ponticianus, and by the story of Antony's effect on the imperial officials at Trier, but the example of Antony returns at the very moment of Augustine's final decision. It seems clear enough that the life of Antony was not only important

---

[19] This digression – which contains many interesting points, to which I shall return – can be considered to run from *Conf.* 8.8.20 as far as the end of *Conf.* 8.11.27.
[20] *Conf.* 8.12.28: 'ego sub quadam fici arbore straui me nescio quomodo.'
[21] *Conf.* 8.12.29. The story is told at *VA* 2.3, and discussed in ch. 3, above.
[22] *Conf.* 8.12.29. The passage from Romans is given in Chadwick's translation as: 'Not in riots and drunken parties, not in eroticism and indecencies, not in strife and rivalries, but put on the Lord Jesus Christ and make not provision for the flesh and its lusts.'
[23] As Augustine points out, Alypius endured none of the agonies of hesitation he himself had suffered.

in 386, but was also part of Augustine's design as he wrote his *Confessions* in the late 390s, and that in retelling the stories both of Antony and of the friends of Ponticianus he could not but have 'had his own conversion in mind'.[24] At the simplest level, the stories (and especially the friends of Ponticianus) can be understood as doublets for the conversions of Augustine and Alypius – although not always without overstretching coincidences of language and subject matter.[25] Yet relationships in Augustine are never simple, and here he has gone to some lengths to articulate precisely the importance that the life of Antony had during an episode in his own life. Augustine's response, and the responses of others in his series of conversion narratives, can help us to understand what it meant in late antiquity to read the life of Antony. This, then, is a matter of lives, both as they were written and as they were lived.

The need for acceptance

The dramatic conversion undergone by Augustine in his own garden must of course represent the culmination of a longer process of conversion, which some have traced even as far back as his childhood.[26] On this understanding, which the majority of readers now seem to accept as the most psychologically plausible, the experiences related by Augustine in Book 8 of the *Confessions* acted only as a sort of 'catalytic agent' in bringing about the final change.[27] This has rightly led to a certain amount of caution in interpretations of Augustine's conversion at Milan as representing a decisive break in his thought or attitudes; and the entire episode has even been dismissed as 'both anachronistic and apologetic', a misleading account owing more to the conversion of St Paul than to the truth of Augustine's own mental and spiritual state in 386.[28]

---

[24] O'Meara 2001: 189.
[25] Olson (1995: 51–4) seems to overstate the similarities between the two stories; the more extreme suggestions in Courcelle 1968 are dealt with well by O'Donnell 1992: III.59–61. O'Donnell's commentary offers potential linguistic parallels (e.g. at III.40, s.v. 'hortos') without attempting to assert a firm or definite relationship.
[26] Most famously in Nock 1952: 259–66, followed by many other commentators.
[27] Nock 1952: 266.
[28] Fredriksen 1986: 33. O'Donnell (1992: III.xxxi) advises caution regarding 'Augustine's own insistence as to the importance of his own conversion, as recorded in Bk. VIII of

Nevertheless, regardless of the truth of the matter, Book 8 records Augustine's own opinion (albeit his opinion in the late 390s) of what it was that permitted him to opt decisively for the Christian church. Whether we are dealing here with the Augustine of 386 or with Augustine the autobiographer, it is clear that we are also dealing with the impact which the story of one life could have on another. In this case, as Augustine presents it, the life of Antony acted as the effective catalyst. It is important to ask what significance he considered it to have.

To answer that question, it will be necessary to look at the story of Antony as the last in a string of conversion narratives with which Augustine presents his readers. The rest of his narrative has catalogued the development of his beliefs from his involvement with Manichaeanism to a philosophical scepticism and then an increasing interest in neoplatonism; but the structure of the *Confessions* makes it clear that, for Augustine the later author at least, the events of Book 8 do indeed constitute a significant step. In preparation for the changes that he is about to describe, Augustine begins the book by monitoring his own spiritual status in a direct address to God:

Of your eternal life I was certain, though I saw it 'in an enigma and as if in a mirror'. All doubt had been taken from me that there is indestructible substance from which comes all substance. My desire was not to be more certain of you but to be more stable in you. But in my temporal life everything was in a state of uncertainty, and my heart needed to be purified from the old leaven. I was attracted to the way, the Saviour himself, but was still reluctant to go along its narrow paths.[29]

Already by 386, then, Augustine seems to have been convinced of the intellectual merits of Christianity: this development perhaps owed to the influence of Ambrose of Milan, and manifesting itself in a new respect for the writings of the apostle Paul.[30] The developments in Book 8 will therefore take place 'on moral rather

the *Confessions*'. The relevance of Paul's conversion will be discussed in more detail elsewhere in this section.

[29] *Conf.* 8.1.1, quoting 1 Corinthians 13:12.
[30] *Conf.* 7 *passim*, but esp. 7.21.27. This is not the place to discuss the precise neoplatonic content of Ambrose's contemporary sermons and their influence on Augustine, as is done by Courcelle 1968: 172–3 and elsewhere), with discussion by Mandouze (1968: 476–8) and O'Donnell (1992: II.413–44); nor is there space to discuss in detail Augustine's intellectual journey, as traced for example in O'Meara 2001 or Bourke 1945.

than intellectual terrain'.[31] To the question of 'what was still lacking', Augustine provides the answer: not certainty, but stability.[32] What this in turn seems to amount to is Augustine's unwillingness to make a decisive commitment to the 'narrow paths' of the Christian church. In the narrative of the *Confessions* his immediate response is to visit Simplicianus, a Milanese priest whom Augustine describes as a man both of 'saintly zeal' and 'of much experience and much learning'.[33] His subsequent interview with Simplicianus seems designed to prove the value of this combination of zeal and learning through the example, which Simplicianus offers Augustine, of the conversion to Christianity of the neoplatonist Marius Victorinus. The similarities between Augustine and Victorinus – both orators with interests in neoplatonism and Christianity – have often been noted, and it seems likely that they did not elude Augustine himself, whether as one hearing the story for the first time or in retrospect as the author of this account.[34] Victorinus, it seems, is offered here as a model for Augustine's own conversion. Certainly by the end of the story Augustine claims that he was 'fired up to imitate him', and admits that Simplicianus will have had this aim in mind.[35] Yet a closer look at the story suggests that there was in fact little to imitate; and within a few lines Augustine has relapsed into indecision.[36]

A possible explanation for the short-lived nature of this inspiration is that the story of Victorinus is remarkably vague on the details of the decision to convert to Christianity. After years of defending the pagan cults, and also an unspecified (but presumably long) period in which Victorinus claimed to believe – as a neoplatonist – in the same things as the Christians, the account of his development ends with what seems an abrupt change of heart:

But after his reading, he began to feel a longing and drank in courage. He was afraid he would be 'denied' by Christ 'before the holy angels'. He would have felt guilty of a grave crime if he were ashamed of the mysteries of the humility of your Word and were not ashamed of the sacrilegious rites of proud demons, whose pride he imitated when he accepted their ceremonies. He became ashamed of the

---

[31] O'Donnell 1992: II.391.   [32] O'Connell 1996: 210.
[33] *Conf.* 8.1.1.   [34] As noted by O'Donnell 1992: III.21.
[35] *Conf.* 8.5.10: 'exarsi ad imitandum: ad hoc enim et ille narrauerat'.
[36] *Conf.* 8.5.10.

emptiness of those rites and felt respect for the truth. Suddenly and unexpectedly he said to Simplicianus (as he told me): 'Let us go to the Church: I want to become a Christian.'[37]

The significance of this moment has been prepared by Augustine, so that the crucial step in Victorinus' conversion is clear. He had earlier joked with Simplicianus that he was a Christian outside the church, one who failed only to attend mass – a position which Simplicianus refused to accept as valid.[38] The change here is that Victorinus has finally abandoned pagan practice in order to participate fully in Christian cult. He has also accepted the consequences of that action: indeed, we are told that Victorinus, as a Christian, was subsequently unable to pursue his career as a teacher.[39] Intellectual assent was evidently not sufficient to persuade Simplicianus: he demanded that Victorinus should make this kind of complete and public affirmation. The story thus reinforces the point Augustine had made at the start of the book, where he had identified the need to add stability in God to his existing intellectual certainty.

Yet if the example of Victorinus makes clear what a Christian conversion must look like, it does little to explain how the decision is to be arrived at. It is true that Augustine, or Simplicianus, offers a series of reasons for making the change: fear, guilt, and shame rank highly among them. This is the language of feeling, and again it confirms that an intellectual decision to convert to Christianity must, for Augustine, be accompanied by an element of 'moral choice'.[40] But the abruptness of this change is also emphasised in Augustine's telling of the story. Victorinus decided 'suddenly and unexpectedly'; Augustine goes on to record the 'joy' felt by Simplicianus and the church and the 'amazement' of Rome.[41] This example makes clear that conversion is possible for a man like Augustine, and it is not difficult to see that it might well serve as an inspiration. But this sudden change brought about by obscure developments in the thoughts and feelings of Victorinus is not

---

[37] *Conf.* 8.2.4, quoting Luke 12:9.   [38] *Conf.* 8.2.4.
[39] *Conf.* 8.2.3. The barrier was apparently the Emperor Julian's *Edict on Teaching* issued in 362: *C.Th.* 13.3.5; cf. Julian, *Letter* 42 (36).
[40] O'Donnell 1992: III.21.
[41] *Conf.* 8.2.4: 'mirante Roma, gaudente ecclesia'.

an exemplum that can easily be imitated. There is no mechanism proposed, no change that Augustine might make in his own life that might allow him to achieve the same result. The only practical advice that Victorinus seems to offer is to read: for his longing followed on from his reading. And reading is, of course, what Augustine has been doing since Book 7 when he took up the letters of Paul.

So while the example of Victorinus might present an image of Augustine's future, it could not in itself bring about the requisite change in his life, nor in his habits of mind. The example of Victorinus has been said to have 'prepared the way for the decisive stroke of grace' which did finally prompt Augustine's conversion, but it did so in an almost entirely negative way.[42] Within the structure of the *Confessions*, and perhaps also in Augustine's own mind, Victorinus' conversion does little to advance the argument: indeed, it stands as an example of something which emphatically did not succeed in bringing about the conversion of Augustine. Instead, the purpose it served was to narrow the issue down to a single point: as O'Meara delicately puts it, 'his will on continence'.[43]

Thus Augustine blames his failure to imitate Victorinus on his own 'cupidity', and goes on to say that he will narrate the means by which 'you delivered me from the chain of sexual desire'.[44] The situation has not changed significantly since the beginning of Book 8, where Augustine had explicitly disowned his old attachments to money and worldly success, but added that:

I was still firmly tied by a woman. The apostle did not forbid me to marry, although he exhorted me to something better and very much wished that all men were unattached as he himself. But I being weaker chose a softer option, and because of this one factor I was inconstant in other respects and was wasting away with nagging anxieties.[45]

An inability to reject sexual desire – or perhaps more importantly, marriage – nevertheless seems an odd thing to focus on as an

---

[42] Portalié 1960: 13.   [43] O'Meara 2001: 174.

[44] *Conf.* 8.5.12: 'cupiditati'; 8.6.13: 'concubitus'. While 'cupiditas' in particular can refer to an unhealthy attachment to worldly things in general, 'concubitus' is unambiguously sexual in meaning.

[45] *Conf.* 8.2.2.

impediment to Christian conversion.[46] Paul himself had remained celibate but, as Augustine admits, he did not forbid marriage to others. Augustine, however, was not willing to settle for an inferior commitment to Christianity, such as even Victorinus had made: he sought to imitate directly the purity of the apostle Paul. Sexual restraint, for Augustine, was a token of a broader renunciation of the quotidian world.[47] The example he sought to follow was a biblical one.[48]

Paul's words, then, have convinced Augustine that a life as an ascetic Christian is an attractive possibility – but again, while he grasps this as an intellectual conviction, it still waits upon the will.[49] Paul himself has been able to achieve this aim; but at this moment Augustine turns to another biblical example of the life he is hoping to lead:

From the mouth of truth I had heard that there are 'eunuchs who have castrated themselves for the kingdom of heaven'. But, he says, 'let him who can accept this accept it'.[50]

This stark image of voluntary asceticism is put forward in Matthew 19:12, and is immediately followed by the gnomic comment which Augustine also quotes. The fact that Augustine expresses himself here, even more than usual in the *Confessions*, in terms taken directly from Scripture, perhaps hints at the significance of this passage as a transition.[51] Augustine seems to admit to a continuing

---

[46] Augustine immediately goes on to refer to the other disadvantages of 'married life', suggesting that his concerns were not entirely a matter of physical desire.

[47] Thus O'Donnell (1992: III.34) who, while wishing to maintain the importance of Augustine's struggle with sexual continence, emphasises its status as a 'sign' of a more generalised submission of the will.

[48] No doubt Augustine was in fact influenced in this attitude by certain of his contemporaries: restraint was emphasised not only by Ambrose in Milan, but also by the neoplatonists and the Manichees with whom Augustine had long associated: O'Donnell (1992: III.7–10) offers all of these explanations; for philosophy see Brown 2000: 106–7, and for Manichaeanism see O'Meara 2001: 159. Evidence for the prominence of this kind of attitude in Augustine's own circle is provided at *Conf.* 9.3.5 with the example of Verecundus. Nevertheless, Augustine in this section focuses on the biblical model of Paul at the expense of contemporary examples.

[49] Stock 1996: 99.

[50] *Conf.* 8.2.2: 'audieram ex ore ueritatis esse spadones qui se ipsos absciderunt propter regnum caelorum, sed "qui potest", inquit, "capere, capiat".'

[51] This passage introduces a string of quotations from Scripture, with virtually no direct narrative from Augustine himself until he returns to his intention to visit Simplicianus in *Conf.* 8.2.3.

difficulty with the Christian scriptures: 'let him who can accept this accept it' suggests that Augustine, at this point, could not. This is different in kind from any difficulty he might have previously encountered with Paul. Since he returned to Paul's writings at the end of Book 7 there has been no hint that Augustine has found himself unable to accept or to understand them. Instead, and throughout Book 8, he treats Paul as a source of self-evident wisdom and advice, which he recognises and knows that he ought to follow.[52] What seems to change more dramatically over the course of this crucial period, and what seems to be intimately bound up with the narrative of his own conversion, is rather his attitude towards the Gospel of Matthew.

Here, at the beginning of Book 8, it continues to elude his grasp. When Augustine heard Matthew tell of the existence of 'eunuchs for the kingdom of God', he found himself unable to accept it. It is not that the meaning of the passage is obscure, nor that Augustine suspected it of being straightforwardly false; nor is it likely that he understood it literally as demanding actual castration.[53] It must mean, I think, that Augustine was simply unable to grasp the information: that he could not fully understand the implications of the passage, and could not see what it implied for him in particular. If he fell short at this point of being fully Christian, as he immediately goes on to explain, it was not because of a lack of belief in the Christian God nor because of a lack of knowledge about him.[54] These are the things that his reading – and above all, his acceptance – of Paul had given him. What remained was an acceptance of the rest of the Bible, and the startling claims of the gospels in particular.

Looking back, Augustine identified this difficulty as focusing on the mystery of the Incarnation, which in Book 7 had represented the final barrier preventing him from gaining 'strength enough to enjoy you', and which he 'was not yet humble enough'

[52] Augustine's attitude to Paul here is very well characterised in these terms in Stock 1996: 98–9.
[53] Although if he knew of the legend of Origen's auto-castration, then this was perhaps a possibility.
[54] *Conf.* 8.2.2; 7.21.27.

to acknowledge.[55] Yet in the process of conversion described in Book 8, the deeper mystery of Christ was implied by this smaller matter: Augustine's inability to grasp the relevance to his own life of Matthew's 'eunuchs for the kingdom of heaven'. The gospels, as much as the example of Paul, revealed to Augustine the real possibility of an ascetic life of the kind he wanted for himself. At this point in his spiritual development he could not accept the importance of the passage: he could understand it, intellectually, but he could not seize the example in order to apply it in his own life.[56] The gap between understanding and action was the gap between Augustine and the world of the Bible.

Thus at the end of this brief introduction to Book 8, while attempting in retrospect to describe the nature of his dilemma, Augustine reaches out once again to Matthew. Again he reiterates that he was intellectually convinced; and again he declares his inability to follow an example from the gospel: 'Now I had discovered the good pearl. To buy it I had to sell all I had; and I hesitated.'[57] The merchant in this parable made no such hesitation: and his decision, coming as it does towards the end of the string of famous parables in Matthew 13, refers both forwards and backwards within the gospel itself. Most obviously it connects to the parable of the sower, and he who 'hears the word of the kingdom and does not understand it': another hint, perhaps, at Augustine's inability to accept Matthew's 'eunuchs for the kingdom of heaven'.[58] Yet it also connects to the precise difficulty that Augustine was having in putting his understanding into action – and in response not only to parables and examples but to a direct imperative: for a few chapters later comes the demand which above all others justified asceticism in late antiquity. It came in the story of the rich young man who asked what he required to enter the kingdom of heaven: 'Jesus said to him: "If you would be perfect, go, sell what you have give to

---

[55] *Conf.* 7.18.24; see also the comments of O'Donnell 1992: II.459–60 here, with Courcelle 1954: 63–71 and O'Meara 1959: 160–2.

[56] The meanings 'seize', 'grasp', 'understand' and others are all embraced by the verb 'capere' here: I will continue to favour the word 'accept', used by Chadwick in translating Augustine's quotation of the biblical passage.

[57] *Conf.* 8.2.2, evoking Matthew 13:46.

[58] Matthew 13:19 [RSV].

the poor, and you will have treasure in heaven; and come follow me.'"[59]

The quotations from Matthew in Book 8 of the *Confessions* therefore help to establish the nature of the remaining barriers in the way of Augustine's conversion to Christianity. His problem is not that he lacks knowledge of Christian doctrine; nor is there any difficulty for him in giving it his intellectual assent; nor is it that he lacks knowledge of what the scriptures say. It is a problem of interpretation of the scriptures: Augustine's difficulty lies simply in recognising that scriptural examples and imperatives apply to him personally. Thus even after he has felt himself inspired by the story of Victorinus, Augustine continues to paint himself in terms directly recalling Matthew's rich young man, unable to abandon his worldly possessions: 'I was as afraid of being rid of all my burdens as I ought to have been at the prospect of carrying them.'[60] It is not that he is unaware of the call; but that he cannot accept the need to follow it. His continuing refusal to allow himself to be converted to Christianity was the result of his inability – or his unwillingness – to follow the ascetic imperative presented in Matthew's gospel.

Put in these terms, Augustine's primary difficulty at the beginning of Book 8 was not the issue of marriage or sexuality in particular, nor even the total renunciation of his secular interests and ambitions. As Augustine portrays it in retrospect, the most significant matter was the broader principle that all this represented. A successful conversion could only be the result of a submission of the will: it was primarily a question of 'humility' and 'obedience'.[61] Above all, this meant for Augustine an absolute humility before the scriptures and an absolute obedience to its demands. Configuring Augustine's situation in this way might suggest that Paul is to be seen as representing 'the letter', when what was lacking was 'the spirit' which would give him life in Christ.[62] To gain that required Augustine to submit himself not only to Paul's intellectual appeal but also to 'an Authority which guaranteed the truth

[59] Matthew 19:21 [RSV]. Vulgate: 'ait illi Iesus si uis perfectus esse uade uende quae habes et da pauperibus et habebis thesaurum in caelo et ueni sequere me.'
[60] *Conf.* 8.5.11.
[61] Morrison (1992: 28) notes the role of obedience (among other things) in Augustine's conversion.
[62] This analogy is drawn at Stock 1996: 98.

of mysteries which [he] could not be expected to understand'.[63] Like Victorinus, he had to abandon his status as a teacher and allow himself to be taught.[64] Confronted with Scripture, he had to let go of the intellectual pride which had led Victorinus to accept pagan rites, and Augustine to misunderstand the simplicity and humility of Christian teachings.[65]

Spiritual progress therefore depended on Augustine's development as a reader of Scripture. As Peter Brown has pointed out, relations with Scripture 'came to form a constant theme throughout the *Confessions*' – perhaps as a result of Augustine's understanding of his new role as a bishop – and the major shifts in his intellectual attitudes tend to be associated with a changing attitude to the Bible.[66] In this case, the change was firmly predicated on his willingness to accept the claims and challenges offered by Matthew. This indeed is vividly illustrated with the arrival of Ponticianus, whose life-changing intervention is provoked by the discovery of Paul's writings abandoned on a gaming-table: these writings may have been an object of deep study for Augustine, but they remained fruitless when it came to prompting the final step to conversion.[67] Reading and even accepting the arguments of Paul was not enough. Augustine had to learn how to grasp the existence and the significance of Matthew's 'eunuchs for the kingdom of heaven'.

Lives as conversion texts

The example of Victorinus therefore failed to bring Augustine to the moment of his final crisis; and so in the sixth chapter of Book 8 he sets out to describe how he was finally delivered 'from the chain of sexual desire . . . and from the slavery of worldly affairs'.[68] Not just from sexuality, then, but from all of the things which prevented

---

[63] O'Meara 2001: 167.   [64] *Conf.* 8.5.10.
[65] *Conf.* 8.2.4: the verb translated as 'accept' here is 'accipio'. The role of pride and its association with paganism is emphasised by Augustine throughout the story of Victorinus, and especially at *Conf.* 8.2.5 and 8.4.9. Augustine's recognition of the humility of the scriptures and his changed view of them is discussed throughout Book 7, and especially at 7.5.7–8.
[66] Brown 2000: 162.   [67] *Conf.* 8.6.14.
[68] *Conf.* 8.6.13: 'de uinculo quidem desiderii concubitus . . . et saecularium negotiorum seruitute'.

him following the biblical ascetic imperative. Again we are reminded that this is the essential step for Augustine: it would not be enough to present him, as in the story of Victorinus, with the example of a mysterious and dramatic conversion. Nor would it be enough to present him with a contemporary Christian with a similar background to his own who yet combined high office with unquestioned faith – for this is what Ponticianus offers, as he arrives on his errand to Augustine. Ponticianus was the kind of Christian who must have been very familiar to Augustine from his time in Rome and Milan – for of course in a Christian court a large number of attendants and officials will have shared the emperor's faith.[69] What finally brings Augustine to the point of conversion is not the example of a contemporary convert, but the stories told by Ponticianus of conversions within Christianity itself from participation to asceticism. They are stories describing Christian responses: to Scripture, and to Christian biography.

Although Augustine relates Ponticianus' stories in rather less detail than he devotes to the conversion of Marius Victorinus, it would be difficult to dispute that his exposure to the stories of Antony and of the friends of Ponticianus at Trier represents the most significant episode in Book 8, and perhaps in the whole of the *Confessions*.[70] It is clear from his own account that they 'affected Augustine profoundly', or at least that he judged them to have done so in retrospect: this, as O'Meara remarks, 'is quite simply what the *Confessions* says'.[71] The lack of detail, however, means that when more profound questions are asked the work becomes less easy to interpret. Augustine tells us that Ponticianus 'dwelt on the story [of Antony] instilling in us who were ignorant an awareness of the man's greatness', but it is not clear what aspects Ponticianus emphasised as he (presumably) summarised the main

---

[69] The importance of Ponticianus' own example as a Christian is generally minimised in commentary, and probably rightly: for Augustine would have been familiar with successful and educated Christians even had he not been brought up in North Africa with a Christian mother. However, O'Donnell (1992: III.38) – citing Mandouze (1968: 195 n. 9) – suggests that Ponticianus may still have had an impact: 'for someone in office to speak this way would probably have greater effect on [Augustine], still impressed by such people'.

[70] The stories are told at *Conf.* 8.6.14–15: cf. the story of Victorinus, which occupies *Conf.* 8.2.3–5 and 4.9.

[71] O'Meara 2001: 189.

points of the story from memory.[72] Indeed, it is not even clear what the main points of Antony's story would have been for a fourth-century audience, let alone when the story was to be told by a North African courtier to two highly educated compatriots in the imperial city of Milan. One of the risks here is that of assuming that Ponticianus' understanding of the *Life of Antony*, as he chose to pass it on to his colleagues, followed the same lines as modern interpretations, or as our own private understandings of the text.

Many commentators have seemed to assume this, however, and have speculated with varying degrees of confidence as to what exactly Ponticianus will have said. Olson considers it 'probable' that his account focused on four main areas: Antony's reaction to the initial call; his resistance to temptation by 'beasts and grotesques'; his rejection of Arianism; and his rejection of philosophy.[73] Most other authors, perhaps unsurprisingly, pick up Augustine's references to sexuality and see the message of the *Life of Antony* almost exclusively from this perspective. Thus O'Meara epitomises Antony as 'that great champion of chastity'; and Morrison too sees Ponticianus' story as 'the account of Anthony's conversion to a life of chastity'.[74] These readings, although they take their cue from what Augustine says about his own condition in 386, seem to reflect too modern an attitude towards asceticism to be safe assumptions about the reception of a desert saint such as Antony by his contemporaries. The same is true of references to the saint's 'paradigmatic celibacy' or, more broadly, to Antony as 'that paradigm of the contemplative life': they are too simplistic and too comfortably modern to do justice to what must have been a complex range of responses to such an unorthodox and transgressive figure.[75] Direct contemporary responses to the story of Antony remain in short supply: the closest possible attention must therefore be paid to the precise nature of the evidence offered by Augustine.[76]

---

[72] *Conf.* 8.6.14.   [73] Olson 1995: 51.   [74] O'Meara 2001: 189; Morrison 1992: 18.
[75] Morrison 1992: 18; O'Connell 1996: 236.
[76] As I have argued in a previous chapter, the subsequent production of saints' lives – not least those by Jerome – can be seen as a set of responses to the appearance and popularity of the *VA*, but these are at best indirect. Evagrius' translation provides a direct response to the original Greek work, but he makes no real comment in his prefatory dedication

Some of what Ponticianus must have stressed can be recognised in the way Augustine describes his immediate response, and in the way he recalls Antony later in the story of his own conversion. Augustine recalls that Ponticianus told the story of Antony, and describes the source of his and Alypius' astonishment:

We were amazed as we heard of your wonderful acts very well attested and occurring so recently, almost in our own time, done in orthodox faith and the Catholic church.[77]

Antony's orthodox position on doctrine and practice was evidently emphasised at the time, or else is being emphasised in retrospect by Augustine – and it is of course a significant theme of the *Life of Antony* itself. Yet this was not the cause of Augustine's amazement. The key elements in Augustine's response can instead be addressed under the three headings of divine intervention, historicity and contemporaneity: 'your [i.e. God's] wonderful acts'; 'very well attested'; 'occurring so recently'.[78] This brief sentence is easily passed over, but it is worth a real effort of exegesis, so as to do justice to the complexity not only of Antony's story but of Augustine's reaction to it.

First of all, then, Augustine found Antony's story remarkable for the wonderful acts or 'miracles' – *mirabilia* – it contained. Exactly which miracles Ponticianus mentioned is not specified, although Augustine later refers explicitly to the circumstances of Antony's initial call to the ascetic life.[79] We might assume with Olson that Ponticianus also told of Antony's struggle with demons, or perhaps that he mentioned incidents such as his taming of wild animals or the miraculous discovery of water in the desert.[80] Whether he mentioned these miracles or not, however, it is important to note that Augustine makes no definite reference to them, nor indeed to any episode of Antony's life after the call. That event by itself was perhaps sufficiently miraculous to prove the point that Augustine

and his few innovations in the text are limited to historical commentary and corrections: see the NPNF edition of Athanasius, *VA* 82 n.16.

[77] *Conf.* 8.6.14.

[78] They appear in a different order in the Latin text: 'tam recenti memoria et prope nostris temporibus testatissima mirabilia tua'.

[79] *Conf.* 8.12.29: for further discussion of this, see below.

[80] Examples at *VA* 15, 51, 54.

evidently took from it: that the story of Antony's life was above all the story of God's active intervention in the world.

In itself, this idea was nothing new to Augustine. Miracle stories and tales of divine intervention abounded in the Bible, in both the Old Testament and the New. What was it, then, that made the miracles in Antony's life more impressive than, for example, Paul's conversion to Christianity? The explanation must lie in the other aspects that Augustine picks out in his immediate response: the historicity of the story, and its setting in Augustine's own modern world. Regarding the latter point, it is certainly true that in comparison to Paul, Antony is 'nearer in time', and is perhaps therefore a more plausible model for Augustine to choose to imitate.[81] But the matter is not merely one of chronology. The modern world of Augustine was different in kind to the world of the Bible, which in effect was confined within the pages of the canonical Christian books. These described a world cut off from the normal rules of contemporary everyday life: a distant world in which God intervened on a regular basis, and a world which ended with the last of Paul's letters.

Antony's miracles suggest that he belongs in the world of Paul, in the world of the Bible; and yet he is a recent figure, situated 'almost in our own time'. His story, if true, showed that miracles continued to occur in the post-biblical world, beyond the Bible and well into recent times. It demonstrated the continued presence – and active intervention – of God in the lives of men, collapsing together the world of Paul and the world of Antony, which was also the world of Augustine. It showed that the events described in the Bible did not take place under a special dispensation, a unique set of rules that had long since ceased to apply. Instead, the rules that applied to the characters in Scripture could be seen to have a place in contemporary experience, to apply to the men of Augustine's own age. The closing of the biblical canon had not after all meant the end of miracles. The story of Antony held out the hope that God might act directly upon Augustine himself.

The example of Antony thus brought the biblical world within range of Augustine's experience – but only as long as the story

---

[81] As argued at Stock 1996: 99.

itself were true. It was because Augustine, when he heard it in 386, believed the story to be 'historically accurate' that he allowed it 'to define the meaning of his own life'.[82] This, then, is the third aspect of his response that he emphasises in recounting the incident for his *Confessions*: that the story was remarkable in part because it was so 'very well attested' (*testatissima*). At first glance this assertion of Augustine's might seem strange. He has just heard for the first time about Antony, and at second- or (more likely) third-hand at best: for Ponticianus could hardly have known the saint personally and was presumably taking his information from the written *Life*.[83] Ponticianus, moreover, was a relative stranger to Augustine, only a compatriot rather than a colleague. In modern terms this would seem close to the height of unreliability; but this would be to ignore the way in which information was transmitted, and friendships maintained, in late-antique circles such as that of Augustine.

This kind of interaction is well captured by Peter Brown in his biography of Augustine. By the time he wrote the *Confessions*, and no doubt long before, 'Augustine had come to live in a circle of men who shared a lively curiosity about other people'.[84] They communicated by letter, but also seized upon any extra news that the letter-carriers could bring.[85] In an empire in which friends might be separated by thousands of miles, and so by months of travel, the testimony brought by a mutual acquaintance might be the nearest available substitute for an actual meeting. Even the closest friendship might be conducted at second-hand, and an oral report from a trusted intermediary was a rare and most welcome occurrence. In such cases the bearer of the news 'represents the one who has sent him, and much may be inferred from his actions'.[86] Ponticianus' description of Antony can be fitted neatly into this

---

[82] Olson 1995: 50.

[83] As suggested in Monceaux 1931: 63, Ponticianus was most likely to have been familiar with the Latin translation of the *Life of Antony* carried out by Evagrius, usually dated to between 371 and 375. That Augustine had this version in mind when writing the *Confessions* is suggested by the linguistic parallels at *Conf.* 8.12.29, as noted by O'Donnell 1992: III.40–1.

[84] Brown 2000: 158.

[85] Brown 2000: 158–9, quoting Augustine, *Letter* 31.2.5.

[86] Conybeare 2000: 38. I must acknowledge David Scourfield's help in encouraging my thinking on this point in particular.

context, and can be imagined to have had a far greater impact than a reading of the *Life of Antony* alone. A book or a treatise might risk making Antony an inaccessible, literary figure: a total stranger at the opposite end of the Roman world.[87] The conversation with Ponticianus could bring Antony within the reach of Augustine's own circle of friends.

For Augustine, then, knowledge did not have to be first-hand to be reliable. He had already described his thinking on this point in a previous book of the *Confessions*:

I considered the innumerable things I believed which I had not seen, events which occurred when I was not present, such as many incidents in the history of the nations, many facts concerning places and cities which I had never seen, many things accepted on the word of friends, many from physicians, many from other people. Unless we believed what we were told, we would do nothing at all in this life.[88]

This is the later Augustine describing his decision to abandon the Manichees; but it is not to be taken as a process which was completed in that single moment. His growing belief that a stance of absolute scepticism was untenable, and his increasing acceptance of the Bible, is portrayed as an ongoing development: 'My belief in this was sometimes stronger, sometimes weaker,' he says; 'I began to believe . . .'; 'I wavered and you steadied me.'[89] Augustine seems still to be working out these ideas at the beginning of Book 8, when he tells of his frustration at being unable to accept Matthew; and it is these ideas precisely which are reinforced by Ponticianus' story of Antony.

This independent and reliable testimony to the reality of miracles in his own time not only had an effect on Augustine's attitude to the contemporary world, but also enabled him to take a different attitude to the Christian scriptures. The gospels too claimed to be eyewitness reports, and Paul wrote in the first person; but these authors were themselves distant figures in comparison to Ponticianus and the men he might have named as his sources:

[87] As characterised by Brown 2000: 159.   [88] *Conf.* 6.5.7.
[89] All three quotations here are taken from *Conf.* 6.5.8.

Evagrius, and perhaps Athanasius.[90] Nevertheless, the consistency of the tales told in Scripture and about Antony suggested that the two could be treated together, from the same point of view. His straightforward acceptance of the truth of Antony's story offered a new way for Augustine to understand Scripture: to accept the Gospel of Matthew just as he had immediately accepted Ponticianus' story. Antony is the catalyst for Augustine's conversion because it is through his story that Augustine is at last able to grasp the significance of the Bible for his own life. In effect, the life of Antony offers Augustine the option of reading Scripture as history: to have faith in it in the same way as he has faith in what Ponticianus has told him.

This general point can be derived simply from Augustine's acceptance of the reality of the story, but the crucial moment seems to come in the one episode from Antony's life which we can be sure was related on this occasion. At the very moment of his conversion, in the penultimate chapter of Book 8, Augustine explicitly recalls,

how Antony happened to be present at the gospel reading, and took it as an admonition addressed to himself when the words were read: 'Go, sell all you have, give to the poor, and you shall have treasure in heaven; and come, follow me.' By such an inspired utterance he was immediately converted to you.[91]

This was the decisive significance of Antony's story for Augustine: for he was an example of a contemporary figure who took Scripture literally, to the extent of his following a biblical imperative overheard by chance as though it had been intended directly for him. We may be so familiar with the story, and with the idea of divine intervention, as to take Antony's reaction for granted – which would rather underrate the unexpectedness of his response. It depends wholly on Antony's willingness to think in this particular way, an interpretative leap which set him apart from his fellow Christians, and culminating in an extraordinary belief:

---

[90] The heading of the *VA*, derived from the Evagrian version, ascribes the original work to Athanasius, and neither Ponticianus nor Augustine will have had any reason to doubt this: O'Donnell 1992: III.38 n.9.

[91] *Conf.* 8.12.29, quoting Matthew 19:21.

The event of a human being standing in a church reading another human being's report of how yet another human being once told a rich young man to give his possessions to the poor and become a disciple: by way of that event, God then and there said to Antony: Antony, give up your possessions to the poor and become a disciple of Jesus.[92]

There is no warrant for assuming that such thinking was natural for Augustine, nor for anyone else in late antiquity. The idea itself must have been 'audacious'; and it can help demonstrate how the story of Antony could serve 'more than anything else in revealing to [Augustine] God's Providence over him and all mankind'.[93] It is in this sense that Antony offered himself as a model for Augustine to follow.

In receiving his vocation, Antony simultaneously adopts an interpretation of Scripture and an interpretation of contemporary experience, running them together as though they belonged to the same order of reality. God spoke through Christ to the rich young man in the distant and vanished biblical age; he continues to speak through the scriptures, but more specifically through the arrangement of events which had led to Antony's overhearing precisely these words. Augustine undoubtedly accepted the first of these points already; but it was his acceptance of the presence and active intervention of God in the contemporary world – a lesson he was taught through the story of Antony – which was responsible for the shape of his conversion experience. Where Antony's call was a single decisive moment, Augustine's conversion divided it into two distinct elements. First of all, having retreated to his garden, he overheard an unexpected voice crying 'tolle, lege' – 'pick up and read'.

At once my countenance changed, and I began to think intently whether there might be some sort of children's game in which such a chant is used. But I could not remember having heard of one. I checked the flood of tears and stood up. I interpreted it solely as a divine command to me to open the book and read the first chapter I might find.[94]

---

[92] Wolterstorff 1995: 7. It is not clear to me whether an understanding of Christ as divine, rather than as a 'human being', would increase or decrease the extraordinary nature of this belief.
[93] Wolterstorff 1995: 8; O'Meara 2001: xxi.   [94] *Conf.* 8.12.29.

At first Augustine reaches for a mundane explanation, in the form of a children's game – and it is important that he never rules out this possibility.[95] The example of Antony, however, has encouraged an alternative means of interpreting this experience, and he explicitly takes Antony as his model in choosing – rightly or wrongly – to take it as a divine command. He begins to see himself, that is, as another recipient of God's intervention, like Paul in Acts or Antony in Ponticianus' story.

It is Paul whose writings he immediately takes up – and again he follows the example of Antony, imitating him here by engaging in 'the practice of bibliomancy'.[96] He reads the famous passage from Romans – 'put on the Lord Jesus Christ' – and understands it to apply to himself just as Antony understood the passage from Matthew: Augustine is ready to believe that God was instructing him '*here and now*' to give himself over to Christianity.[97] Like Antony, he is now able to respond immediately to a scriptural imperative: not directly to the ascetic imperative itself, but certainly to 'the corresponding positive injunctions . . . [to] abandon the flesh and put on Christ'.[98] This is perhaps, compared to the story of Antony, a disappointingly vague and generalised kind of advice, although it seemed to Augustine to strike a chord with his own spiritual situation.[99] Yet the important matter here is not the text itself, nor any unusual facet it displays, but the conjunction of events and the new approach to Scripture which Augustine had learned from the story of Antony.

---

[95] O'Donnell 1992: III.61, considering both his immediate reaction and his 'mature' reaction. There has been plenty of debate over whether or not Augustine's account of his conversion is true, and over whether there could have been any ordinary circumstance which might explain what Augustine claims to have heard: see the judicious remarks of O'Donnell (1992: III.59–69) – in particular on the claims of Courcelle (1963: 91–197) – and especially s.v. 'uocem', 'tolle lege' and 'ludendi'; and also O'Meara (2001: 186–94). What matters in this case is that Augustine presents us with his uncertainty – real or fictional – and with his subsequent decision to reach for a supernatural explanation.

[96] Presented as a direct imitation of Antony by Morrison 1992: 19.

[97] Romans 13:13–14; Wolterstorff 1995: 7 (italics in original).

[98] O'Meara 1997: 34.

[99] Stock (1996: 109) prefers to see the passage from Romans not as a direct imperative but rather as 'an epistle in which Paul himself is engaged in an interpretative conversation with an implied audience [of Christians]', but the point seems to remain the same: that Augustine's response to this particular text is due to a change in his approach to the reading of Scripture.

If Antony was a paradigm of anything in late antiquity, it was of the unsophisticated consumer of Scripture. The point is stressed not only in his response to the gospel, but from the very first chapter of the *Life of Antony* in which he is established as wilfully illiterate.[100] This refusal to engage in philosophical discussion was a distinctive trait of many late-antique ascetics, and among other things allowed them to be firmly contrasted with philosophers and professors of rhetoric whose pedantry could be presented as blinding them to the simple truth.[101] Augustine himself had drawn this contrast when discussing his attitude to Scripture in Book 6 of the *Confessions*; and the same transformation from a proud rhetorician to a humble consumer of church teaching is at work in his presentation of the conversion of Marius Victorinus.[102] The example of Antony allows Augustine to understand the character of this humility: the need to abandon his sophisticated literary sense, his professional attitude to philosophy and rhetoric, and to accept the injunctions of Scripture at face value. He is drawn towards a literal understanding of Scripture, of the kind he will demonstrate in the final books of the *Confessions*.[103]

Prompted by Ponticianus' story, then, and at the very beginning of the crisis which precipitated his conversion, Augustine recalls bemoaning his position in exactly these terms:

I turned to Alypius and cried out: 'What is wrong with us? What is this that you have heard? Uneducated people are rising up and capturing heaven, and we with our high culture without any heart – see where we roll in the mud of flesh and blood . . .'[104]

Again the contrast is between men of high culture, such as Augustine and Alypius, and the 'unlearned' who are able to rise above mundane concerns. The crucial Latin phrase here – 'surgunt indocti et caelum rapiunt' – has been held to apply exclusively to the friends of Ponticianus whose story Augustine has also just heard, but the

---

[100] *VA* 1 (and also compared to Jacob, as noted in a previous chapter).
[101] A development traced in Lim 1995, esp. ch. 6: cf. examples from the *Life of Antony*, ch. 3, above.
[102] *Conf.* 6.5.8; *Conf.* 8.2.4.
[103] *Conf.* 11–13: this 'literal' interpretation of the scriptures does not rule out figurative interpretation, which Augustine considered to apply only to the *events* literally recorded there: see Kirwan 1989: 12–13, and esp. Markus 1996: ch. 1.
[104] *Conf.* 8.8.19.

adjective seems to apply rather more naturally to Antony and to contemporary ascetics in general.[105] The similar explanation which Augustine provides in describing his conversion long before the *Confessions*, writing at Cassiciacum, seems to suggest the same thing. In his treatise *Against the Academics*, he again recalls the effect that the stories of Ponticianus had on him: 'For truly, I said to myself, these men would never have been able to do such great things, nor lived as they evidently did live . . . opposed to this so great a good.'[106] The emphasis on miracles and on an extraordinary way of life seems to evoke Antony and the desert ascetics. It was 'the example of the eastern monks' and of Antony in particular which had made the strongest impression on Augustine, and it was that on which he patterned his own conversion.[107]

Antony's example provided Augustine with a model in more ways than one. His response to the ascetic imperative in the Gospel of Matthew 'underscored the effect of divine intervention' in the contemporary world. It helped to justify the belief that God might deign to intervene in Augustine's own life.[108] Indeed, the story of Antony offered an interpretative framework outside of which the subsequent events in Augustine's Milanese garden would make no sense – in retrospect, but crucially even as they were experienced. This is not therefore just a matter of literary patterning, but the record (fictional or otherwise) of a definite shift in Augustine's understanding of the world around him. Furthermore, Antony recognised no distinction between the world of the Bible and the contemporary world – and in this way he also served as a model for Augustine as a reader of Scripture. Ultimately, it was Antony's example that enabled Augustine to finally accept the relevance of

[105] O'Donnell (1992: III.47) suggests that the phrase 'probably' refers to the friends of Ponticianus, but this seems an odd epithet for Augustine to apply to a pair of imperial *agentes in rebus* whom he has never met, and in the presence of a (presumably educated) friend of theirs in Ponticianus. Mandouze (1968: 115 n. 9) proposes that the term has a wider application; but in this case the argument is further complicated by the controversy sparked by Courcelle (1968: 183–7), who sought to identify the two friends with Jerome and Bonosus, a position which Theiler (1953: 122) attempted to refute by applying to them this passage. O'Donnell (1992: III.39–40) provides a succinct account of this controversy, but the fact that Augustine's phrase has been dragged into this wholly separate discussion has perhaps resulted in its application being unnecessarily restricted.
[106] *Contra Academicos* 2.5, quoted in O'Meara 2001: 191.
[107] Ladner 1959: 354; see also O'Meara 2001: 189 and Olson 1995: 53–4.
[108] Morrison 1992: 10.

the scriptures to his own life. The text he had available in Milan was a copy of the letters of Paul; but as with Antony, the change was marked by his new attitude to Matthew. Antony heard the ascetic imperative and applied it to his own life; in his example of a contemporary renunciation of the world, Augustine could finally accept the reality and the relevance of Matthew's 'eunuchs for the kingdom of God'. His cry to Alypius – 'surgunt indocti et caelum rapiunt' – was itself an echo of Matthew: 'From the days of John the Baptist until now the kingdom of heaven suffereth violence and the violent take it by force.'[109]

The imitation of Antony

Augustine's story therefore attests to the power of 'this wonderful work, the reading of which suffices to instil an ascetic vocation on the spot'.[110] The irony here, of course, is that in fact for Augustine it does no such thing. Although he may initially have been inspired to imitate the life of Antony, not even in this first flush of enthusiasm did he make any attempt to remove himself to a 'genuinely "monastic" environment'; he did not set out in search of his own private desert.[111] Augustine's first idea was the kind of retreat he soon adopted with his friends and family at Cassiciacum, not far removed from the plan he had cherished in his days as a neoplatonist – and some distance from 'the heroic example' of Antony.[112] Nor did Antony's brand of asceticism make any lasting positive impression on Augustine, who in his later writings consistently rejects the anchoritic lifestyle as a model for zealous Christians.[113] Ultimately Augustine preferred to adopt the communal life of a cenobitic monastery, at least for the monks whom he organised under his rule.[114] His response to the *Life of Antony* was an 'intimate . . . readjustment' which 'did not need to be expressed in histrionic gestures', and can therefore be distinguished from the

---

[109] Matthew 11:12 [AV]. Vulgate: 'a diebus autem Iohannis Baptistae usque nunc regnum caelorum uim patitur et uiolenti rapiunt illud.'
[110] Monceaux 1931: 62, 'ce merveilleux ouvrage, dont la lecture suffisait pour déterminer sur l'heure les vocations ascétiques'.
[111] O'Donnell 1992: III.66; Monceaux 1931: 68.   [112] Brown 2000: 113.
[113] Monceaux 1931: 68ff.   [114] Ladner 1959: 355; Monceaux 1931: 69.

reactions of 'the less balanced admirers of the monks, the learned Jerome among them'.[115]

It is an interesting question whether the response of Jerome or that of Augustine was more typical of contemporary readers of hagiography: although most likely, both were too idiosyncratic to be taken as representative even of a particular class. But Augustine also records the responses of two other contemporaries to the *Life of Antony*, in the story that Ponticianus tells of his friends from the court at Trier.[116] The immediate effect of a reading of the *Life of Antony* on the two *agentes in rebus* is a clear model for its subsequent effect on Augustine and Alypius, and no doubt it was with this in mind that Ponticianus initially told the story and Augustine included it in the *Confessions*. Yet this is more than a matter of literary stylisation, and the linguistic and material elements said to be shared by the two scenes rarely amount to much: to take a single example, the public gardens outside Trier offer a very different scene to Augustine's private garden in Milan.[117] Rather, the most significant commonality is in some respects a negative one. Like Augustine, the friends of Ponticianus fail to adopt the life of a desert ascetic which the *Life of Antony* portrays.[118] In this respect they presented Augustine with a more valuable example than has often been recognised.

Despite his claim that during this story he turned his attention away from Ponticianus and on to himself, Augustine provides a detailed account of the incident of the men at Trier.[119] Although they discovered a house apparently used by a Christian community, they seem not to encounter any living Christian ascetics: their

---

[115] Brown 2000: 114.

[116] *Conf.* 8.6.15. The summary at O'Donnell 1992: III.39–40 does not prove that the two friends of Ponticianus could not have been Jerome and Bonosus, but since there seems no way of settling the question I have assumed that they were not.

[117] That the conversion of the friends of Ponticianus was little more than a doublet of Augustine's own conversion is suggested by Courcelle (1963: 186); O'Donnell (1992: III.40) [s.v. 'hortos'] notes the parallel of the two gardens, but O'Meara (2001: 188–9) rightly comments that many of the connections seem 'forced' and frequently rely on a partial and tendentious presentation of events.

[118] Olson (1995: 51) offers the rather misleading parallel that, like Antony, the friends of Ponticianus chose to 'live in a hut', but goes on to admit the lack of any direct imitation.

[119] *Conf.* 8.7.16: inspired by this passage, O'Connell (1996: 236) has Ponticianus 'droning on' here, which understates the evident importance Augustine ascribed to the conversation.

contact is mediated entirely through a reading of the *Life of Antony*. The one who took up the book to read it 'was amazed and set on fire', but – unlike in the story of Victorinus – Augustine is very specific concerning the process of reasoning that brought about a decision.[120] The primary issue was not sexuality or marriage, for when Augustine adds that the two converts were married he does so seemingly only as an afterthought, and with no hint that it was a cause for concern.[121] Instead the *agentes in rebus* concentrate on the vicissitudes of a secular career:

Tell me, I beg of you, what do we hope to achieve with all our labours? What is our aim in life? What is the motive of our service to the state? Can we hope for any higher office in the palace than to be Friends of the Emperor? And in that position what is not fragile and full of dangers? How many hazards must one risk to attain a position of even greater danger? And when will I arrive there? Whereas, if I wish to become God's friend, in an instant I may become that now.[122]

Augustine describes the inner process of conversion which follows on from this outburst, but again in terms of generalised secular concerns, until at last 'his mind rid itself of the world'.[123] Immediately the first courtier's companion agreed to join him, again having been persuaded of the benefits of exchanging secular ambition for serving God.[124] The two of them chose to remain behind and join the community they had discovered.

The terms in which Augustine presents this momentous and exemplary decision therefore sound surprisingly cynical, appearing to add up to little more than a cost-benefit analysis. Nor is it obvious that these *agentes in rebus* were men closer to Augustine's own position than was Marius Victorinus, or Ponticianus himself. As with Victorinus, the point was partly the immediacy of the change, but also its fullness: the friends of Ponticianus had abandoned all of their secular concerns and 'given themselves wholly to you for healing'.[125] But above all, the lesson for Augustine lay in the text which inspired them, and in the nature of that inspiration. The conversion of the *agentes in rebus* was evidently prompted

---

[120] *Conf.* 8.6.15.
[121] *Conf.* 8.6.15: 'When later their wives heard this, they also dedicated their virginity to you.' The term 'sponsa', which Chadwick here translates as 'wife', can also mean simply 'fiancée'.
[122] *Conf.* 8.6.15.   [123] *Conf.* 8.6.15.   [124] *Conf.* 8.6.15.   [125] *Conf.* 8.7.17.

by the *Life of Antony*, but in such a way that it served more as 'a metaphorical rather than as a literal exemplum' – since there was, as has been seen, no spontaneous rush to the desert.[126] Yet as Augustine describes it, the encounter with the *Life* led them to question their present lifestyle. Its value was as a kind of counter-example.

On this reading, then, the *Life of Antony* presented the friends of Ponticianus with an alternative vision of the contemporary world. It allowed them to look beyond the confines of their dependence on the imperial system, and indeed substituted the rule of God for the rule of the Roman emperor. There is no suggestion that this was a conversion to Christianity from another religious belief, and it seems likely that the men were already Christians, combining their faith with a secular career. But just as it would for Augustine, the example of Antony held out the possibility of a new kind of Christian life. The story of his conversion, and of his miracles above all, was to suggest a whole new interpretative framework within which the contemporary world could be understood: it suggested that late-antique Christians inhabited a world in which God was not only present but in which he continued to intervene. In Augustine's account of the friends of Ponticianus, therefore, it is significant that he never claims that they set out to imitate Antony. Instead, he sees the effect of the *Life of Antony* in their obedience to the familiar command: 'both men, already yours, were building their tower at the right cost of forsaking all their property and following you'.[127] Under such conditions the story of Antony might seem to have a very clear moral: not that the life of a desert ascetic was obligatory for all modern Christians, but that the strictures and imperatives of the biblical world continued to apply.

Ponticianus' friends are thus shown to anticipate Augustine's own response to an encounter with the *Life of Antony*: focusing less on the details of Antony's life than on the example of his attitude to Scripture. If Antony served as an inspiration for Augustine then it was by demonstrating the potential to live a contemporary life

---

[126] Olson 1995: 52.

[127] *Conf.* 8.6.15: the references are to Luke 14:28 and Matthew 19:21 – and probably also to Peter's response to the ascetic imperative at Matthew 19:27, as noted by O'Donnell (1992: III.42).

in obedience to the scriptures: to live in the late-antique world as though the conditions familiar from the Bible still applied. The failure to live as an anchorite was therefore not as complete a rejection of Antony as it might seem: for although it is true that Augustine 'did not sell all he had, give to the poor, and follow Jesus', it would be misleading to suggest that he simply 'went home, and lived very comfortably'.[128] The immediate and significant change was his decision to adopt Christianity, overcoming the difficulties that had beset him at the beginning of Book 8. Yet by the end of 388, Augustine had embarked on a way of life which imitated that of Antony not in its details but in tracing its source to the Bible. The life he planned for himself and his colleagues at Thagaste, back home in Numidia, was not the product of direct, individual obedience to Matthew's imperative, but grew out of Augustine's acceptance of a different biblical model. What he admired above all was the community at Jerusalem as described in the Acts of the Apostles.[129] This was the kind of biblical life he set out to adopt for himself.[130]

The significance of the example of Antony was that he inspired Augustine's attempt to apply biblical principles to his own life. Antony's uncomplicated acceptance of Scripture effectively erased the gap that separated late-antique life from the Bible, eliding the historical developments that might otherwise have seemed an insurmountable barrier. His miracles were evidence that God continued to work on behalf of modern men; and the friends of Ponticianus had shown what changes might be wrought by the acceptance of that proposition. As Augustine has the allegorical figure of Continence tell him in the midst of his turmoil:

Are you incapable of doing what these men and women have done? Do you think them capable of achieving this by their own resources and not by the Lord their God? . . . Why are you relying on yourself, only to find yourself unreliable? Cast yourself upon him, do not be afraid. . .[131]

Thus the model of asceticism which Augustine adopted owed little in the end to Antony, or to the alternative contemporary models

---

[128] O'Donnell 2005: 72.   [129] Acts of the Apostles 4:32.
[130] Monceaux 1931: 71; Monceaux (1931: 68–72) traces the early development of Augustine's ideas on Christian asceticism.
[131] *Conf.* 8.11.27.

of pagan and Jewish asceticism, but 'was born directly from the Gospel: from the contrast between the dictates of the Gospel and the social realities of the time'.[132] This in some ways implies a criticism of Antony, and must in part account for Augustine's lack of enthusiasm for the saint in his other works. The lesson that Antony's example taught him, however, was the one he happened to need in 386: that there existed the scope for a biblical life even in the contemporary world.

The ascetic indicative

It may be hazarded that this kind of response to the *Life of Antony* – and to hagiography in general – was by no means as eccentric as it might first appear. In the light of Jerome's example, it would be easy to assume that the conventional effect of encountering the life of a saint was a rush to imitate it: that hagiographies were essentially 'model lives . . . carefully presented to others for their imitation'.[133] This understanding should not be lightly dismissed, and can indeed be supported by the explicit claims of some of the texts in question. Theodoret of Cyrrhus, writing in the mid-fifth century, explains the intention behind the lives collected in his *Religious History* with an appropriate analogy:

Just as painters look at their model when imitating eyes, nose, mouth, cheeks, ears, forehead, the very hairs of the head and beard . . . so it is fitting that each of the readers of this work choose to imitate a particular life and order their own life in accordance with the one they choose.[134]

This is a clear prospectus setting out an intention to convert readers into saints themselves – or at least ascetics. Yet it is possible to doubt whether many of 'those who heard or read these texts' ever in fact 'read them in this way themselves'.[135]

Augustine, as we have seen, apparently felt no obligation to mimic the precise details of Antony's life; and that this was not a wholly unprecedented response is suggested by his example of Ponticianus' friends. Moreover, Jerome's response to the *Life of*

---

[132] Monceaux 1931: 64, 'Celui-ci est né directement de l'Evangile: du contraste entre les leçons de l'Evangile et les réalités sociales du temps.'
[133] Cameron 1999: 37.   [134] *HR* 30.7.   [135] As proposed at Cameron 1999: 37.

Antony is not a clear-cut example of a man inspired to recreate the saint 'not on paper but in his own being'.[136] All of these instances are notable, indeed, for the literary nature of their experience: all encountered Antony first through the *Life*, at various distances from the original Greek and far from its Egyptian setting; and both Jerome and Augustine engaged with Antony's example primarily in literary terms – Augustine by inscribing his reaction to it in the *Confessions*, Jerome in his lives of Paul and Hilarion.[137] Nor did the subjects of Jerome's lives choose to imitate Antony in every detail, which was exactly what made them worth writing about, or inventing. None of these can be called an 'ordinary' response, and it is, of course, in the nature of the evidence that even supposedly ordinary responses are generally to be found within a highly literary context. Nevertheless, it remains difficult to identify many historical examples of readers who were inspired by hagiographies to a direct imitation of their heroes. That the desert had become a city of ascetics was ultimately a claim made for rhetorical effect, but one which makes it easy to overestimate 'the sheer numbers who . . . followed Antony into the desert'.[138]

The available instances of contemporary responses to the lives of the saints suggest a different picture – and this is true not only of the protagonists of late-antique stories but also of those only glimpsed at the margins. The friends of Ponticianus might stand as one such example of the response invited by an encounter with a saint, and we may recall the equally revealing story told in the *First Greek Life of Pachomius*. Pachomius had gone to read at the church in the nearby village of Tabennesi (in Upper Egypt), and 'when the men of the world saw a man of God in their midst, they were very eager to become Christians and faithful'.[139] The encounter is direct, and not mediated by a written account as it was for Ponticianus' friends and for Augustine. Nonetheless, there is the same immediately apparent opposition between the 'men of the world' and the 'man of God', and there is an interesting

---

[136] Harpham 1987: 42.

[137] For Jerome's lives and their links to Antony, see above, ch. 3.

[138] The impact of the claim made at *VA* 14 may be seen in the title of Chitty (1966); the quotation is from Burton-Christie 1993: 8.

[139] *VP* 30.

and comparable effect. The consequence is not that the men from the village become ascetics, or join the community established by Pachomius. Instead, they are converted to Christianity, or rather to a more steadfast engagement with Christianity. As in the case of Augustine, the example of Pachomius inspired the villagers to reconsider their own relationship to the world and to their religion. This kind of change was perhaps not so dramatic as a complete and immediate renunciation of life in the world. But it was far more practicable, and likely to have been far more common.

For if the primary aim of hagiography was to inspire mass imitation of the saints, then it must be considered a failure.[140] No doubt some who read the story of Antony were inspired in precisely this way, but the vast majority of those who encountered the tale must have been more like the villagers of Tabennesi, or the friends of Ponticianus, or like Ponticianus himself. These kinds of responses were surely more typical in late antiquity, and it is not necessary to see them as a betrayal of the intentions of the authors and popularisers of the various lives. The *Life of Antony* was explicitly addressed to the monks outside of Egypt, and its purpose is described in appropriate terms:

You asked me to give you an account of [Antony], that you also may direct yourselves to imitate him . . . And I know that in hearing about him, along with marvelling at the man, you will also want to emulate his purpose; for Antony's way of life provides monks with a sufficient picture of ascetic practice.[141]

The creation of new monks was evidently part of the plan, and attention is directed to the practical matter of what an ascetic life ought to look like. Yet there would undoubtedly be some, such as Augustine, who would reject this detailed advice, but who might nevertheless emulate Antony in their own fashion.

The definitive statement at the beginning of the *Life of Antony* is perhaps therefore open to a wider interpretation than simply as providing 'a model for others to imitate'.[142] Even if its readers were not themselves monks, and did not immediately become monks, the text may still be seen to have had a pronounced effect. An

---

[140] As pointed out at Coon 1997: 9: 'Holy biographies inspired [only] a minority of Christians to act out the ascetic and miraculous deeds of God's saints.'
[141] *VA* pref. 3.   [142] Brakke 1995: 258.

attractive way of considering this effect is to alter the terms of the discussion. It is too limiting to characterise hagiographies as merely 'imitable models of exemplary conduct', which present their readers with a direct 'ascetic imperative'.[143] Without wishing to lose what seems the important element here – what has been called 'the argument from *Life* to action' – it is possible instead to imagine a more complicated relationship than one of obedience and command.[144]

These lives perhaps functioned not in the imperative but rather in the *indicative*. They represented a proposition about the world in which their readers lived – a vision of the contemporary world and the way it worked which departed from common experience. They described a world in which miracles occurred, in which God actively intervened, and in which contemporary Christians like them were adopting a lifestyle more familiar from the Bible. Without offering imperatives themselves, they demonstrated the possibility of living up to the ascetic imperative, and the other models of behaviour, presented in the Christian scriptures. This is what those who encountered the lives of the saints were challenged to accept, and to apply in their own lives.

The vital elements were precisely those which Augustine identified in Ponticianus' account of Antony: a combination of miracles and verisimilitude, proof that wonderful events were occurring in the present day. The heroes of the lives did not have to be real, and their stories could incorporate a certain amount of unreality, as long as they took place in a recognisable contemporary world and were at least seemingly historical.[145] What mattered was that the lives described a biblical world which could yet be identified with the world their readers inhabited. Ascetics and saints brought the Bible into the contemporary world, and their biographies made it 'accessible' throughout the empire.[146] Antony was a living example of the biblical life, no less than was Pachomius when he appeared in the flesh at Tabennesi. Nor was it by chance that, in the *History of*

---

[143] Harpham 1987: 4.   [144] Cameron 1991: 147.

[145] The best-known example of apparently wanton unreality in late-antique hagiography is the centaur in Jerome's *VPauli* 7: there are good discussions (offering a slightly different approach from that given here) in Miller 1996 and Merrills 2004. See also my discussion in ch. 3, above.

[146] Brown 1983: 10.

the Monks in Egypt, Apa Apollo was described as being 'like some new prophet and apostle dwelling in our own generation'.[147]

Hagiographies therefore provided their readers with a generalised inspiration more than with a set of step-by-step instructions, and it was as reasonable a response for the friends of Ponticianus to bring asceticism out of the desert as it was for the villagers of Tabennesi, who were already in the desert, to decline to become ascetics. Saints such as Antony were not models to be imitated in every detail so much as 'pioneers', whose lives offered a 'guarantee that renunciation of the world was possible' even in the later Roman empire.[148] It was in this sense that Christian biography offered an imperative, insofar as this new understanding of the world demanded a commensurate change in the reader. 'This is what the world is like,' said these texts, with the implication: 'Where do you fit in?' The challenge for the reader was to adapt his or her life to a world which included Antony. They were required to 'live up' to this world in which they already lived.

That Augustine was not inspired by the example of Antony to head immediately for the desert does not mean that the story told by Ponticianus did not have a powerful effect – and plausibly one which was typical of the impact of Christian biography in late antiquity. The importance of Antony's story for Augustine lay in the saint's testimony to the continuing presence of God and the continuing relevance of Scripture in the contemporary world. With this in mind, the conclusion of the *Life of Antony* suggests a better analogy for the workings of Christian biographies and for the influence of distant ascetics:

For although they carry out their work secretly and desire to remain unnoticed, still the Lord shows them forth like lamps to all people, so that even those who only hear about them may know that the commandments can lead to reformation, and so may receive zeal for the way to virtue.[149]

This might encourage a better understanding of the relevance of saints' lives in late antiquity: for if saints are like lamps, then they do not exist to be imitated, and nor can they be ends in themselves.

---

[147] *HM* 7.8, as translated by Brown 1983: 18. [148] Rousseau 1978: 94.
[149] *VA* 93, as translated by Brakke 1995: 252–3.

Instead, their purpose is to light up the world and make its true character visible. This was the role which the story of Antony played in Augustine's conversion. Antony was the lamp which enabled Augustine to recognise the true nature of the world, and which let it shine forth for him in its true, biblical colours.

5

THE END OF SACRED HISTORY

'You know how to interpret the appearance of earth and sky; why then do you not know how to interpret the present time?' (Luke 12:56). In this saying of Jesus, the 'signs of the times' must be understood as the path he was taking, indeed it must be understood as Jesus himself. To interpret the signs of the times in the light of faith means to recognize the presence of Christ in every age.

(Joseph Cardinal Ratzinger, 'Theological Commentary' in *The Message of Fatima* (Press release: Congregation of the Doctrine of the Faith, Vatican City, 26 June 2000))

Augustine was scrupulous, in his *Confessions*, to name and give credit to the people whom he regarded as the most influential in guiding him towards his conversion to Christianity.[1] One of those named was, as we have seen, the Egyptian ascetic Antony: and Antony's role in the *Confessions* thus offers a valuable example of how the life of a saint might be understood by a group of readers and hearers in the contemporary late-antique world. The evident impact of the *Life of Antony*, both indirectly on Augustine and on Alypius, and directly on the friends of Ponticianus and on Ponticianus himself, attests to the popularity and the potential power of this relatively new tradition of Christian biography. Augustine and his friends were perhaps in many ways an unusual audience – a group often self-conscious in its spirituality and willing to engage with the lives of others, receptive to spiritual biography and ultimately 'ripe for autobiography'.[2] Nevertheless, the presence of the *Life of Antony* in the *Confessions* offers a way to approach Augustine's work as in itself a response to the tradition of Christian biography and, at the same time, a contribution to that literary tradition in its own right. For Augustine was not only a reader of

---

[1] As pointed out by Crosson 1999: 30.
[2] Brown 2000: 158–9, offering as evidence a letter from Paulinus of Nola to Alypius enquiring about precisely this kind of change: Paulinus, *Letter* 24.2.

the *Life of Antony* but also an imitator of it, in life and in literature. The significance of this exemplary life extended far beyond the single moment of his conversion; its implications, in fact, might be traced throughout Augustine's career.

To begin with, Antony's recent and remarkable conversion to the ascetic life not only prompted but was recapitulated in Augustine's conversion to Christianity; and both were conditioned by the sudden recognition that Scripture could be re-enacted in the present day. Certainly the portrait in the *Confessions* of Augustine's conversion to Christianity makes it clear that in 386 he interpreted that experience as 'the unfolding of a supernatural process' in which God had intervened directly in his life.[3] This interpretation of the events – and in particular, his response to the overheard chant of 'tolle, lege' and to a random passage from the letters of Paul – was inspired by the story of Antony's response to the ascetic imperative in the Gospel of Matthew. Augustine imitated Antony, then, not by going into the desert and adopting his ascetic lifestyle, but by taking a new attitude to Scripture: by ignoring the barriers, historical, geographical and phenomenological, which separated his familiar world from the world of the Bible, and so recognising a genuine continuity between events recorded in the scriptures and events in the contemporary Roman empire. For Augustine, at least at the time of his conversion, the presence of an ascetic holy man such as Antony in his own late-antique environment allowed him finally to grasp the significance of the 'eunuchs who have castrated themselves for the kingdom of heaven's sake'.[4] The re-enactment of Scripture in the contemporary world guaranteed the truth of the Bible and the triumph of the Christian faith.

Yet in the *Confessions* – even in only Book 8 of the *Confessions* – there is more than this single decisive moment. Augustine's own response to the *Life of Antony* is only one of a series of exemplary conversions, which allow a sustained consideration of the effect of this reappraisal of Scripture on himself and on his friends and contemporaries. The literary structure of the *Confessions* drew these various, relatively undramatic occasions – Marius Victorinus in conversation with a Milanese priest, Augustine and Alypius in

---

[3] Morrison 1992: ix.   [4] *Conf.* 8.2.2; Matthew 19:21.

their garden, the friends of Ponticianus in Trier – into a kind of typological relationship 'in which foreshadowing and fulfilment take place . . . between secular figures, guided by Providence'.[5] This sequence need not end with Augustine and Alypius but can be extended to include all the readers of the *Confessions*, 'down to and including ourselves', so that the re-enactment of Scripture might be presented as a personal challenge to be taken up even by the most hesitant of Christians.[6] What had applied to the lives of emperors, bishops and monks now applied to the life of the ordinary Christian reader.

Augustine's account thus takes its place in the tradition of late-antique Christian biography, but also reflects on that tradition; in addition to offering a set of responses to the contemporary world and to Scripture, it further 'directs us to how we are to read biographical texts, including Augustine's own'.[7] Augustine's *Confessions* thereby functioned in part as a guide to their own interpretation. The complexity of Augustine's text, however, should serve as a warning that his account of his own life is not to be approached in exactly the same way as its models and inspirations. Indeed, despite Augustine's apparent confidence in 386 that God could be seen to be acting in the world – and that his own experiences might reflect this just as Antony's evidently had – it seems clear that by the time he came to look back on his conversion he had begun to doubt that such a claim could be made with any real certainty. Augustine remained confident that God continued to act in the world, and there is no reason to imagine that he would have wished to deny that divine influence in the events of his own life. All the same, there seems to have been a genuine shift in his understanding of how the events of his time should be understood. The sacred history that he could confidently see all around him at the time of his conversion would appear, as Augustine reflected on events, to be rather more open to interpretation. Rather than a reliable record of the irruption of the divine into the contemporary world, Augustine would come to see Christian biographies – and even his own autobiography – as merely provisional, unauthorised lives.

5 Stock 1996: 77.   6 Stock 1996: 77.   7 Olson 1995: 51.

Christian times

At the time of his conversion in 386, then, the young Augustine
evidently believed that the intervention of God in the world could
not only be taken for granted but could also be reliably recognised
and understood. In this way, Augustine's self-portrait in the *Confessions* can be seen to have reflected the characteristic concerns
of late-antique Christian biography. The Augustine of 386 was
presented as responding to a divine command; for him, God was
acting in the present day just as he had in the world of Scripture –
and just as he did in the Christian biographies which purported
to describe the lives of his contemporaries. This, then, is much
more than simply a belief in the vital importance of 'divine providence and divine grace'.[8] In itself, such a belief would hardly have
been surprising; and there is certainly no reason to imagine that
Augustine, as a Christian, ever doubted the dominion of God over
everything – even, as he would remind his readers, over the fall of
a sparrow.[9] All history had, after all, been prophesied in Scripture,
and 'there is nothing that is not subject to the administration of
divine providence'.[10] Rather, the young Augustine seems to have
believed – and to have continued to believe even into the 390s –
in a much stronger version of this position. For a few years, that
is, Augustine seems to have believed that his own times could be
interpreted as part of 'a definite phase in the history of salvation'.[11]

This belief, as attributed to Augustine, has been labelled with
the phrase 'tempora christiana', and it has caused a certain amount
of controversy.[12] Nevertheless, it seems clear that for a short time
at least, Augustine picked out his own period at the end of the

---

[8] Harrison 2000: 204.
[9] Augustine, *De Genesi ad litteram* 5.21.42, citing Matthew 10.29.
[10] Thus Markus 1988: 11, citing Augustine, *De libero arbitrio* 1.5.13. The point is pursued
by Madec 1996: 99 and restated at Markus 2000: 202–3.
[11] Markus 1988: 37; see also Markus 1988: 31, 'a distinct phase in the history not only of
the Roman Empire, but of salvation'.
[12] There is, for instance, little doubt that Augustine employed the phrase 'tempora christiana' in a number of different senses, as was originally made clear in Markus 1988:
esp. 27–37. There is a close discussion of the idea in Bonner 1971; objections made in
Madec 1996 are subsequently discussed in Markus 2000. Recent authors – e.g. Harrison
(2000: 203) – seem prepared instead to use the term to refer to a looser set of connected
ideas about Christian history.

fourth century as an exceptionally meaningful age. His conversion in Milan in 386 had been followed a few years later by the decree of the Emperor Theodosius I which reconfirmed the pre-eminent position of Christianity in the empire; and Augustine could add to the miracles recorded in the *Life of Antony* his own personal experience of powerful Christian leaders such as Ambrose in Milan.[13] It is perhaps hardly surprising that Augustine's writings in this period should display something rather more far reaching than merely 'a tendency to applaud the Theodosian settlement'.[14] They seem to propose instead 'a prophetic interpretation of the Theodosian age', in which the proper recognition and interpretation of contemporary events could even come to serve as 'an essential component of the basic catechesis of converts.'[15] Thus for Augustine, the sacred history narrated to converts was to extend, albeit selectively, from the beginning of the book of Genesis 'down to the present times of the Church'.[16]

In his earliest writings, then, Augustine was willing to accept that contemporary events could be incorporated into an ongoing sacred history, which could in turn be understood in a manner consistent with the interpretation of the scriptures. Modern events could be presented as fulfilments of specific biblical prophecies; and salvation was not only on hand but on display, to be seen and recognised by all.[17] A general belief in the operation of providence was supplemented by a more specific belief that the contemporary world could be read and understood in terms that might otherwise be restricted to Scripture: that it presented itself as a kind of living Scripture.[18] This approach was taken up with enthusiasm by historians such as Augustine's protégé Orosius, and it can be detected in other histories of the period such as that composed by Rufinus of Aquileia.[19] Rufinus, of course, was explicitly intending to continue

[13] The 391 law of Theodosius I banning pagan practice in effect established Christianity as the norm for public worship: *C.Th.* 16.1.2.
[14] Bonner 1971: 234. [15] Markus 1988: 36, 32.
[16] Augustine, *De catechizandis rudibus* 3.5.
[17] Markus 1988: 30; Augustine, *Enarrationes in Psalmos* 6.13; *De consensu euangelistarum* 1.14.21. Cf. also Markus 2000 for an emphasis on the 390s in particular, with additional evidence provided from Augustine's contemporary sermons.
[18] Markus 1988: 32.
[19] Bonner 1971: 234; Markus 2000: 207 gives the example of Rufinus.

the *Ecclesiastical History* of Eusebius of Caesarea, and this connection is surely significant. Rufinus and Orosius took their place in a Eusebian tradition of historical and biographical writing which tended to understand the new Christian empire – whether assigned to Constantine or to Theodosius – 'as being in some special sense, the instrument for the extension of God's Kingdom upon earth'.[20] So too, for a time, did Augustine.

This Eusebian tradition was not the only model available even to Christian historians, but it remained a dominant one throughout the fourth century and into the fifth; and it was sufficiently influential that it has even been said that 'theologians were generally agreed in regarding the conversion of Constantine as the inauguration of a new period of sacred history'.[21] Whether this idea was ever fully accepted is perhaps open to debate, but it seems clear that the same set of assumptions also underlay contemporary Christian biography. The important, if implicit, claim made throughout such lives was that the scriptural parallels which undoubtedly existed could, furthermore, be easily recognised and interpreted by the reader. Thus it was established that the lives of certain individuals were clearly perceptible as involving the re-enactment of Scripture; that God himself had arranged matters so as to make these patterns clear; and that the patterning of these lives by God himself permitted a return to that 'privileged strand of history' in which divine intentions could be authoritatively discerned, and which had previously been confined to the 'biblical narrative of God's saving work among his chosen people'.[22] God's habit of speaking through interpretable signs might have been thought to have lapsed with the last of the biblical authors. Between Eusebius and Augustine, Christian biography suggested that the habit could be seen to continue.

Yet although Rufinus and Orosius would extend this tradition with enthusiasm in the realm of Christian history, and although Christian biographies would go on to record further examples of what seemed to be divine intervention, it is possible to argue that Augustine in the 390s was already beginning to retreat from any such position. This is not to say that Augustine ever rejected entirely the possibility that miracles might take place in the modern world,

[20] Bonner 1971: 234.   [21] Harrison 2000: 202.   [22] Markus 1988: 9.

191

or that God had continued to take any part in human history other than the distant watchfulness implied by divine providence. Such an understanding of Augustine's attitude has indeed been proposed, and is usually based on passages taken from his treatises *On True Religion* and *On the Value of Belief*, both datable to the 390s. These works are then often contrasted with the apparent credulity shown by the older Augustine in his later writings, and in particular his *City of God*.[23] The result has been a superficially plausible – but ultimately unconvincing – picture of the rigorous young Augustine growing more credulous in his old age; or if not 'credulous' exactly, then naïve or superstitious, or else merely recognising the ingrained credulity of more ordinary Christians.[24]

Yet Augustine can be found placing his trust in miracles at every stage of his career. The portrayal of the young Augustine in the *Confessions* shows him inspired by the stories of miracles performed by Antony in the desert; and as then responding with immediate acceptance to apparent divine intervention on his behalf. Thus in 386, his belief in miracles was powerful enough to convert him to Christianity. This young man must surely have had more than a little in common with the Augustine who would go on to extol, years later in his treatise on the *City of God*, 'that wonderful operation of [God's] power whereby, being eternal, he is active in temporal events'.[25] This is not to imply that Augustine's views on these difficult matters were wholly consistent throughout his life. Instead, what can be seen is a gradual development in his attitude, from the certainty with which he interpreted the signs around him in 386 to a more nuanced understanding of miracles and of sacred history in general. Augustine continued to believe that God had retained the power and the will to intervene in the contemporary world; but he became more and more sceptical that these

[23] The relevant passages (discussed in detail below) are Augustine, *De uera rel.* 25.47; *De util. cred.* 15.34; *De ciu. dei* 22.8. Some of the more prominent examples of modern authors interpreting the texts in the way I describe include Van der Meer 1961: 539–57; Brown 2000: 413–22; O'Daly 1999: 227 n. 54; and De Vooght 1934, who provides a tabulation of Augustine's apparently changing views. There is also a careful discussion of the question at Pegon 1982: 492–4.
[24] Van der Meer (1961: 553–6) and Brown (2000: 415) both raise objections to the charge of credulity: Van der Meer prefers to speak of Augustine's 'superstition', while Brown suggests that Augustine was taking into account the popular beliefs of his congregation.
[25] *De ciu. dei* 22.9 (describing miracles in general).

interventions could be securely recognised and interpreted. Miracles and wonders were not always to be relied upon.

This, then, is the argument of the two treatises of the 390s in which Augustine raised the question of miracles – and in which his primary concern was with the problem of religious authority. His work *On True Religion* thus sets itself quite clearly in opposition to the arguments of heretics and other opponents of Augustine's own orthodox church, but in this case not chiefly on logical grounds. Indeed, Augustine explicitly disavows any intention to refute the opinions of his opponents, and specifies instead that he will focus on demonstrating that the true Christian religion has other, stronger foundations.[26] His appeal is to authority in contrast to reason; or rather, he appeals to a reasoned view of what constitutes acceptable authority.[27] Truth is the greatest source of authority, of course, but Augustine notes that it is not always possible to apprehend the truth directly: it remains, therefore, 'for us to consider which men and which books are to be believed with regard to the proper worship of God'.[28] The discussion of miracles, then, centres around the extent to which they can be considered to be authoritative in themselves. In answering this question, Augustine draws a clear distinction between the miracles given to the earliest Christians and the circumstances of his own day; and he has been understood to say that miracles no longer take place.[29]

Augustine's point, however, is surely more subtle. He recognises that 'our ancestors, at that early stage in their progression from temporal to eternal concerns, followed miraculous signs' because, as he notes, 'they could do nothing else', and that 'this was done for them so that it would not be necessary for their descendants'.[30] What Augustine is ruling out for the contemporary world is therefore the kind of miracle that compelled immediate belief. The authenticity of these early miracles could not be in doubt, for they overturned all that was believed at the time, and yet resulted in mass adoption of

---

[26] *De uer. rel.* 9.17.   [27] *De uer. rel.* 24.45.

[28] *De uer. rel.* 24.45–6: 'sed nostrum est considerare, quibus uel hominibus uel libris credendum sit ad colendum recte Deum'.

[29] *De uer. rel.* 25.47.

[30] *De uer. rel.* 25.47: 'maiores nostros eo gradu fidei, quo a temporalibus ad aeterna conscenditur, uisibilia miracula (non enim aliter poterant) secutos esse: per quos id actum est, ut necessaria non essent posteris'.

Christianity – and for Augustine, this argument from sheer weight of numbers was among the most important.[31] But for precisely this reason, spectacular miracles of this sort were not necessary and indeed were not to be permitted in the modern world once Christianity had been established – for they would not only begin to lose their impact, but could easily become a distraction. Rather, the role of the miracle in the modern world was to instil belief in the minds of those who had not yet learned how to reason about the divine; and the task now was to examine whether a miracle was indeed compatible with the reasoned opinion of a purified mind – or in effect, with the settled opinions and traditions of the orthodox church.[32] Miracles demonstrated what ought to be believed; but the necessary core of the Christian faith was now much better known. If modern miracles appeared to contradict conventional wisdom, then they had simply been misinterpreted, most probably as a result of that pride which led heretics and schismatics to delight in opposition for its own sake.[33] Miracles persisted – but were less spectacular and less authoritative in themselves. Now, instead of overturning the established order, they merely confirmed the truth of the faith.

The distinction that Augustine wished to draw therefore depended significantly on a definition of miracles which allowed them to occur in the contemporary Roman empire but nevertheless to remain in some way ambiguous. This is precisely the question addressed around the same time by Augustine in his treatise *On the Value of Belief*.[34] Here again Augustine insists that the truth can be recognised through the reason of a purified mind, but acknowledges that this will be unattainable for all but the best; for the remainder, authority is provided either in the sheer number of believers or in the performance of miracles.[35] That belief encouraged by miracles can be more true and more valuable than an attachment to

---

[31] *De uer. rel.* 25.47 (authenticity); 25.46 (weight of numbers).

[32] *De uer. rel.* 25.46: 'nunc enim agitur quibus credendum sit, antequam quisque sit idoneus ineundae rationi de diuinis et inuisibilibus rebus; nam ipsi purgatioris animae, quae ad perspicuam ueritatem peruenit, nullo modo auctoritas humana praeponitur'.

[33] *De uer. rel.* 25.47.

[34] Justification for treating the two texts together comes not only in their mention of miracles, but also in Augustine's consecutive treatment of them in his *Retr.* 12 and 13.

[35] *De util. cred.* 15.34.

spurious and misguided reasoning is made clear in the very title of
the treatise, and Augustine is able to offer the example of the miracles of Christ in the gospels.[36] It is important for Augustine's point,
however, both that the authority of these biblical miracles should
persist and that miracles should continue to occur; and although he
admits that miracles 'of [the biblical] sort' might no longer seem
to take place, he does not rule them out altogether.[37] In any case,
miracles are explicitly understood to continue, even if they are not
immediately overwhelming or impressive.

The key here is Augustine's famous definition of a miracle as
'something difficult or strange which seems beyond the expectations or the capacity of the one who marvels at it'.[38] By thus placing
the emphasis on the observation and interpretation of a miraculous
event, Augustine allows that miracles may be continuing unrecog-
nised – indeed, he goes on to suggest that familiarity has rendered
unexceptional the regular miracles of nature:

Take the alternation of day and night, the unvarying order of the heavenly bodies,
the annual return of the four seasons, the leaves falling and returning to the trees,
the endless vitality of the seeds, the beauty of light, colour, sounds, odours, the
varieties of flavours. If we could speak to someone who saw and sensed these
things for the first time, we should find that he was overwhelmed and dizzy at
such miracles. But we make light of all these things, not because they are easy
to understand – for what is more obscure than their causes – but because we are
continually aware of them.[39]

Miracles need not break the laws of nature; they need not be compelling, or overwhelmingly impressive. Indeed, insofar as a true
miracle will only confirm what is already understood and accepted
by the majority of Christians, and what is preserved in the orthodox
tradition of the church, they may even seem distinctly unimpres-
sive. But for Augustine, again, this is not a weakness but a strength.
The fact of a miracle is less important than its interpretation; and
just as right reason could only be compatible with orthodox belief,
so too did orthodox belief define what could count as a genuine
miracle.

[36] *De util. cred.* 15.32.   [37] *De util. cred.* 15.34: 'cur, inquis, ista modo non fiunt?'
[38] *De util. cred.* 15.34: 'quidquid arduum aut insolitum supra spem uel facultatem mirantis
apparet' (based on the translation of Burleigh).
[39] *De util. cred.* 15.34 (tr. Burleigh).

Augustine's concern in each of these works was with the limits and the weaknesses of pure reason and with the role played by authority and belief in religion. His response was to recognise the power of pure reason but also the difficulty in achieving it; and to emphasise instead the importance of a belief in the authority of others. And yet it was also necessary to consider carefully the grounds for any such belief, and in particular its effects – for if it was seen to challenge the traditions of the church and the majority of other believers, then it was to be looked upon with suspicion. Augustine in the 390s was therefore in no way attempting to deny the existence of divine providence, nor the continuing occurrence of miracles in the world of late antiquity. He had been content in 386 to convert to Christianity on the basis of an apparent miracle, and to do so under the influence of the story of the *Life of Antony*; and he was evidently prepared to believe for some time that the new Roman empire of Theodosius could be understood as a new era of sacred history. He had continued, that is, to believe not only in the intervention of God in the world, but in the possibility of interpreting his purposes. But it seems likely that with his treatises *On True Religion* and *On the Value of Belief* we begin to see Augustine retreating, not from a belief in miracles as such, but from any certainty regarding their interpretation. It remained the case that God's providential care of humanity could be read and understood 'through history and prophecy'; and yet it might not be known for sure.[40] After all, he would now add, such faith in temporal things as histories and historians was inevitably 'more a matter of belief than a matter of knowledge'.[41]

Faith in facts

Thus when Augustine, perhaps thirty years later, came to offer a catalogue of miracles as part of the final book of his *City of God*, it is notable that he focused attention on two aspects in particular.[42] The

---

[40] *De uer. rel.* 25.46: 'quid autem agatur cum genere humano, per historiam commendari uoluit, et per prophetiam'.
[41] *De uer. rel.* 25.46: 'temporalium autem rerum fides, siue praeteritarum, siue futurarum, magis credendo quam intellegendo'.
[42] *De ciu. dei* 22.8.

first thing to note is that the miracles he records are almost all relatively unspectacular, and would have left room for an explanation in purely natural (as opposed to supernatural) terms. The second is that Augustine's main concern is not with the truth of the stories but with his desire that they should become better known. This is not, therefore, the triumph of superstition over rationality; rather, it is an exploration of the potential value of a modern miracle which nevertheless takes into account Augustine's understanding of the limits of interpretation. It is not true to say that the later Augustine 'believes everything he hears at third or fourth hand from anyone who says it is so, or anything he reads in a work of any serious author', nor that 'religious tales that were generally believed in he himself accepted without question'.[43] Rather, Augustine continued to be interested in the problem of authority just as he had been in his treatises of the 390s; and he continued to depend on an important distinction between knowledge and belief.

In the *City of God*, then, an absolute scepticism on the model of the New Academy was rejected and replaced with certain reliable routes to knowledge.[44] Reason could of course be trusted, although its use was limited by the difficulty of achieving the necessary purity of soul; and the scriptures too offered a guaranteed source of true knowledge. Once that had been taken into account, however, the rest of knowledge was more provisional:

[for] regarding certain things which we have perceived neither through the senses nor through reason, and which have not been revealed to us in the canonical scriptures nor have become known to us through witnesses whom it would be absurd not to believe, we may, without just reproach, be in doubt.[45]

Besides reason and Scripture, then, the evidence of the senses could be relied upon – but it seems clear that this could only attest to events and not to their meanings. Similarly, witnesses might well be considered trustworthy with regard to the facts of a case, and yet not represent a reliable guide to its proper interpretation. Applied to miracles, then, and more generally to the record of God's active

---

[43] Van der Meer 1961: 555–6.   [44] *De ciu. dei* 19.18.
[45] *De ciu. dei* 19.18 (my translation): 'de quibusdam rebus, quas neque sensu neque ratione percepimus neque nobis per scripturam canonicam claruerunt nec per testes, quibus non credere absurdum est, in nostram notitiam peruenerunt, sine iusta reprehensione dubitamus.'

intervention in the world, this necessarily allowed plenty of room for doubt. Thus Augustine might admit the reported facts of a story to be true, although he was equally capable of reserving judgement: 'perhaps this is true, perhaps it isn't'.[46] More frequently, however, he would accept the historical account but reject what appeared to be an implausible interpretation.

An example is his discussion of the tomb of John the Evangelist at Ephesus, in which unpromising situation the saint was believed to be still living on, visibly disturbing the earth with his movement and breathing. Augustine was sceptical – not of the phenomenon itself, but of the proposed explanation.[47] Whether the earth was indeed particularly disturbed in that place he would leave it to those who knew the area to judge; and Augustine was careful not to rule out such a claim, which he had himself heard from witnesses who were not unreliable.[48] Nevertheless, Augustine is unwilling to engage with those who assign the phenomenon to John's continuing earthly life – judging it 'superfluous to contend with such an opinion' – on the grounds that he finds it incommensurate with Scripture.[49] The possibility remains that this is indeed a genuine miracle, and Augustine goes on to insist that God is perfectly capable of such things; and yet there might always be other explanations.[50]

A distinction was therefore to be drawn between event and interpretation – both the interpretation of an event as a miracle at all, or as an example of divine intervention, and then (even if that were granted) the interpretation of the meaning of any such miracle. Augustine's catalogue of wondrous events in the *City of God* should not be considered, then, as offering proofs, but rather examples and illustrations. He tells stories but does not insist on their status as miracles; he allows others to provide explanations, and does not entirely ignore the jeerers and the sceptics. Thus in the

[46] Van der Meer 1961: 556, citing Augustine's scepticism about the pelican wounding itself to feed its young at *Enarrationes in Psalmos* 101.1.8: 'uos sic audite, ut si uerum est, congruat; si falsum est, non teneat.'
[47] Van der Meer 1961: 555; the discussion arises in the commentaries on John's gospel, which have been dated to 406.
[48] *Io. eu. tr.* 124.2: 'uiderint enim qui locum sciunt, utrum hoc ibi faciat uel patiatur terra quod dicitur; quia et reuera non a leuibus hominibus id audiuimus.'
[49] *Io eu. tr.* 124.2: 'huic opinioni superuacaneum existimo reluctari.'
[50] *Io eu. tr.* 124.3.

story of the tailor Florentius, his initial prayer for his cloak to be recovered is mocked by local youths as an inappropriate request for money.[51] Their presentation of this as illegitimate is challenged when Florentius discovers a fish unexpectedly cast up on the shore, and their scepticism is apparently overturned when a gold ring is found in its belly – so that the cook who finds it and returns it to him can say 'See how the Twenty Martyrs have clothed you!'[52] Augustine, however, as narrator, makes no explicit comment here; although his approval is of course clear, the act of intepretation is performed by a character within the tale. The people involved were left to draw their own conclusions, and so too is the reader. Nevertheless, if there is an intepretative model in these miracle stories, it is most likely to be the physician confronted with a female cancer patient who had made a sudden and remarkable recovery without his help:

He questioned her with some force as to what remedy she had employed . . . But when he heard what had happened, he is said to have replied, with scrupulous politeness, but in a voice of scepticism and with a manner which made her fear that he was about to revile Christ, 'I thought you were going to tell me some great thing!' When he saw that she was shocked at this, he at once added, 'What great thing is it for Christ to heal a cancer, when he raised a man who had been four days dead?'[53]

The physician would have found remarkable an account which threatened to 'overturn the opinion of Hippocrates'; the claim that a miracle had occurred, by contrast, merely confirmed him in his Christian faith.[54]

Augustine's stance was evidently that even if the interpretation of an event as a miracle is not intellectually rigorous, it might nevertheless be persuasive and valuable. When he heard for himself the story of the woman unexpectedly cured of cancer, he accepted it as a miracle and indeed was 'extremely angry that so enormous a miracle should have been kept hidden' – and yet his response was not to offer any more elaborate interpretation.[55] Instead, he rebuked the woman for remaining silent and encouraged her to

---

[51] *De ciu. dei* 22.8.   [52] *De ciu. dei* 22.8.
[53] *De ciu. dei* 22.8; Augustine uses a similar argument at *Io. eu. tr.* 124.3, as discussed above.
[54] *De ciu. dei* 22.8.   [55] *De ciu. dei* 22.8: ' . . . tam ingens miraculum sic latere'.

make the story public; and 'my brief questioning now caused her
to describe the manner in which the whole sequence of events
had come to pass; and those who heard her listened in great wonder, glorifying God'.[56] The story stood alone without Augustine's
recommendation: as soon as the lady's friends heard the tale they
immediately understood it, rightly or wrongly, as a convincing
example of divine intervention in the contemporary world. The
concern of this chapter of the *City of God* was not to pin down
the meaning of these miracles but to attest to the fact that they
continued to occur, and to bring them to wider attention.[57] His justification for telling these stories is not primarily that they are true,
but that they offer valuable confirmation of the existing orthodox
Christian faith; and also that most ordinary Christians find them
compelling.

The *City of God* thus reveals a real commitment to the principles
of his earlier treatises *On True Religion* and *On the Value of Belief*,
in which true reason was frequently unattainable, and the value of
a miracle could be judged by whether it was consonant with the
majority of Christians and the tradition of the established church.
This is Augustine's reason for hoping that the accounts may come
to be more widely known: because whether they are true miracles
or not – that is, whether God's hand can truly be seen behind them,
and whether or not his purposes in performing them can be reliably understood – the events have shown themselves to be effective
in encouraging an appropriate piety. The popular interpretation of
these miracles cannot be guaranteed to be true, but it is universal and immediate; they serve no partisan purpose, no inducement
to pride in a heresy or a schism; and even in the absence of certainty, they offer stability and security in the Christian church. For
Augustine, then, these miracles can safely be left uninterpreted.
They were to be accurately recorded, but left to speak for themselves. If any additional meaning were required, it would make
itself known without the intervention of a human interpreter.[58]

That this was Augustine's approach in his pastoral teaching is
further suggested in the most famous of these miracle stories, cen-
tring on his own church at Hippo and surviving not only in the

---

[56] *De ciu. dei* 22.8.   [57] *De ciu. dei* 22.8.   [58] As Augustine argues at *De ciu. dei* 22.7.

account in the *City of God* but also in the sermons he preached at the time.[59] The notable feature as events unfold is Augustine's apparent reluctance to interpret them as bishop and instead to go along with the crowd. A brother and sister had arrived at Hippo afflicted by a palsy, and on Easter Sunday the brother was suddenly and very publicly cured at the shrine of Stephen (the proto-martyr). Immediately witnesses went to inform Augustine, who was preparing to celebrate mass.[60] As Augustine recalls, he then performed the mass, but in place of a sermon offered only a brief comment: 'for I desired them not to listen to me, but rather to reflect on the eloquence of God, as it were, evinced in this divine work'.[61] In the sermon as it survives he pleads exhaustion to justify the brevity of his address, but otherwise makes the same point to his congregation directly:

We are accustomed to hearing the *libelli* which describe the miracles God performs through the prayers of the most blessed martyr Stephen. This man's *libellus* is the sight of him; first-hand knowledge instead of some writing, his face presented to you instead of a document.[62]

Augustine is willing to let the Christians of Hippo make up their own minds. He does not to try to explain the miracle or its meaning, nor even to narrate the event in the style of a martyr act or any other inspirational *libellus*. This may well have been effective crowd control.[63] It seems also to point to a potentially awkward gap between events and their interpretation.

In the next sermon, on the following day, Augustine seems to have changed his mind, and announces that the young man who was cured has in fact been encouraged to provide a written account of his story.[64] Some context is thereby provided for the miracle, although no compelling explanation.[65] Indeed, after reading aloud this new *libellus* Augustine seems to show himself surprised – and perhaps more than a little doubtful – about certain of the details,

[59] *De ciu. dei* 22.8; Augustine, *Sermons* 320–4. The events and Augustine's response to them are discussed at McLynn 2003: 259–61.
[60] *De ciu. dei* 22.8.   [61] *De ciu. dei* 22.8.
[62] Augustine, *Sermons* 320 (tr. Hill, slightly adapted).
[63] McLynn (2003: 260) notes the possible presence of neophytes for baptism at an Easter service, and points to the likelihood that Augustine would have been dealing with a rather distracted congregation.
[64] Augustine, *Sermons* 321.   [65] Augustine, *Sermons* 322.

and in particular the claim that he himself had appeared in a dream to the brother and sister guiding them towards the shrine at Hippo: 'After all, what am I, that all unknowingly I should have appeared to these two?'[66] This is not to present Augustine as wholly sceptical, as he was quite prepared to accept that a miracle had occurred; but it is perhaps significant that his comments on the story rapidly become an account of miracles performed by Stephen elsewhere, as if to show that Hippo need not be too proud of itself for hosting an event for which the causes and reasons would no doubt remain unknown.[67] By the end of this short sermon, Augustine had come to focus his attention on a line from the Psalms, which he recalls rather than explains, and which perhaps represents a retreat from present uncertainty to the security of Scripture.[68]

For as if to reaffirm the unpredictability of these kinds of events, Augustine had once again been interrupted, this time by the miraculous healing of the young man's sister, and the hurried conclusion he made to his sermon attests again to his desire to give precedence to the events themselves, and to his congregation's understanding of them.[69] His later account in the *City of God* ends with the cheering of the crowd and with the narrator's rhetorical question: 'what was in the hearts of those people as they rejoiced but the faith of Christ, for which Stephen had shed his blood?'[70] Further interpretation here would only be a distraction; or so it would seem. And yet in his original sermons Augustine had returned the following day to complete the theme he had previously abandoned: ending not with an account of the miracles that had just been witnessed, nor with an attempt to explain their meaning to his congregation, but with 'the bishop's plodding reaffirmation of the efficacy of those [relics] kept in the nearby town of Uzalis'.[71] Augustine was in one sense reasserting control of the story, but he was not directing it. Instead, he chose to emphasise the mysterious nature of the whole affair – and he ends with the mystery that God who could have cured these

---

[66] Augustine, *Sermons* 323.2.

[67] Note esp. Augustine, *Sermons* 323.2, in which the congregation is reminded of miracles performed at Ancona, but also of the uncertainty regarding the reasons for the presence of a memorial shrine there.

[68] Augustine, *Sermons* 323.4; McLynn (2003: 260) detects here 'an almost apologetic note'.

[69] Augustine, *Sermons* 323.3–4; cf. *De ciu. dei* 22.8. [70] *De ciu. dei* 22.8.

[71] McLynn 2003: 260; Augustine, *Sermons* 324.

people anywhere should have waited to cure them at Hippo.[72] Similarly, in the chapter of the *City of God* following the catalogue of miracles Augustine would again insist that miracles occur and that they attest to 'that faith which preaches the resurrection of the flesh to life eternal'; but when it came to explaining particular miracles he would allow only that 'some things are done in one way, others in another, and mortals can in no way comprehend this'.[73]

Augustine towards the end of his life thus believed that miracles occurred; and there is no good reason to think that he had ever doubted this. What seems to be evident in texts from the 390s onwards, instead, is an insistence on distinguishing between the fact of a miracle and its meaning – between event and interpretation. It is this distinction that should be kept in mind, I believe, when considering Augustine's attempt to clarify his earlier beliefs through the *Retractationes* he composed in the 420s.[74] Here he looks back at his earlier treatises and, with regard to his work *On the Value of Belief*, insists that he had intended to say that 'such great and numerous miracles [as in the Bible] no longer take place, not that no miracles occur in our times'.[75] Making the same point with regard to the treatise *On True Religion*, he explains that:

Not even now, when a hand is laid on the baptised, do they receive the Holy Spirit in such a way that they speak with the tongues of all nations; nor are the sick now healed by the passing shadow of the preachers of Christ. Even though such things happened at that time, manifestly these ceased later. But what I said is not to be so interpreted that no miracles are believed to be performed in the name of Christ at the present time.[76]

He goes on further to explain that at the original time of writing he had recently witnessed the famous healing of a blind man in Milan.[77] That, he might have added, took place in the same year as his conversion to Christianity, a time when he was equally receptive to the miracle stories of the *Life of Antony*, and was willing to admit the influence of divine intervention in his own life. Augustine seems never to have doubted the continuing occurrence of

---

[72] Augustine, *Sermons* 324.   [73] *De ciu. dei* 22.9.
[74] Augustine, *Retr.* (dated by O'Donnell to 425–7).
[75] Augustine, *Retr.* 13.5.   [76] Augustine, *Retr.* 12.7.
[77] Augustine, *Retr.* 12.7; for the healing of the blind man at Milan see also: *De ciu. dei* 22.8; *Conf.* 9.7; Augustine, *Sermons* 286 and 318; Ambrose, *Letters* 22 and *Hymns* 10.

miracles; but he does seem to reveal an increasing awareness of the difficulties of interpretation.

There has been some scepticism about the value of Augustine's *Retractationes* as a guide to his original intentions, and it is perfectly possible that the elderly Augustine, whether consciously or otherwise, misrepresented his earlier beliefs. Certainly there must have been a powerful desire to produce definitive versions of his writings and, by the apparently innocent means of correcting his own errors, to control others' readings of works long ago sent out into the world.[78] And yet the emphasis in these two corrections on the essential difference between the miracles recorded in Scripture and those taking place in the contemporary world can indeed be found in the original texts themselves. It was a theme to which Augustine would repeatedly return, and which he would express most fully in his magisterial *City of God*. There he was prepared to insist that the truth of the scriptures 'has now been proved' and that as the word of God they can never be thought to lie. The important difference between the Bible and the contemporary world was precisely the reliability of the narrative: for unlike modern accounts of miraculous events, the biblical miracles are 'written in books which contain the whole truth, both as to the miracles which were wrought and as to the belief for the sake of which they were wrought'.[79] Scripture was unique in its capacity not only to relate events with absolute accuracy, but also to make available the authoritative interpretation. In the modern world, even when the facts were correct, the explanation could only be provisional; and this, as Augustine came to realise, marked the end of sacred history.

Closing the canon

This developing doctrine of Augustine's must therefore complicate the response related in the *Confessions*, when in 386 he seemed to

---

[78] See, for example, the remarks of O'Donnell 1992: 1.1.

[79] *De ciu. dei* 20.30: 'scripturis sanctis, quarum iam ueritas multis modis adserta est'; *De ciu. dei* 22.8: 'in eisdem quippe ueracissimis libris cuncta conscripta sunt, et quae facta sunt, et propter quod credendum facta sunt.

accept the *Life of Antony* as evidence for the continuing contemporary relevance of the scriptures – indeed, for the continuation of a kind of biblical narrative in the present day. Increasingly it was important to Augustine to keep modern saints and miracles apart from their biblical models. Thus when Antony appears again, very briefly, in the preface to Augustine's work *On Christian Teaching*, it is not as a miraculous figure in his own right or as a paradigm of biblical holiness, but as a reader of Scripture, 'who, though lacking any knowledge of the alphabet, is reported to have memorised the divine scriptures by listening to them being read, and to have understood them by thoughtful meditation'.[80] Here Antony has been turned into a man of his time – one who depends on the scriptures but whose relationship with them goes no further than careful study. His capacity as an uneducated man to remember the scriptures may be miraculous, but it is a miracle which carries with it no authority of its own. Antony, in other words, submits to the authority of the scriptures; his contemporary holiness is entirely dependent upon them. The modern world has been subordinated to the world of the Bible; and above all, to the *words* of the Bible.

This is the key to Augustine's understanding of the Bible and of its relation to his own world. For him, the unique nature of the biblical narrative lay not only in the actions it recorded but also in the fact that they had been recorded reliably. The value of Scripture as proof of God's interventions on behalf of humanity was that it could be guaranteed to provide a true and unmediated account of the miraculous events it described. The reason was divine inspiration: 'the belief that when [the authors of Scripture] wrote these books God was speaking to them, or perhaps we should say through them'.[81] The reliability of the scriptures, moreover, lay not only in the fact that they recorded accurate facts – for a good historian might manage that much – but also in the fact that through divine inspiration the authors were directed in their selection and interpretion of the events they chose to recount. For Augustine, what distinguishes an inspired author from his non-inspired counterpart is 'his judgement, his interpretation of [events] in terms of the pattern of redemptive history into which divine

---

[80] *Doct. christ.* pref. 8.   [81] *De ciu. dei* 18.41.

inspiration vouchsafes him insight'.[82] To write the history of a prophetic age demanded a sure grasp of the significance of every miracle and every sign, so that in interpreting them the inspired author could be seen to have been effectively 'reading the mind of God'.[83]

Yet as has been seen from the examples of Christian biography discussed in previous chapters, events in the post-biblical world had begun to be drawn into this web of meaning and prophecy, with the contemporary re-enactment of Scripture functioning as the herald of a new prophetic age. Augustine may have been willing for a time to interpret his own age as if reading the Bible: but it was a position which necessarily gave rise to a number of unwelcome implications, and it was one he would soon come to reject. In doing so, however, he was raising a challenge to the tradition of Christian biography in which the *Confessions* might otherwise have taken its place. For the implicit claim made by Eusebius and the other authors of contemporary Christian biographies, when they portrayed their heroes in terms of biblical typology and re-enactment, was inescapably a textual one. It was also one which threatened to compromise the uniqueness of the scriptures.

For these lives of contemporary saints and emperors adopted many of the literary conventions of Scripture, its characteristic patterns of interpretation and narrative. Each author picked out the significant events of a life, and organised and described them in such a way as to make reference to biblical models and precursors – establishing a close relationship between these written accounts of post-biblical lives and the 'unified structure of narrative and imagery' to be found in Scripture.[84] The evident consistency of the scriptures – the sense that they all belonged as part of a single, integrated composition – had been a powerful argument in favour of the unique authority of the Christian canon.[85] By mimicking the textual features of Scripture, by proving themselves consistent with it, late-antique Christian biography might usurp some of that authority for itself. The relationship might be intrinsic to the actual

[82] Markus 1988: 14.   [83] Froehlich 1977: 35; cf. Markus 1996: 3–4.
[84] Frye 1982: xvii.   [85] *De ciu. dei* 18.41; see also Kirwan 1989: 13.

events described, in the sense that God might design an individual's life in order to cast light on the history of salvation.[86] Yet the evident agreement of their stories with the inspired canonical texts might be taken further, to imply that modern biographers had themselves been inspired in the construction of their narratives. The most significant feature of biblical narrative was, after all, 'its claim to divine authorship or inspiration'; and so the extension of typology and re-enactment beyond the Bible and into late-antique literature helped to imply an equivalence in this respect too between post-biblical biography and the divinely authorised history set down in Scripture.[87]

It was the use of typology in particular which made this claim so powerful. Since the argument from typology rested on the recurrence of events in the historical world, it required the reader to place a high level of trust in the author of the written text. The essential claim, after all, was that any patterns that were to be found in the course of human history attested to an organising intelligence: a non-human Author who could communicate his meanings 'not only with words, as do human beings, but also with deeds'.[88] Each text therefore had to be regarded as unfailingly accurate in its selection and depiction of historical events, and to be read, in effect, as though it were transparent. Any suspicion that an author had interfered with the pattern would undermine entirely the significance of what was recorded. Thus the claim that correspondences had been found between contemporary events and those recorded in Scripture, and that such correspondences were proof of God's continued active intervention in the course of history, was simultaneously a claim on the part of the modern author to the 'outstanding authority' possessed by the canonical scriptures.[89] If God's role as author of the historical events was to be recognised, it had also to be admitted that the author of the text had presented an accurate unmediated account, free of the treacherous human devices of artifice and allusion.

---

[86] A relationship brought out at Stock 1996: 76.
[87] Vanhoozer 1990: 177; this kind of relationship is also proposed for post-biblical literature by Charity (1966: 152, 167ff.), in particular with regard to the *Divine Comedy* of Dante Alighieri.
[88] Markus 1996: 3, paraphrasing Augustine, *Letters* 102.33.   [89] *De ciu. dei* 11.3.

This claim is explicitly made in the fifth-century collection of exemplary biographies compiled by Theodoret of Cyrrhus, and conventionally known in English as the *Religious History*.[90] Written around AD 450, two decades after Augustine's death, the work established itself as a continuation of the Bible in both historical and literary terms. The monks whose lives Theodoret recounts are connected to Scripture in conventional fashion: James of Nisibis, the first to be mentioned, is immediately labelled 'this new Moses', while the second, Julian Saba, is compared to Moses twice and also to Peter and John the Baptist.[91] Here too there is the assertion that the monks in general appeared 'like the apostles and prophets'.[92] There is established, then, a biblical world among the ascetics of Syria, and one to which Theodoret – who might otherwise have seemed a rather undistinguished provincial bishop – could claim special access. The Bishop of Cyrrhus comes across as an 'intrusive narrator' who 'insinuates his own presence . . . at every turn', and it is strictly through him that his readers gain access to these contemporary prophets and apostles.[93] The effect is to parade his episcopal authority, acknowledged by his heroes throughout.[94] At the same time, he is able to claim for his work some of the authority of Scripture itself.

That the miracles performed in the *Religious History* are not either pale imitations of Scripture nor attempts to diminish its superior status is made clear in Theodoret's account of Symeon Stylites, who has just performed a healing miracle in clear imitation of Christ:

But let no one call the imitation usurpation, for [Christ's] is the utterance, 'He who believes in me will himself do the works that I do, and greater than these will he do.'[95]

Christ's prophecy not only provides the excuse for Symeon's miracles, but also permits him to position his own work as part of the biblical tradition. By means of this prediction the lives of the

---

[90] The recent translation of the *HR* by Price prefers to translate the title as the *History of the Monks in Syria*, implying a generic relationship to the *Historia Monachorum in Aegypto*; but see Urbainczyk 2002: 33–4 for a discussion of the nomenclature here.
[91] *HR* 1.5, 2.4, 2.8, 2.11. For these examples and more, see Krueger 1997: 404–11.
[92] *HR* 6.5; cf. *HM* prol. 9.   [93] Lim 2003: 465.
[94] Urbainczyk 2002: 130–1, 151–2.   [95] *HR* 26.17, quoting John 14:12.

Syrian holy men are already contained within Scripture: they have a place prepared for them in the biblical framework of typology and re-enactment. Moreover, as with earlier collections of lives, the *Religious History* made this familiar structure a central feature of its own literary form. These Syrian ascetics re-enacted the Bible but served in addition as 'types for each other'.[96] In mimicking both the content and the form of the scriptures, Theodoret is able to present his text as a new instalment in a single ongoing narrative: a new chapter of a unified work. Indeed, in its imitation of Scripture the *Religious History* could gain authority just as contemporary ascetics did from their imitations of Moses and Christ. It was not that his text was simply *like* the Bible: it was a true continuation of Scripture.[97]

The implications for the text and for Theodoret himself were profound, and he did not shy away from them. He was perfectly willing to claim for his own work the authority that belonged to the Bible; so that he could assert in the prologue that:

Quite obviously, he who will disbelieve what we are about to tell does not believe either in the truth of what took place through Moses, Joshua, Elijah and Elisha, and considers as a myth the working of miracles that took place through the sacred apostles.[98]

There is a clear similarity here to Eusebius' claim that the life of Constantine had proved the story of Moses to be more than a myth.[99] In each case there is the implication that the modern text is to be treated with the same seriousness as Scripture; and that the author too is divinely inspired in the same way as those who wrote the Bible. Theodoret therefore turns to Moses as a model not only for his ascetics but also for himself, invoking at the very start of the work the Patriarch's example as one who 'wrote down the way of life of the holy men of old' as a result of divine inspiration.[100] The 'complex typological system' found in this work – and which has already been recognised thoughout late-antique Christian biography – thus allowed modern authors to claim similar inspiration.[101] Their works were no longer to be

---

[96] Krueger 1997: 409.   [97] This point is also made in Krueger 2004: 27–9.
[98] *HR* prol. 10.   [99] *VC* 1.11.1.
[100] *HR* 1.1; see also the discussion at Krueger 2004: 30–1.   [101] Krueger 2004: 31.

understood as mere products of contingent circumstance, but were nothing less than the word of God.

Thus the presence of typology in a post-biblical work paradoxically increased the writers's authority by effacing his or her role in the construction and arrangement of the text. Simply by claiming the ability to recognise accurately the interventions of God in human affairs, and to interpret the significance of these interventions, was to place oneself on a par with the biblical authors whose divine inspiration had given them such an insight. This, then, was the implication of the late-antique readiness to see in Constantine a re-enactment of the role of Moses, or to see in Antony a new Elijah. It was also the implication of Augustine's recognition of his own times as part of sacred history – which is to say, his early confidence that events in the modern world could be securely interpreted as the fulfilment of biblical prophecies.[102] Yet, as has been seen, by the time he came to write the *City of God* Augustine had definitively rejected this view. It is not so much that he 'never came to accept' the idea, as that his thought on these matters shows clear signs of development – or more bluntly, that he changed his mind.[103] Augustine's attitude to miracles was only one facet of this change: the fundamental shift was in his understanding of the status of Scripture.

Thus Augustine's view in the *City of God* is clear. To interpret the contemporary world in terms of typology and re-enactment was no longer a viable proposition. Augustine repeatedly emphasises the special nature of the canonical scriptures which, owing to God's superintendence, are to be considered 'writings of outstanding authority'.[104] The Bible, he reminds his readers, 'never lies'.[105] The canon of the scriptures, he went on, was 'fixed and final', and he would later provide a list of the contents of the authoritative Old and New Testaments, and an explanation of the appropriate method for deciding what ought to be included.[106] His comments elsewhere make clear, too, that history outside of the scriptures

---

[102] For a full discussion of Augustine's idea of sacred history, see in particular Markus 1988: 1–44.

[103] Bonner 1971: 234.   [104] *De ciu. dei* 11.3.

[105] Kirwan 1989: 13, citing *De ciu. dei* 18.41; another famous example at *De ciu. dei* 11.6: 'litterae sacrae maximeque ueraces'.

[106] *De ciu. dei* 18.41; *Doct. christ.* 2.24–9.

was not to be put on the same footing. Augustine was prepared to grant history a prominent place among human traditions, and indeed did not consider it a wholly human institution, since 'what has already gone into the past and cannot be undone must be considered part of the history of time, whose creator and controller is God'.[107] Nevertheless, although it 'relates past events in a faithful and useful way', it remains the case that it allows no definite insight into the divine purpose: for 'so many, in fact almost all, of the just judgements of God are hidden from mortal perception and understanding'.[108] The point is summed up in one of the early chapter headings preserved in manuscripts of the *City of God*, for the chapter in which Augustine comments on 'the diversity of human fortunes': it shows 'God's judgement not absent, but untraceable'.[109]

What this amounts to, as Robert Markus has commented, is a 'radical agnosticism about God's purposes in human history' – and about anyone's ability to record accurately the way those purposes have played out.[110] Although God acted in the contemporary world just as he did in Scripture – and although Augustine was willing to draw attention to the most prominent instances in which his power seemed to manifest itself, in modern miracles – nevertheless, this could not justify understanding the world as if it could be read as the continuation of Scripture. Miracles and other apparent evidence of God's activity could not be made the basis for a secure account of contemporary history as 'sacred history'. On the contrary, Augustine argued that 'the special quality' possessed by sacred history 'resides in the narrative' and not in the events narrated.[111] God could be seen to act in all history, but 'the prophetic quality required by "sacred history"' was restricted to those authors who could be guaranteed by external evidence to be divinely inspired: not by virtue of what they described but by virtue of who they were.[112] For Augustine, writing the *City of God*, this was a status which had been revealed to apply only to the authors

---

[107] *Doct. christ.* 2.109 (tr. Green).   [108] *De ciu. dei* 20.2.
[109] *De ciu. dei* 20.2 – these chapter headings belong to the earliest manuscript tradition and may be Augustine's own.
[110] Markus 2000: 207.   [111] Markus 1988: 14–15.   [112] Markus 1988: 16.

of the canonical scriptures: and thus 'sacred history is simply what is in the scriptural canon'.[113]

Such assertions about the uniqueness of the scriptures undermined the idea that the life of a particular contemporary Christian would be able to shed significant light on God's purposes, or on the eschatological progress of Christianity. It cast doubt on the claim that late-antique Christian biography constituted a part of sacred history, or was a continuation of that history as it was narrated in the scriptures. It did permit the belief that 'our personal narratives' – and those of others – 'imitate the master narrative of scripture', but went on to insist that 'we cannot understand their underlying logic through the evidence of our senses'.[114] Thus the elevation of contemporary heroes to the status of biblical figures could not safely be understood as anything more than a literary technique, almost a figure of speech. Such lives might be useful and edifying, but they carried no scriptural authority; and they could not in themselves provide significant evidence for the continued intervention of God in the world. A narrative recording a pattern in contemporary events which resembled those found in the scriptures was quite possibly nothing more than the result of empty ingenuity.

Indeed, there was a real risk that such a preoccupation with the contemporary world would distract from the true value of the scriptures, which lay in their capacity to provide trustworthy information 'concerning those things which we need to know for our own good, and yet are incapable of discovering for ourselves'.[115] The scriptures were valuable not only because they were the result of divine inspiration but because in encountering them the reader learns that 'he is entangled in a love of this present age, that is, of temporal things' – and that it is necessary to overcome this involvement in the contemporary world in order to lead a truly Christian life.[116] Thus in their claim to be demonstrating the continuing power and presence of God, biographies of contemporary Christians might enable readers to develop an appropriate awe and

---

[113] Markus 1988: 16. Markus locates the firm statement of this position in chapter 12 of Augustine's *De Genesi ad litteram*, which he dates to 414 – with its conclusions absorbed into the *De ciu. dei*.
[114] Stock 1996: 76.   [115] *De ciu. dei* 11.3.
[116] *Doct. christ.* 2.19: 'amore huius saeculi, hoc est temporalium rerum'.

humility; but these alone cannot make Christians in the absence of true knowledge guaranteed by revelation. It is only upon reading and understanding the scriptures that 'the fear which makes him ponder the judgement of God, and the piety which makes it impossible for him not to admit and submit to the authority of the holy books, compel him to deplore his own condition'.[117] Without this awareness there is no recognition of where true authority lies: instead, the chance events of the contemporary world risk being put on a level with the holy scriptures, and distracting from or even diminishing their authority.

An unauthorised life

It seems clear, then, that by the time Augustine came to write the *City of God* and *On Christian Teaching* he had developed a much more complex understanding than he had possessed in 386 of how he might respond to the biblical text, and a greater sensitivity as a reader to different levels; and it is interesting that he once again in this context returns to the passage of Matthew which refers to men becoming 'eunuchs for the kingdom of God'.[118] Thus in discussing the various possible ways of understanding scriptural precepts, Augustine notes that:

It often happens that someone who is, or thinks he is, at a higher stage of the spiritual life regards as figurative instructions which are given to those at a lower stage. So, for example, one who has embraced a life of celibacy and castrated himself for the sake of the kingdom of heaven might maintain that any instructions given in the sacred books about loving or governing one's wife should not be taken literally but figuratively.[119]

This recognition of multiple levels is something of which Augustine seems to approve; and he is perfectly willing to incorporate it

---

[117] *Doct. christ.* 2.19: 'tum uero ille timor quo cogitat de iudicio dei, et illa pietas qua non potest nisi credere et cedere auctoritati sanctorum librorum, cogit eum se ipsum lugere'.

[118] Matthew 19:12; cf. *Conf.* 8.2.2, discussed in ch. 4, above.

[119] *Doct. christ.* 3.58: 'saepe autem accidit ut quisquis in meliore gradu spiritalis uitae uel est uel esse se putat figurate dicta esse arbitretur quae inferioribus gradibus praecipiuntur; ut uerbi gratia si caelibem amplexus est uitam et se castrauit propter regnum caelorum, quidquid de uxore diligenda et regenda sancti libri praecipiunt, non proprie sed translate accipi oportere contendat.'

as a precept that 'some instructions are given to all people alike, but others to particular classes of people'.[120] This admission, combined with the re-use of the same passage of Matthew which played such a prominent role in Book 8 of the *Confessions*, perhaps suggests a way of understanding that work in the light of Augustine's later commitments. For the Augustine who was converted in 386 was not the same Augustine who related that experience in the *Confessions*, written ten or so years later. At the time, he perhaps required a contemporary example of Matthew's 'eunuchs for the kingdom of God' – a biblical paradigm that he found in his own world in Antony. But by the time he came to record the events themselves, he had perhaps reconsidered this view. Certainly the narration in the *Confessions* can be seen to display a distinct unwillingness to commit to the claims made by the younger Augustine.

As a result, Augustine's account of his own life must have struck many readers as unsatisfactory. Rather than a triumphant conversion to Christianity, they were confronted with 'the self-portrait of a convalescent'.[121] The euphoria of his conversion, and of his encouragement of Alypius, had been replaced already in the narration with a definite desire to remain sceptical; and there is a distinct suggestion that enthusiasm may have contibuted more to his conversion than any outside help or any genuine insight. That there was a change in Augustine's views between his conversion and his mature work is not to be denied; but this would seem to be a hint that this change was underway as early as the final years of the fourth century, when he first came to write the *Confessions*. The Augustine of 386 was not the same man who in the 390s chose to write about the circumstances of his conversion.[122] Already by then, Augustine was retreating from any claim to the ability to interpret God's role in the contemporary world. This is not to say that Augustine will have in any way regretted his conversion or felt it to be in any way compromised; in writing his *Confessions*,

---

[120] *Doct. christ.* 3.59: 'alia omnibus communiter praecipi, alia singulis quibusque generis personarum'.
[121] Brown 2000: 177. The reaction of Pelagius – who was apparently 'deeply annoyed' – is adduced as evidence for this reception.
[122] O'Donnell (1992: I.xviii) focuses on the importance of recognising the presence of two Augustines in the *Confessions*, as character and author.

however, he was prepared to admit that he might have reached the truth by a more difficult and less spectacular route.

The change in tone between the heroic lives of the saints and Augustine's stubbornly flawed, incompletely Christian life was therefore not just the inevitable result of a shift from hagiography to autobiography, but is also a sign of what seems an increasing scepticism about the conventions of this style of writing. The best example is Augustine's persistent retreat into narrative uncertainty through his repeated use of indefinite expressions. His general fondness for referring to 'a certain Cicero' or 'a certain Aeneas' becomes most marked of all in the conversion scene in Book 8, and it seems to be more than a mere affectation.[123] Thus even the guest who precipitates his crisis of faith is described as 'a certain Ponticianus'; later Augustine will throw himself down in his garden 'under a certain fig tree'.[124] Most famously, when he recalls hearing a voice saying 'Pick up and read', he records his uncertainty of the time – which was rapidly resolved into action – without offering a definitive explanation.[125] This retrospective refusal to insist on a single interpretation of even such a significant event establishes an interesting tension, in which 'no event . . . is brought about by a situation inexplicable in terms of natural causes', and yet still 'those events are not adequately accounted for'.[126] There is room for a miracle; but there is also room for doubt.

The presentation of events in Augustine's *Confessions* seems therefore rather more complex and ambiguous than in other contemporary Christian biographies. In the *Life of Antony*, the possibility of divine intervention was taken for granted by both hero and author, and the correctness of Antony's response to the gospel reading he overheard was guaranteed by his subsequent marvellous life. Similarly, in the narrative of the *Confessions*, the young Augustine

---

[123] As noted by O'Meara 2001: xxiv–xxv.   [124] *Conf.* 8.6.14, 8.12.28.

[125] *Conf.* 8.12.29: 'quasi pueri an puellae, nescio'. Augustine's irresolution here has inspired much of the debate over the historicity of this scene and of the *Confessions* in general, usefully summarised through the comments of O'Donnell (1992: III.59–66); O'Meara 2001: xxv) argues that the rhetorical approach used here has no bearing on the authenticity of the scene, and he is surely correct. Sturrock (1993) emphasises the literary nature of the scene and stresses the contingency of Augustine's interpretation, as does Crosson (1999: 32).

[126] Crosson 1999: 31–2.

in his Milan garden hesitated only briefly before he chose, after the example of Antony, to interpret the voice as bearing a message meant specifically for him.[127] But the later Augustine – the author of the *Confessions*, and a conspicuous presence in the text – steps back from this interpretation. His use of indefinite language at these crucial moments implies a more complex attitude to the nature of that providence which had so disposed events that he might be converted to Christianity. This need not amount to a rejection, and indeed the lack of substantiating detail adds to the impression of the randomness of these decisive events, in turn perhaps highlighting providence as the real organising principle.[128] Yet it also leaves room for the 'mature' Augustine to express a greater level of uncertainty, a greater 'nuance, caution, and . . . reserve'.[129] It allows for the possibility of an error, and offers some ironic distance from the younger Augustine's unreflective enthusiasm: 'I interpreted it solely as a divine command . . .'

Augustine therefore presents his own example but, as author, fails to endorse it fully. The interpretation he seized upon in 386 is not forced upon his readers, who are instead left to use their own judgement as to the extent of the role played by providence. The indefinite language makes the same point over and again throughout the *Confessions*: that Augustine's past is uncertain, that the truth of his version cannot be guaranteed. Arguably this approach is a necessary result of the very presentation of the work as a confession, a literary form by which Augustine 'disclaims authority for his own text' by invoking God as a higher authority.[130] He knows he will not be believed when he talks about himself, and even finds scriptural warrant for this reaction:

Why do they demand to hear from me what I am when they refuse to hear from you what they are? And when they hear me talking about myself, how can they know if I am telling the truth, when no one 'knows what is going on in a person except the human spirit which is within'?[131]

---

[127] Miles 1982: 356.   [128] As suggested by O'Meara 2001: xxiv–xxv.
[129] O'Donnell 1992: III.64.   [130] O'Donnell 1992: II.4.
[131] *Conf.* 10.3.3 (quoting 1 Corinthians 2:11): 'quid a me quaerunt audire qui sim, qui nolunt a te audire qui sint? et unde sciunt, cum a me ipso de me ipso audiunt, an uerum dicam, quandoquidem nemo scit hominum quid agatur in homine, nisi spiritus hominis qui in ipso est?'

This is presented as a matter of fact: a simple confession can never be sure to be accepted by others who have no way of determining its truth. Augustine's own account of himself will be believed only by those whose ears are opened to him already, by love or charity: above all, his friends and fellow-Christians.[132] It will never be taken as authoritative by those who are not already disposed to believe it.

This is not to say that Augustine is attempting 'to freeze out the hostile or sceptical reader' – in fact, he explicitly states his intention to write even for those 'to whom I cannot prove that my confession is true'.[133] In this case, however, the most important contribution will not be Augustine's story, but God's intervention:

> But if they were to hear about themselves from you, they could not say 'The Lord is lying.' For what is to hear about oneself from you except to understand oneself? And who in turn understands himself and says 'That is false,' unless he himself is a liar?[134]

It is difficult to see this as a claim that Augustine's writings were 'divinely inspired', or that God was in any strong sense 'the co-author of the *Confessions*'.[135] Instead, Augustine seems to envisage God acting outside the *Confessions* as a kind of independent confirmation of any truth that they might contain. Throughout this opening section of Book 10 he plays down the significance of his own life story, denying potential accusations of self-indulgence or pride.[136] Moreover, he cannot be sure that the story as he presents it is complete or even correct, for 'there is something of the human person which is unknown even to the "spirit of man which is in him"' – depths of the soul which only God can know.[137] He hopes, to be sure, that God will allow him to confess all that is needed, but the mood is uncertain and knowledge is inevitably postponed:

---

[132] *Conf.* 10.3.3: 'sed credunt mihi quorum mihi aures caritas aperit.'
[133] O'Donnell 1992: II.4; *Conf.* 10.3.3.
[134] *Conf.* 10.3.3: 'si autem a te audiant de se ipsis, non poterunt dicere, "mentitur dominus". quid est enim a te audire de se nisi cognoscere se? quis porro cognoscit et dicit, "falsum est", nisi ipse mentiatur?'
[135] Morrison 1992: 10, and his n. 54.
[136] For example, *Conf.* 10.2.2: 'When I am evil, making confession to you is simply to be displeased with myself. When I am good, making confession to you is simply to make no claim on my own behalf, for you, Lord, "confer blessing on the righteous" but only after you have first "justified the ungodly".'
[137] *Conf.* 10.5.7.

'Accordingly, let me confess what I know of myself. Let me confess to what I do not know of myself.'[138] This uncertainty is the dominant theme of the section, with the truth of the story dependent on the collaboration of God – which is desired rather than asserted.

This is all of a piece with Augustine's approach to biblical exegesis, as demonstrated in the *Confessions* and in his other contemporary works. Although Augustine is convinced that Scripture was divinely inspired, it is far from clear that he makes anything like the same claim concerning his own private interpretations of the biblical text. Certainly Augustine attempts to enlist the help and inspiration of God in his work, but it is difficult to locate any 'explicit' assertion that 'his allegorical exposition is divinely inspired'.[139] Just as in the passages downplaying the significance of the *Confessions* as a whole, Augustine contrasts God's complete and absolute wisdom with his own necessarily untrustworthy and provisional interpretations. He allows the possibility of divine inspiration in his exegesis, but at the same time alerts his readers to the alternative:

With you inspiring me I shall speak the true things which you have wished to be drawn out of these words. Nor do I believe that I shall speak truly if anyone other than you is inspiring me, since you are the truth but every man is a liar, and for that reason 'he who speaks a lie speaks from himself'. Therefore I speak from you so that I may speak the truth.[140]

Again, this passage falls short of certainty. The truth of any interpretation depends on divine inspiration, and although Augustine will offer his exegesis 'without fear', he explicitly admits the possibility

---

[138] *Conf.* 10.5.7. Note the subjunctive mood of the repeated main verb (*confitear*) – a request rather than a demand. Chadwick's translation of the final lines of 10.2.2 neatly captures the same uncertainty: the phrase 'neque enim dico recti aliquid hominibus' is well expressed by the conditional 'If anything I say to men is right . . .'

[139] McMahon 1989: 27, 28.

[140] *Conf.* 13.25.38 (quoting John 8.44): 'uera enim dicam te mihi inspirante quod ex eis uerbis uoluisti ut dicerem. neque enim alio praeter te inspirante credo me uerum dicere, cum tu sis ueritas, omnis autem homo mendax, et ideo qui loquitur mendacium, de suo loquitur. ergo ut uerum loquar, de tuo loquor.' McMahon chooses to translate the beginning of the second sentence as 'For under the inspiration of none but you do I believe myself to speak the truth . . .' (1989: 27–8); my own translation here is based on that of Chadwick.

of error.[141] The language Augustine uses here – especially when taken together as part of the wider context of the *Confessions* as a prayer to God – means that the boundary is not very clear between 'declaring' and 'petitioning'.[142] Augustine 'hopes' and 'strives' for God's endorsement of his ideas, and perhaps 'feels' or believes that it has been granted.[143] But he cannot and does not confirm or demonstrate God's complicity in his own unavoidably provisional interpretations of Scripture. He believes in it; he relies upon it; but there will nevertheless be those to whom he cannot prove it to be true.

Thus the issue of Augustine's beliefs must be separated from his claim to authority. Augustine no doubt believed that God had guided, inspired or authorised not only his readings of Scripture in the *Confessions*, but also the narrative he had imposed on his own life. But he did not require, nor even expect, his readers to agree. Some would read him from a charitable viewpoint, but others would not; and although the former would derive a greater benefit from the *Confessions*, only God's additional intervention could prove the latter wrong.[144] It is too strong to say that Augustine excludes the uncharitable reader entirely.[145] More often than not, he invites scepticism to the extent of even giving it a scriptural pedigree. As he would later demonstrate in the *City of God*, it was always possible to move from a general understanding of the world's unpredictability – so that, for example 'we do not know by what decision of God this good man is poor' – to a positive statement of faith, with scriptural backing: 'The judgements of God become the more inscrutable and his ways the more untraceable.'[146] Even if Augustine had once believed himself to have discerned the truth about God's actions in the world, his subsequent reflections led him to decide that Paul had been right all along: 'how unsearchable are His judgements, and His ways past finding out'.[147]

[141] *Conf.* 13.25.38: 'dicam nec uerebor'.
[142] McMahon 1989: 28, 'declaring, not petitioning'.
[143] These terms are those used by McMahon (1989: 29), and it seems unnecessary to go beyond them.
[144] This seems to me the most sensible reading of *Conf.* 10.2.2–10.6.8.
[145] Despite O'Donnell 1992: II.4.   [146] *De ciu. dei* 20.2.   [147] Romans 11.33.

Truth and consequences

Thus in contrast to the confidence the Eusebian approach, in which the activity of the Christian God could be clearly identified in the actions of contemporaries, and could be reliably captured in their biographies, Augustine brought late-antique Christian readers face to face with 'the intractable ambiguity of what is happening and will happen'.[148] Christian biographies claimed to be telling the truth, both about their protagonists and about God, and about the progression of sacred history. This claim was made not only through their content but through their form: for just as the events they described were frequently identifiable as re-enactments of Scripture, so too (in a different sense) were the biographies themselves. A modern Moses might not be out performing miracles in the wilderness; he might instead be an author, like Theodoret, divinely inspired to write a modern equivalent of the Pentateuch. For Augustine, however, human interpretations and writings paled in comparison to divine Scripture, which for Augustine was uniquely authoritative. Ordinary literature (*litterae*), his own writings included, was to be contrasted with 'a single and unitary text (*scriptura*)', defined in the *City of God* as:

that Scripture which, not by the chance impulses of mortal minds but manifestly by the guiding power of supreme providence, stands above the literature of all peoples and, excelling in divine authority, has subordinated to itself every kind of human ingenuity.[149]

The Bible presented the one and only 'authorised' interpretation of events; its truth was guaranteed by the 'immediate divine authority' which no other historical writing could claim for itself.[150] Augustine could not be an authority even on his own life; and the only truly authorised lives were those narrated in Scripture.

It is vital therefore to maintain a firm distinction between the status of Augustine's own writings and the status of Scripture.[151] There are inevitable similarities in how the two might

---

[148] Harrison 2000: 205.
[149] Vessey and Pollmann 1999: 8, quoting Augustine, *De ciu. dei* 11.1.
[150] Vessey and Pollmann 1999: 21; Bittner 1999: 346.
[151] A point made by Solignac (1962: 13–14), with which McMahon half-concurs: (1989: 29).

be read, not least because both require interpretation and so risk misinterpretation; and in each case the most rewarding approaches will be those characterised by Christian charity. With regard to Scripture, however, Augustine insists that this kind of approach is not only desirable but essential: with Scripture, 'any interpretation that breaches the command of charity cannot be a correct understanding'.[152] This is not true of the *Confessions*. An uncharitable reader might refuse to accept Augustine's account as authoritative, and might (as some no doubt did) dismiss the work as a farrago of self-love and vainglory. Augustine himself would of course be disappointed with such an interpretation, and he would certainly disagree; but the reading would not represent a challenge to the truth of his Christian faith. His own work was not divinely inspired, as the scriptures had certainly been; his own authority was merely human, and he might very easily have failed to communicate his message. When it came to his own works, Augustine was in one sense utterly, and perhaps unusually, undogmatic.

A nice example of this attitude might be noted towards the end of Augustine's life, as he looked back over his published works in his *Retractationes*. Whether Augustine was here trying to impose a retrospective unity on his writings, or whether – if it is indeed a different thing – he was honestly labouring to correct errors and misapprehensions, the effect was ultimately to admit to an absence of authority. Despite his efforts, his works would continue to be read and exploited in ways that he could neither prevent nor foresee. If he remained unable to impose an authoritative interpretation on his readers, however, he could at least deny them the final say by insisting on an undecidability 'in which the authority for the text is ultimately removed from the reader's control'.[153] In the absence of any guarantee of divine inspiration, Augustine evidently regarded even his most successful works as provisional and incomplete.[154] Thus his *Confessions*, he writes, were intended 'to lift up the understanding and affection of men' to God.[155] But even this much success cannot be taken for granted:

---

[152] Markus 1996: 17, describing the argument of the *Doct. christ.*
[153] Stock 1996: 278.   [154] Augustine, *Retr.* prol.   [155] Augustine, *Retr.* 2.6.1.

As far as I am concerned, they had this effect on me while I was writing them and they continue to have it when I am reading them. What others think about them is a matter for them to decide.[156]

---

[156] Augustine, *Retr.* 2.6.1 (tr. Bogan): 'interim quod ad me attinet, hoc in me egerunt cum scriberentur, et agunt cum leguntur. quid de illis alii sentiant, ipsi uiderint.'

CONCLUSION: AUTHORISED LIVES

We cannot look, however imperfectly, upon a great man, without gaining something by him. He is the living light-fountain, which it is good and pleasant to be near. The light which enlightens, which has enlightened the darkness of the world; and this not as a kindled lamp only, but rather as a natural luminary shining by the gift of Heaven; a flowing light-fountain, as I say, of native original insight, of manhood and heroic nobleness;– in whose radiance all souls feel that it is well with them. On any terms whatsoever, you will not grudge to wander in such neighbourhood for a while.

(Thomas Carlyle, *On Heroes, Hero-Worship and
the Heroic in History.* London, 1872: 2)

Evidently a little embarrassed by the novel form of piety devised by Symeon Stylites – whose column in the Syrian desert had already reached a height of thirty-six cubits – Theodoret of Cyrrhus constructed a revealing defence:

> I appeal to fault-finders ... to consider how frequently the Lord has contrived such things for the good of the indifferent. He ordered Isaiah to walk naked and without shoes; Jeremiah to put a girdle around his loins ... Hosea to marry a prostitute ... Ezechiel to lie down on his right side for forty days and one hundred and fifty on his left ... So, just as the God of the universe providentially ordered each one of those things done for the good of those living carelessly, so he arranged this extraordinary novelty to draw everyone by its strangeness to the spectacle and make the proffered counsel persuasive to those who come.[1]

The transition from the Old Testament world of the prophets – and, it would soon become clear, from the New Testament world as well – had not brought with it any dramatic changes in the style or substance of God's interventions in worldly affairs. His actions could be as easily recognised and interpreted as if the Bible were playing itself out once again in the world of late antiquity. And of

---

[1] *HR* 26.12 (tr. Doran, slightly adapted).

course, this new dispensation had its faithful scribes and evangelists in the likes of Theodoret himself – so this new sacred history that was on display out in the world was safely recorded and interpreted in contemporary Christian writings. As I have argued in previous chapters, this characterisation of contemporary Roman life was a common feature of late-antique Christian biography. The consistent application of biblical parallels to a life in the modern world can already be seen as a structural principle in the *Life of Constantine* by Eusebius of Caesarea, and there it can perhaps be considered a response to the new historical situation. With the accession and conversion of Constantine, Christianity was suddenly a world-historical force, and this turn of events required instant interpretation. It might perhaps seem natural that Constantine would be greeted by Christians as a new Moses or even a new Christ. Nevertheless, the implications were profound. Moses and Christ were great figures, at least for Christians, primarily because they marked moments at which the Christian God had intervened in human affairs. In assimilating Constantine to the pattern of life of these predecessors, Eusebius had the emperor re-enact their role in Christianity's cosmic drama. The biblical architecture of the *Life of Constantine* implied a belief about the world of Eusebius: that in the modern world of the author, God continued to direct events as he had in the scriptures.

Thus for Eusebius of Caesarea, the Emperor Constantine was above all responsible for presenting Christ to the world of late antiquity. This emperor did, not only insofar as he 'continually announced the Christ of God with complete openness to all' – that is, not only in his ministry and his evangelism – but also by means of a more personal *repraesentatio Christi*, by which it was possible to '[make] Christ present by one's own life in one's own region'.[2] Eusebius was able to identify those aspects of Constantine's life which marked him out as a new Moses and, both by typological convention and by direct association, a new Christ for the later Roman empire; and in his *Life of Constantine* he developed the implications of these connections. The most important revelation was that the life of the emperor represented a point of

[2] *VC* 3.2.2; Brown 1983: 8.

contact between the biblical past and the new Christian present. Through Constantine it was possible to rediscover the world as it had appeared in the Christian scriptures. At the heart of the *Life of Constantine* was the claim that the emperor's life could be understood as conforming both to the vanished conventions of Scripture and to the realities of the contemporary world.

When the lives of contemporary Christians, then, were presented as re-enactments of scenes from the scriptures, the effect was to assert an equivalence between the two historical situations. Late antiquity was a new biblical era, showing the Bible to be historical fact. The point had already been made in the *Life of Constantine* that modern miracles proved Moses to be more than a myth; and this approach was taken further by Gregory of Nyssa in his *Life of Moses* and *Praise of Basil*. Basil was a modern Moses, and to that his brother Gregory could attest; the implication was that Moses had been a biblical Basil. Thus if modern life conformed to the patterns laid down in Scripture, then Scripture in turn could be understood with reference to the familiar features of modern life. Modern biographies could offer a new interpretation of scriptural phenomena on the basis of late-antique experience; and indeed the lives of the biblical prophets soon came to be modelled on contemporary holy men, so that (for example) the late-antique legend of Daniel was able to transform the prophet into 'a fine expression of Byzantine piety'.[3] Like a biblical scene painted in modern dress, the past was brought vividly to life by assimilating it to the present; but in the same way, the present was rendered a little more unfamiliar.

The irruption of Scripture into everyday life, after all, meant more than identifying Moses with Basil. With his brother as a kind of Moses, Gregory in turn could become a kind of Aaron; but the Bible was richer still than any single story, and the opportunities were endless. Contemporary holy men took their cues from Elijah and Elisha, or from the New Testament with John the Baptist; and as the desert filled up with ascetics it began to offer an alternative vision of life as it might be lived on biblical principles. Nor was it

---

[3] Satran 1995: 96, part of a detailed discussion of this phenomenon in the Byzantine collection of lives of the prophets.

only in their lifestyles that the desert ascetics imitated Scripture, but in their sheer number and variety. The point was made most clearly in collections of lives such as the *History of the Monks in Egypt*, in which monks made due obeisance to the Bible but also imitated and re-enacted one another. The richness and depth of the scriptures, the web of allusions and interconnections brought out in the study of biblical typology, was present too in these contemporary lives. More than being simply dependent on Scripture, the lives of the desert ascetics offered a recreation of it as it existed in the modern world: a new source of the same intoxicating liquor. Thus Christian biography and the re-enactment of Scripture forced a reconsideration of late-antique life. It allowed the world of the later Roman empire to be re-imagined as one in which even ordinary Christians had a part to play in the explication of the divine plan.

On one level, this was a matter of *demonstratio euangelica*, proof of the veracity of the gospels and of the biblical tradition in general. The story of Moses was shown to be plausible through its re-enactment by Constantine in the present day; and at the same time, the modern world was proved amenable to the re-establishment of the values and behaviours known from the scriptures.[4] As Peter Brown has pointed out, this development in late-antique Christianity can be understood to a large extent in relation to the characteristically classical approach to exemplarity and imitation, in which the cultivation of virtue in any form was understood as requiring the successful imitation of an exemplary predecessor.[5] Moreover, the familiarity of these exemplars is an important element here, for in classical culture a success was most often understood as a restoration: thus to imitate Cato the Elder, for example, was to restore the vanished era of which he was perhaps the most outstanding representative. Cato exemplifies the virtues of his time, and to live as he did is to revive in the diminished present at least some part of that authoritative golden age. The faith that this could

---

[4] See *VC* 1.12.2 for the life of Constantine as proof of the biblical account of Moses, and Moses in turn proving the reliability of Eusebius' account of Constantine.
[5] This observation is dealt with in detail in the first section of Brown's discussion of saints as exemplars: see esp. Brown 1983: 1–10. Some of these ideas were later developed in Brown 1995: esp. 58–60.

indeed be done was founded on a classical idea of continuity. A decline may perhaps have occurred, but 'the exempla of the past' had not been 'rendered irreversibly obsolescent'.[6] The greatness or otherwise of the age was not owed to the influence of external factors; it was merely a consequence of the greatness or otherwise of the men who lived in it, and of *how* they lived.

Applied to Christianity, this provides an important distinction between what I have called 're-enactment', along with the understanding of history it implies, and a more typically medieval 'imitation of Christ'. The distinction is again brought out well by Peter Brown, who notes that 'late medieval and modern devotion' was most likely to involve a profound sense of historical discontinuity: it required 'the projection of the imagination and the sensibility of the believer on to a relatively fixed and delimited image of the historical Jesus and the circumstances of His life and Passion'.[7] This medieval idea required a significant distinction between the modern and the biblical world – 'a thrilling but real chasm, demanding to be crossed by the Christian heart' – which is arguably less characteristic of Christianity in late antiquity.[8] There was for Eusebius, and for Constantine, no uncrossable chasm between the modern emperor and his biblical model; there was instead an implied continuity. The world of the Bible had vanished: but to restore it did not require adapting it to a world that was now totally alien. The past could be mapped on to the modern world, at least on certain occasions, to reveal a true and direct correspondence.

Nevertheless, this is not to explain the Christian re-enactment of Scripture as merely a predictable and largely inconsequential expression of a broader secular phenomenon. For one thing, it required at the very least a reorientation of one's outlook. The authoritative past, the golden age of all the virtues, was not for Christians Republican Rome or the reign of Trajan, but the comparatively marginal world of the Old and New Testaments. Instead of looking to the life of an elite politician such as Cato the Elder, the re-enactment of Scripture recollected the lives of illiterate

---

[6] Brown 1983: 3.

[7] Brown 1983: 7. His examples include Margery Kemp and, implicitly, the work of Thomas à Kempis.

[8] Brown 1983: 7.

shepherds and fishermen at the eastern edge of the Mediterranean. This was no less familiar a social and historical world than the other: across the empire there were no doubt many more in late antiquity who lived as Simon Peter had than who lived the life of a Roman gentleman farmer. That there was continuity was not to be denied. But Christianity focused attention on a different continuity, and offered as an example for the modern world a very different understanding of the virtues of the past.

Even more than this, however, there remained a definite gap between the world of the Bible and the world of late antiquity. It was, in a sense, a narrative gap. What had been lost was the thread of the story, an account of the centuries that separated contemporary life from the last of the events related in the Christian scriptures. With Eusebius in particular, and his *Ecclesiastical History*, this began to be rectified, and a Christian history was constructed that would take the story as far as Constantine. And yet the example of Eusebius shows that there was another possible solution to the problem. In his *Ecclesiastical History* the events of the Roman empire are retold from the point of view of the Christian church; but in the *Life of Constantine*, the centuries between Christ and Constantine are, in effect, ignored altogether. In fact either solution was adequate, for it was not the events themselves that mattered but the manner of their interpretation. The narrative that had run through the scriptures described the development of sacred history, the significant events which demonstrated the active presence of the Christian God in the world. As long as this story was resumed, the length of the gap was of lesser significance. Beginning with Eusebius, then, Christian biography in the fourth and fifth centuries supplemented Christian history as 'the medium through which Christian writers chronicled the post-biblical intervention of the divine in human affairs'.[9]

A successful re-enactment of Moses or Christ in the world of late antiquity therefore had notably different implications from any parallel revival of the lifestyle and the virtues of a Roman exemplar such as Cato. It implied a restoration not only of the virtues of the

[9] Coon 1997: 2.

past society they embodied, but also of the underlying assumptions on which that past society was founded: in the case of Christianity, the watchful presence of their God. This, then, was the conclusion to be drawn from the very presence of figures in the contemporary world who could be understood as re-enactments of Scripture; but it was bolstered by the representation of these figures in contemporary Christian biography. Indeed, the historical re-enactment that these lives claimed to be recording was supplemented by a kind of textual re-enactment, in which the biographies themselves mimicked the 'unified structure of narrative and imagery' that characterised the scriptures.[10] The continuity of the biblical narrative was guaranteed by the form as well as the content of these Christian biographies, which adopted the rhetoric of sacred texts so thoroughly as to seem close to sacred themselves.

It was to this that Augustine ultimately objected when he came to express his views most forcefully in the *City of God*: the idea that Scripture could be supplemented at all, or in anything like an authoritative fashion. The kind of relevance to his own life that Augustine had apparently once granted the *Life of Antony* was no longer to be permitted, or at least was not to be guaranteed: for the implications of such a contemporary sacred history were likely to prove a challenge to the Bible's unique authority within Christianity. Modern writings were at best merely a commentary on – and at worst a distraction from, or a denial of – what had already been sufficiently revealed. But despite Augustine, these late-antique *Lives* had made, and continued to make, the implicit claim that the activity of God in the world, and the patterns that revealed his intentions, could be recognised and understood. Christian biographies, and their authors, represented themselves as possessing an authority that had otherwise been restricted to the scriptures. It is this claim in particular that I have identified as characteristic of the late-antique genre of Christian biography; and it is this claim, even though it was finally rejected by Augustine, that allows Christian biography to be seen as a distinctive phenomenon.

[10] Frye 1982: xvii.

Reading the present

Christian biography as it was understood – and as frequently contested – between Eusebius and Augustine should thus be understood in terms of these implicit claims and underlying assumptions. The main assumption that most of these biographers shared was that Scripture was to be understood historically: that the Bible was an accurate record of significant actions and events. Thus when interpreting the scriptures, Augustine was very careful to draw a distinction between the words in which an event was narrated – which he insisted could be taken as having only their literal meaning – and the event itself, which might be interpreted figuratively.[11] It was this separation which made it possible for him to say of an event in Genesis: 'this was done for the sake of signifying something; but done it was, just as things said for the sake of signifying something are said'.[12] This, then, is the principle underlying the use of typology and re-enactment in Christian interpretation: it is an early articulation of the dynamic of 'historical recurrence' through which the prophetic meaning of Scripture could be expressed. Augustine's considered opinion, however, seems to have been that the importance of historical recurrence – the meaningful connection made between two similar or identical events – was confined entirely to relationships within and between the Old and New Testaments. Outside of these authoritative texts, events might indeed be significant but that significance could not be guaranteed – and nor could any specific meaning that was assigned to them. To devise on the basis of contemporary events an interpretation concerning the will of God or the development of sacred history would be at best a mistake and at worst a heresy.

And yet Eusebius and others were more confident that events in Scripture could be usefully correlated with events in the post-biblical world. Their use of typology thus extended beyond the Bible, or rather implicitly expanded the canon to include their own

---

[11] Kirwan 1989: 12–13, citing Augustine, *De Genesi ad litteram* I.1.1, on 'res gestae': 'nam non esse accipienda figuraliter, nullus christianus dicere audebit.'

[12] Markus 1996: 5, quoting Augustine, *De Genesi ad litteram* 11.39.52: 'Et hoc significationis gratia factum est, sed tamen factum; sicut illa quae significationis gratia dicta sunt, sed tamen dicta sunt.'

accounts of contemporary Christian lives. The heroes of these lives re-enacted the heroes of Scripture but also, eventually, one another; until in the fifth century collective biographies began to appear in which the lives of a variety of ascetic heroes seemed to amount less to a collection of individual biographies than to facets of a single, ideal 'way of life'.[13] Ultimately the portraits of individual ascetics were so far diminished that a few details came to stand for a fuller portrait, and in everything not noted as distinctive an ascetic was to be assumed to resemble the rest. These lives therefore came to represent not so much a series of responses to Scripture as a supplementary volume: a new New Testament. The biographies became generic: what came to matter was the accumulation of lives, and in particular the evidence they provided for the continuation of the biblical way of life throughout the present day.

There is thus an obvious unity among the most generic and conventional biographies of late-antique and early medieval ascetics, who in many cases seem to represent little more than variations on a theme.[14] Yet the same kind of unity can also be recognised as a feature of the greatest 'literary' Christian biographies of the fourth century, those 'shot through with art and life' – the works, that is, studied here, by the likes of Eusebius, Gregory of Nyssa, Athanasius, Jerome and the young Augustine.[15] These Christian biographies share with one another and with the more generic later tradition not any common, predictable stereotype of the late-antique sacred hero, but a set of assumptions that are taken to govern the world they all portray. Above all, they are united by the acceptance of God's continued intervention in the world of late antiquity, and by the belief that those interventions can be accurately recorded and understood. Each biography provides its own examples, but they are merely many terms in a single argument: they all serve to show the same thing. Singly and together, they imply the renewed existence of a world in which the Bible can be re-enacted.

[13] For a detailed reading along these lines, see Cox Miller 2000: 231–2; she also notes the significance of the singular form in the title given by Gregory of Tours to his *Vita Patrum*.
[14] The narrative similarities of medieval hagiography in particular are demonstrated in the work of A. G. Elliott (1987), where the pattern of Jerome's *Vita Pauli* is found repeated in a wide selection of later lives.
[15] Delehaye 1998: 49.

This, then, is what may be gained from considering these various biographies as part of a single unitary phenomenon. Christian biography between Eusebius and Augustine shared and presented a common understanding of the world of late antiquity and its relation to Scripture. The re-enactments of Scripture they represented, whether in form or in content, extended into the present day the reach of a kind of biblical typology – in effect assimilating their contemporary world to the world of the Bible. Taken together, they offered a polemical redescription of late-antique reality which proved both popular and influential. We have only Augustine's account to rely on for a picture of the various readers of the *Life of Antony* and the effects it had upon them, but that alone must attest to the extent to which these lives were read and received by contemporaries; and certainly, by the late fourth century and the early fifth century the existence of saints, and of biographies of saints, was simply a fact of life. Although Augustine would deny them the status of Scripture, such biographies continued to be written and read and attended to throughout the Christian world; and their effect continued to be felt.

For it is not enough merely to say that the heroes of these Christian biographies were shown to be imitating biblical exemplars; for they in their turn provided an example to their readers, and this requires a subtly different understanding of the question of exemplarity. The most significant difference between these accounts and the exemplary lives recorded in the scriptures is that Christian biographies set forth for imitation the lives of contemporaries. As a result, the apparently biblical world that these figures exemplified was, at the same time, the familiar contemporary world inhabited by their readers. What was being offered in these *Lives*, then, was not a vanished way of life which might come to be restored, but an actual and successful restoration taking place in the present day. The claim was that 'somewhere, in their own times, even maybe in their own region', certain of their own contemporaries had achieved 'an exceptional degree of closeness to God'.[16] These were presented as historical – or rather, biographical – facts, but it was not vitally important that the stories should have been true;

---

[16] Brown 1995: 58–9.

what mattered was that they engaged with the real and familiar world of their readers. They provided their readers with a new perspective on surroundings that might otherwise be taken for granted; and they gave them an opportunity to re-imagine the world in which they already lived.

In effect, then, late-antique Christian biography enlarged the possibilities for living. Indeed, to many readers it is likely to have represented a challenge. A new understanding of the familiar world required a reassessment of one's relationship with it; and a possible result of this process is recorded in the conversion scene of Augustine's *Confessions*. A biography of a holy man thus served, like the holy man himself, as 'a rallying-point' and 'facilitator for the creation of new religious allegiances and new religious patterns of observance'.[17] Given that lives were being lived in the present day on the same principles as in the scriptures, and given that the active intervention of God in the world had been shown to be continuing in late antiquity, there was an evident challenge to 'live up' to the new biblical world that was taking shape all around. Insofar as these *Lives* delivered an imperative, it was not to imitate these heroes directly: rather, it was to fit oneself to the contours of the world they were creating. It was, in some ways, a matter of fulfilling expectations:

Only by living up to the imperative could each man affirm the indicative as applying to him, and so become what, by virtue of the act of God, he was already – a member of God's chosen people, living in the new history which God had given him, according to the way which God had shown him.[18]

Augustine, for once, put the matter most succinctly: why should anyone delay, when even now 'the unlearned are rising up and seizing heaven'.[19]

In this connection, too, then, it was vital that there existed a multitude of individual examples which all collaborated in expressing a single truth. The *Life of Constantine* alone might have convinced its readers that the world operated on biblical principles; but it was surely the many biographies that followed in its wake that provided the inspiration to participate. Indeed, perhaps the most

---

[17] Brown 1995: 60. [18] Charity 1966: 39, 169.
[19] *Conf.* 8.8.19: 'surgunt indocti et caelum rapiunt'.

important aspect of the implicit demand that was made on readers of Christian biography was that, although it might easily seem like an escape from reality, it was easily presentable as quite the reverse. To adapt one's life to the conventions of Christian biography was not necessarily the act of a romantic or a fantasist, a Don Quixote or an Emma Bovary; it was not, that is, to set oneself entirely in opposition to the accepted conventions of the time. On the contrary, a Christian such as Augustine could believe himself to be on the side of progress. To live like the hero of a Christian biography was to collude in the creation of a new Christian future which was already springing up all around. A reader who accepts the challenge might therefore simply be seen as taking advantage of 'the power . . . to conceive himself as other than he is'.[20] The biblical narrative, in this new relationship to the reader's own life, thus 'figures and transfigures the reader's historicity'.[21] In other words, Christian biography functioned perhaps above all as a stimulus to conversion: personal conversion, but in the grander cause of converting the world.

If this kind of conversion is not an escape from world into text, it may nevertheless be understood as in some ways importing textuality into the world. The literary conventions of the scriptures were now available to be recognised in the events of 'real life'; but above all, the presence of these patterns and of events recalling those in the scriptures implied an author. To an extent, those who modelled their own lives on Christian biographies were applying to the real world the process of selection and narration undertaken by a human author; but since these works could easily be understood as the product of divine inspiration, the true Author was the author of the master narrative encompassing the world and everything in it. This kind of relationship between text and life is perhaps the defining feature of late-antique Christian biography, in which the narrative and the morality imparted by the text 'were inseparable from the life of a person who had demonstrated his physical existence in time', and who was in turn identified as an expression of the divine will of the Christian God.[22] Thus to adapt oneself to the

---

[20] Huxley 1936: 30, his definition of 'bovarism'.
[21] Vanhoozer 1990: 199, paraphrasing Paul Ricoeur.   [22] Stock 2001: 18.

conventions underlying Christian biography in this period was to give up control over one's own life and to submit to direction from above: it was to allow oneself to be authored by God. Moreover, it was to find a place for oneself in the history begun in the Bible and proceeding until the end of time: to participate, therefore, in the grand Christian narrative, the authorised version of all human history. It was to take seriously the demands of Christian biography, and to join the ranks of authorised lives.

BIBLIOGRAPHY

Ancient texts

Works are here given their conventional titles: usually in Latin, but I have occasionally preferred a title in English where that seemed to me more familiar. The *Vita Antonii* has been assigned to Athanasius of Alexandria largely for the sake of convenience: the majority of current editions identify him as the author. Abbreviations are used for the standard series of texts and translations as follows:

CCSL	Corpus Christianorum, series Latina
CSEL	Corpus Scriptorum Ecclesiasticorum Latinorum
FC	Fathers of the Church
GCS	Griechischen christlichen Schriftsteller
GNO	*Gregorii Nyseni Opera*
NPNF	A Select Library of Nicene and Post-Nicene Fathers
OCT	Oxford classical Texts
SC	Sources Chrétiennes
TTH	Translated Texts for Historians

Ambrose of Milan, *Letters*, ed. O. Faller and M. Zelzer in *Sancti Ambrosii Opera X: Epistulae et Acta* (*CSEL* 82/1–4: Vienna, 1968–96). English translation by J. H. W. G. Liebeschuetz with C. Hill in *Ambrose of Milan: Political Letters and Speeches* (TTH 43: Liverpool, 2005).

Athanasius of Alexandria, *Vita Antonii*, ed. with French translation by G. J. M. Bartelink in *Athanase d'Alexandrie: Vie d'Antoine* (SC 400: Paris, 1994). English translations by R. C. Gregg, in *Athanasius: The Life of Antony and the Letter to Marcellinus* (New York, 1980), and by T. Vivian and A. N. Athanassakis with R. A. Greer in *The Life of Antony* (Cistercian Studies 202: Kalamazoo, MI, 2003).

Augustine of Hippo, *Confessionum*, ed. J. J. O'Donnell in *Augustine: Confessions* (3 vols., Oxford, 1992). English translation by H. Chadwick in *Saint Augustine: Confessions* (Oxford, 1991).

De ciuitate dei, ed. B. Dombart and A. Kalb in *Sancti Aurelii Augustini episcopi De ciuitate Dei libri XXII* (Teubner: 2 vols., Stuttgart, 1981). English translation by R. W. Dyson in *Augustine: The City of God against the Pagans* (Cambridge, 1998).

De doctrina christiana, ed. with English translation by R. P. H. Green in *Augustine: De doctrina christiana* (Oxford, 1995).

De uera religione, ed. with French translation by J. Pegon in *Oeuvres de Saint Augustine*, vol. *8: La foi chrétienne: De uera religione, De utilitate credendi, De fide rerum quae non uidentur, De fide et operibus* (Bibliothèque Augustinienne: Paris, 1982). English translation by J. H. S. Burleigh in *Augustine: Earlier Writings* (Library of the Christian Classics 6: Philadelphia, PA, 1953).

De utilitate credendi, ed. with French translation by J. Pegon in *Oeuvres de Saint Augustine*, vol. *8: La foi chrétienne: De uera religione, De utilitate credendi, De fide rerum quae non uidentur, De fide et operibus* (Bibliothèque Augustinienne: Paris, 1982). English translation by J. H. S. Burleigh in *Augustine: Earlier Writings* (Library of the Christian Classics 6: Philadelphia, PA, 1953).

Retractationes, ed. A. Mutzenbecher in *Sancti Aurelii Augustini Retractationum libri II* (*CCSL* 57: Turnhout, 1984). English translation by M. I. Bogan in *Saint Augustine: Retractations* (FC 60: Washington DC, 1968).

Basil of Caesarea, *Letters*, ed. with a French translation by Y. Courtonne in *Sainte Basile: Lettres* (Budé: 3 vols., Paris, 1957–66). English translation by A. C. Way in *Saint Basil: Letters* (FC 13 and 28: 2 vols., Washington DC, 1951–5).

Codex Theodosianus, ed. T. Mommsen and P. M. Meyer in *Theodosiani libri XVI cum Constitutionibus Sirmondianis et Leges nouellae ad Theodosianum pertinentes* (2 vols., Berlin, 1905; 2nd edn, 1964). English translation by C. Pharr in Pharr *et al.* (eds.) *The Theodosian Code and Novels and the Sirmondian Constitutions* (Princeton, 1952).

Constantine, *Oratio Constantini ad sanctos*, ed. I. Heikel in *Eusebius Werke I: Vita Constantini, De laudibus Constantini, Constantini imperatoris oratio ad sanctorum coetum* (GCS 7: Leipzig, 1902). English translation by M. J. Edwards in *Constantine and Christendom: the Oration to the Saints, the Greek and Latin Accounts of the Discovery of the Cross, the Edict of Constantine to Pope Silvester* (TTH 39: Liverpool, 2003).

Eusebius of Caesarea, *Demonstratio Euangelica*, ed. I. Heikel in *Eusebius Werke VI: Demonstratio Euangelica* (GCS 32: Leipzig, 1923).

Historia Ecclesiastica, ed. E. Schwarz and T. Mommsen in *Eusebius Werke II/ 1–3: Historia Ecclesiastica* (GCS 9/1–3: Leipzig, 1903–9). English translation by G. A. Williamson in *Eusebius: The History of the Church from Christ to Constantine* (Harmondsworth, 1989).

Vita Constantini, ed. F. Winkelmann in *Eusebius Werke I/1: Über das Leben des Kaisers Konstantin* (GCS NF 7/1: Berlin, 1975). English translation by Av. Cameron and S. G. Hall in *Eusebius: Life of Constantine* (Oxford, 1999).

Gregory of Nazianzus, *Oratio 43*, ed. with a French translation by J. Bernardi in *Grégoire de Nazianze: Discours 42–43* (SC 384: Paris, 1992). English translation by L. P. McCauley in M. R. P. McGuire (ed.) *Gregory of Nazianzus and Ambrose of Milan: Funeral Orations* (FC 22: Washington DC, 1953).

Gregory of Nyssa, *De uirginitate*, ed. with a French translation by M. Aubineau in *Grégoire de Nysse: Traité de la virginité* (SC 119: Paris, 1966).

In Basilium fratrem, ed. O. Lendle in *Sermones* 2 (*GNO* 10.2: Leiden, 1990). English translation by J. A. Stein in *Encomium of Saint Gregory, Bishop of Nyssa, on his Brother Saint Basil, Archbishop of Cappadocian Caesarea* (Washington DC, 1928).

Letters, ed. P. Maraval in *Grégoire de Nysse: Lettres* (SC 363: Paris, 1990).

Vita Gregorii Thaumaturgi, ed. G. Heil in *Sermones* 2 (*GNO* 10.2: Leiden, 1990). English translation by M. Slusser in Slusser (ed.) *St Gregory Thaumaturgus: Life and Works* (FC 98: Washington DC, 1998).

Vita Macrinae, ed. with a French translation by P. Maraval in *Grégoire de Nysse: Vie de Sainte Macrine* (SC 178: Paris, 1971).

Vita Moysis, ed. with French translation by J. Daniélou in *Grégoire de Nysse: Vie de Moïse* (SC 1: 2nd edn, Paris, 1968). English translation by A. Malherbe and E. Ferguson in *Gregory of Nyssa: The Life of Moses* (Cistercian Studies 31: New York, 1978).

Historia monachorum in Aegypto, ed. with French translation by A.-J. Festugière (Subsidia Hagiographica 53: Brussels, 1971). English translation by N. Russell in *The Lives of the Desert Fathers* (Cistercian Studies 34: London and Oxford, 1981).

Jerome, *De uiris illustribus*, ed. with Italian translation by A. Ceresa-Gastaldo in *Gerolamo: Gli uomini illustri* (Nardini: Biblioteca Patristica 12: Florence, 1988). English translation by T. P. Halton in *Saint Jerome: On Illustrious Men* (FC 100: Washington DC, 1999).

Letters, ed. with French translation by J. Labourt in *Saint Jérôme: Lettres* (Budé: 8 vols., Paris, 1949). English translation by J. Parker in *Jerome: Letters and Select Works* (NPNF 6, 1893).

Vita Hilarionis, ed. A. A. R. Bastiaensen, plus Italian translation by C. Moreschini and L. Canali in C. Mohrmann (ed.) *Vita dei Santi 4: Vita di Martino, Vita di Ilarione, In memoria di Paola* (Milan, 1975). English translation by C. White in White (ed.) *Early Christian Lives* (Harmondsworth, 1998).

Vita Malchi, ed. C. C. Mierow in R. E. Arnold (ed.) *Classical Essays presented to James A. Kleist, S. J.* (St. Louis, 1946). English translation by C. White in White (ed.) *Early Christian Lives* (Harmondsworth, 1998).

Vita Pauli, ed. H. Hurter in W. A. Oldfather (ed.) *Studies in the Text Tradition of St Jerome's Vitae Patrum* (Urbana, Illinois, 1943). English translations by P. B. Harvey in V. L. Wimbush (ed.) *Ascetic Behavior in Greco-Roman Antiquity: a Sourcebook* (Minneapolis, MN, 1990) and by C. White in White (ed.) *Early Christian Lives* (Harmondsworth, 1998).

Lactantius, *De mortibus persecutorum*, ed. with English translation by J. L. Creed (Oxford Early Christian Texts: Oxford, 1984).

Menander Rhetor, ed. with English translation by D. A. Russell and N. G. Wilson (Oxford, 1981).

Pachomii uita altera, ed. F. Halkin in Halkin (ed.) *Sancti Pachomii Vitae Graecae* (Subsidia Hagiographica 19: Brussels, 1932).

Pachomii uita prima, ed. F. Halkin in Halkin (ed.) *Sancti Pachomii Vitae Grae-cae* (Subsidia Hagiographica 19: Brussels, 1932). English translation by A. Veilleux in *Pachomian Koinonia: The Lives, Rules, and Other Writings of Saint Pachomius and his Disciples, vol. 1* (Cistercian Studies 45: Kalamazoo, MI, 1980).

Palladius, *Historia Lausiaca*, ed. C. Butler in *The Lausiac History of Palladius* (Texts and Studies 6: 2 vols., Cambridge, 1904). English translation by R. D. Meyer in *Palladius: The Lausiac History* (Ancient Christian Writers 34: London, 1965).

XII panegyrici latini, ed. R. A. B. Mynors (OCT, Oxford, 1964). English translation by C. E. V. Nixon and B. S. Rodgers in *In Praise of Later Roman Emperors: The Panegyrici Latini*, (Berkeley and Los Angeles, 1994).

Rufinus, *Historia ecclesiastica*, ed. T. Mommsen in *Eusebius Werke II/2: Historia Ecclesiastica* (GCS 9/2: Leipzig, 1908). English translation by P. R. Amidon in *The Church History of Rufinus of Aquileia, Books 10 and 11* (New York and Oxford, 1997).

Socrates, *Historia ecclesiastica*, ed. G. C. Hansen in *Sokrates: Kirchengeschichte* (GCS n.s. 1: Berlin, 1995). English translation by A. C. Zenos in *Socrates and Sozomenus: Ecclesiastical Histories* (NPNF 2, 1891).

Sozomen, *Historia ecclesiastica*, ed. J. Bidez (*PG* 67: 844–1032), plus French translation by A.-J. Festugière in G. Sabbah (ed.) *Sozomène: Histoire Ecclé-siastique* (SC 306: Paris, 1983). English translation by C. D. Hartranft in *Socrates and Sozomenus: Ecclesiastical Histories* (NPNF 2, 1891).

Sulpicius Severus, *Vita Martini*, ed. with French translation by J. Fontaine in *Sulpice Sévère: Vie de Saint Martin* (SC 133–5: Paris, 1967). English trans-lation by A. Roberts in *The Works of Sulpitius Severus* (NPNF 11, 1894).

Themistius, *Orationes*, ed. H. Schenkl in G. Downey and A. F. Norman (eds.) *Themistii Orationes quae supersunt* (Teubner: 3 vols., Leipzig, 1965–74). Selected English translations by R. J. Penella in *The Private Orations of Themistius* (Berkeley and Los Angeles, 2000).

Theodoret of Cyrrhus, *Historia religiosa*, ed. with French translation by P. Canivet and A. Leroy-Molinghen in Canivet and Leroy-Molinghen (eds.) *Théodoret de Cyr: Histoire des Moines de Syrie* (SC 257: Paris, 1977). English trans-lation by R. M. Price in Price (ed.) *Theodoret of Cyrrhus: A History of the Monks of Syria* (Cistercian Studies 88: Kalamazoo, MI, 1985).

Modern authors

Alchermes, J. (1994), 'Spolia in Roman cities of the late empire: legislative rationales and architectural reuse', *Dumbarton Oaks Papers* 48, 167–78.

Anatolios, K. (2004), *Athanasius*. London.

Anderson, G. (1994), *Sage, Saint and Sophist: Holy Men and their Associates in the Early Roman Empire*. London.

Ashbrook Harvey, S. (1990), *Asceticism and Society in Crisis: John of Ephesus and the Lives of the Eastern Saints*. Berkeley and Los Angeles.

Auerbach, E. (1952), 'Typological symbolism in medieval French literature', *Yale French Studies* 9, 3–10.

—— (1953), *Mimesis: The Representation of Reality in Western Literature*, tr. W. R. Trask. Princeton, NJ.

—— (1959), 'Figura', tr. R. Manheim in Auerbach, *Scenes From the Drama of European Literature: Six Essays*, 11–71. Gloucester, MA.

Barnard, L. W. (1997), 'Athanasius and the Pachomians', *Studia Patristica* 32, 3–11.

Barnes, T. D. (1975), 'Publilius Optatianus Porfyrius', *American Journal of Philology* 96, 173–86.

—— (1977), 'Two speeches by Eusebius', *Greek, Roman and Byzantine studies* 18, 341–5.

—— (1981), *Constantine and Eusebius*. Cambridge, MA and London.

—— (1982), *The New Empire of Diocletian and Constantine*. Cambridge, MA and London.

—— (1986), 'Angel of light or mystic initiate? The problem of the *Life of Antony*', *Journal of Theological Studies* 37, 353–68; repr. in Barnes, *From Eusebius to Augustine: Selected Papers 1982–1993*. Variorum Collected Studies: Aldershot, 1994.

—— (1989), 'Panegyric, history and hagiography in Eusebius' *Life of Constantine*', in R. Williams (ed.), *The Making of Orthodoxy: Essays in Honour of Henry Chadwick*, 94–123. Cambridge; repr. in Barnes, *From Eusebius to Augustine: Selected Papers 1982–1993*. Variorum Collected Studies: Aldershot, 1994.

—— (1992), 'The Constantinian settlement', in H. W. Attridge and G. Hata (eds.), *Eusebius, Christianity and Judaism*, 635–57. Detroit; repr. in Barnes, *From Eusebius to Augustine: Selected Papers 1982–1993*. Variorum Collected Studies: Aldershot, 1994.

—— (1993), *Athanasius and Constantius: Theology and Politics in the Constantinian Empire*. Cambridge, MA.

—— (1994), 'The two drafts of Eusebius' *Vita Constantini*', in Barnes, *From Eusebius to Augustine: Selected Papers 1982–1993*. Variorum Collected Studies: Aldershot.

—— (2001), 'Constantine's speech to the assembly of the saints: place and date of delivery', *Journal of Theological Studies* 52, 26–36.

Barr, J. (1966), *Old and New in Interpretation: A Study of the Two Testaments*. London.

Bartelink, G. J. M. (1994), 'Introduction', in Bartelink (ed.), *Athanase d'Alexandrie: Vie d'Antoine*, 1–121. Paris.

Bastiaensen, A. A. R. (1994), 'Jérôme hagiographe', in G. Philippart (ed.), *Hagiographies*, vol. I, 97–123. Turnhout.

Baynes, N. H. (1968), *The Political Ideas of Augustine's De Civitate Dei, Historical Association* pamphlet 104. Revised edn.

Bebis, G. S. (1967), 'Gregory of Nyssa's *De Vita Moysis*: a philosophical and theological analysis', *Greek Orthodox Theological Review* 12, 369–93.

Bercovitch, S. (1972) (ed.), *Typology in Early American Literature*. Boston, MA.

Berman, P. G. (2002), *James Ensor: Christ's Entry into Brussels in 1889*. Los Angeles.

Bittner, R (1999), 'Augustine's philosophy of history', in G. B. Matthews (ed.), *The Augustinian Tradition*, 345–60. Berkeley and Los Angeles.

Blackman, E. C. (1948), *Marcion and his Influence*. London.

Bleckmann, B. (1997), 'Ein Kaiser als Prediger: Zur Datierung der konstantinischen "Rede an die Versammlung der Heiligen"', *Hermes* 125, 183–202.

Blowers, P. M. (1997), 'The Bible and spiritual doctrine: some controversies within the Early Eastern Christian ascetic tradition', in Blowers (ed.), *The Bible in Greek Christian Antiquity*, 228–55. Notre Dame, IN.

Bonner, G. (1971), '*Quid imperatori cum Ecclesia?* St Augustine on history and society', *Augustinian Studies* 2, 231–51.

Bourke, V. J. (1945), *Augustine's Quest of Wisdom*. Milwaukee, WI.

(1984), *Wisdom From St Augustine*. Houston, TX.

Borges, J. L. (1986), *Seven Nights*, tr. E. Weinberger. London.

Børtnes, J. and T. Hägg (2006) (eds.), *Gregory of Nazianzus: Images and Reflections*. Copenhagen.

Bowersock, G. W. (1995), *Martyrdom and Rome*. Cambridge.

Bradford, W. (1952), *Of Plymouth Plantation, 1620–1647*, ed. S. E. Morison. New York.

Brakke, D. (1994a), 'The Greek and Syriac versions of the *Life of Antony*', *Le Muséon* 107, 29–52.

(1994b), 'The authenticity of the Ascetic Athanasiana', *Orientalia* 63, 17–56.

(1995), *Athanasius and the Politics of Asceticism*. Oxford.

(2006), *Demons and the Making of the Monk: Spiritual Combat in Early Christianity*. Cambridge, MA.

Brakke, D., M. L. Satlow and S. Weitzmann (2005) (eds.), *Religion and the Self in Antiquity*. Bloomington, IN.

Brenk, B. (1987), 'Spolia from Constantine to Charlemagne: aesthetics versus ideology', *Dumbarton Oaks Papers* 41, 103–10.

Brock, S. P. and S. Ashbrook Harvey (1987), *Holy Women of the Syrian Orient*. Berkeley and Los Angeles.

Brown, P. (1971), *The World of Late Antiquity: From Marcus Aurelius to Muhammad*. London.

(1981), *The Cult of the Saints: its Rise and Function in Latin Christianity*. Chicago.

(1983), 'The saint as exemplar in late antiquity', *Representations* 1, 1–25.

(1989), *The Body and Society: Men, Women and Sexual Renunciation in Early Christianity*. London.

241

(1992), *Power and Persuasion in Late Antiquity: Towards a Christian Empire.* Madison, WI.

(1995), *Authority and the Sacred: Aspects of the Christianisation of the Roman World.* Cambridge.

(1998), 'The rise and function of the holy man in late antiquity, 1971–1997', *Journal of Early Christian Studies* 6, 353–76.

(2000), *Augustine of Hippo: a Biography.* Rev. edn. London.

(2004), *The Rise of Western Christendom: Triumph and Diversity, AD 200–1000.* 2nd edn. Oxford.

Brown, P. *et al.* (1997), 'The world of late antiquity revisited', *Symbolae Osloenses* 72, 5–90.

Browning, R. (1981), 'The "low-level" saint's life in the early Byzantine world', in Hackel (1981) 117–27.

Bruce, F. F. (1968), *This is That: The New Testament Development of some Old Testament Themes.* Exeter.

Brunt, P. A. and J. M. Moore (1970), *Res Gestae Diui Augusti: The Achievements of the Divine Augustus.* Corrected edn. Oxford.

Burckhardt, J. (1949), *The Age of Constantine the Great,* tr. M. Hadas. London.

Burgess, R. W. (1997), 'The dates and editions of Eusebius' *Chronici Canones* and *Historia Ecclesiastica*', *Journal of Theological Studies* n.s. 48, 471–504.

Burridge, R. A. (1995), *What Are the Gospels? A Comparison with Graeco-Roman Biography.* Cambridge.

Burrus, V. (2000), *'Begotten, Not Made': Conceiving Manhood in Late Antiquity.* Stanford, CA.

(2003), *The Sex Lives of Saints: an Erotics of Ancient Hagiography.* Philadelphia, PA.

Burton-Christie, D. (1993), *The Word in the Desert: Scripture and the Quest for Holiness in Early Christian Monasticism.* Oxford.

Cahill, P. J. (1984), 'The unity of the Bible', *Biblica* 65, 404–11.

Cameron, Al. (1969), 'Theodosius the Great and the regency of Stilicho', *Harvard Studies in Classical Philology* 73, 96–102.

(1970), *Claudian: Poetry and Propaganda at the Court of Honorius.* Oxford.

Cameron, Av. (1983), 'Constantinus Christianus', *Journal of Roman Studies* 73, 184–90.

(1989), 'Introduction', in Cameron (ed.), *History as Text: the Writing of Ancient History,* 1–10. London.

(1991), *Christianity and the Rhetoric of Empire: the Development of Christian Discourse.* Berkeley and Los Angeles.

(1997), 'Eusebius' *Vita Constantini* and the construction of Constantine', in Edwards and Swain (1997) 145–74.

(1999), 'On defining the holy man', in Hayward and Howard-Johnston (1999) 27–43.

(2000), 'Form and meaning: the *Vita Constantini* and the *Vita Antonii*', in Hägg and Rousseau (2000) 72–88.

(2005), 'The reign of Constantine, 306–337', in A. K. Bowman, Av. Cameron and P. Garnsey (eds.), *The Cambridge Ancient History, vol.* XII: *The Crisis of Empire, AD 193–337.* 2nd edn. Cambridge.

Cameron, Av. and S. G. Hall (1999) (eds.), *Eusebius: Life of Constantine.* Oxford.

Carcopino, J. (1930), *Virgile et la mystère de la IVᵉ Églogue.* Paris.

Chadwick, H. (1981), 'Pachomios and the idea of sanctity', in Hackel (1981) 11–24.

Charity, A. C. (1966), *Events and their Afterlife: The Dialectics of Christian Typology in the Bible and Dante.* Cambridge.

Chesnut, G. (1977), *The First Christian Histories: Eusebius, Socrates, Sozomen, Theodoret and Evagrius.* Paris.

Chitty, D. J. (1966), *The Desert a City: an Introduction to the Study of Egyptian and Palestinian Monasticism under the Christian Empire.* Oxford.

(1975), *The Letters of Saint Antony the Great.* Oxford.

Clark, E. A. (1984), *The Life of Melania the Younger: Introduction, Translation and Commentary.* New York.

(1986), *Ascetic Piety and Women's Faith: Studies in Late Ancient Christianity.* Lewiston, NY.

(1999), *Reading Renunciation: Asceticism and Scripture in Early Christianity.* Princeton, NJ.

Clark, G. (1993), *Augustine: The Confessions.* Cambridge.

(1995), 'Introduction', in Clark (ed.), *Augustine: Confessions, Books I–IV,* 1–25. Cambridge.

Clausen, W. (1994), *A Commentary on Virgil's Eclogues.* Oxford.

Clebsch, W. A. (1980), 'Preface', in R. C. Gregg (ed.), *Athanasius: The Life of Antony and the Letter to Marcellinus,* xiii–xxi. New York.

Coakley, S. (2002), *Powers and Submissions: Spirituality, Philosophy and Gender.* Oxford.

Coleiro, E. (1957), 'St Jerome's lives of the hermits', *Vigiliae Christianae* 11, 161–78.

Coleman, S. and J. Elsner (1995), *Pilgrimage Past and Present: Sacred Travel and Sacred Space in the World Religions.* London.

Constable, G. (1995), 'The ideal of the imitation of Christ', in his *Three Studies in Medieval Religious and Social Thought,* 143–248. Cambridge.

Conybeare, C. (2000), *Paulinus Noster: Self and Symbols in the Letters of Paulinus of Nola.* Oxford.

Coon, L. L. (1997), *Sacred Fictions: Holy Women and Hagiography in Late Antiquity.* Philadelphia, PA.

Cooper, K. (1996), *The Virgin and the Bride: Idealized Womanhood in Late Antiquity.* Cambridge, MA.

Courcelle, P. (1954), 'Saint Augustin "Photinien" à Milan (Conf. VII,19,25)', *Ricerche di storia religiosa* 1, 63–71.

——(1968), *Récherches sur les Confessions de Saint Augustin*. Paris.

——(1969), *Late Latin Writers and Their Greek Sources*, tr. H. E. Wedeck. Cambridge, MA.

——(1973), *Les Confessions de Saint Augustin dans la tradition littéraire*. Paris.

Cox [Miller], P. (1983), *Biography in Late Antiquity: The Quest for the Holy Man*. Berkeley and Los Angeles.

Cox Miller, P. (1996), 'Jerome's centaur: A hyper-icon of the desert', *Journal of Early Christian Studies* 4, 209–33.

——(2000), 'Strategies of representation in collective biography: constructing the subject as holy', in Hägg and Rousseau (2000) 209–54.

Cracco Ruggini, L. (1977), 'The ecclesiastical histories and the pagan historiography: providence and miracles', *Athenaeum* 55, 107–26.

Croke, B. (1976), 'Arbogast and the death of Valentinian II', *Historia* 25, 235–44.

Crosson, F. (1999), 'Structure and meaning in St Augustine's *Confessions*', in G. B. Matthews (ed.) *The Augustinian Tradition*, 27–38. Berkeley and Los Angeles.

Cullmann, O. (1967), *Salvation in History*, tr. S. G. Sowers. London.

Curran, J. (1994), 'Moving statues in late antique Rome: problems of perspective', *Art History* 17, 46–58.

——(1997), 'Jerome and the sham Christians of Rome', *Journal of Ecclesiastical History* 48, 213–29.

Dagron, G. (1974), *Naissance d'une Capitale: Constantinople et ses institutions de 330 à 451*. Paris.

——(2003), *Emperor and Priest: the Imperial Office in Byzantium*, tr. J. Birrell. Cambridge.

Daniélou, J. (1955a), 'La chronologie des sermons de Grégoire de Nysse', *Revue des Sciences Religieuses* 29, 346–72.

——(1955b), 'La chronologie des oeuvres de Grégoire de Nysse', *Studia Patristica* 7 [= *Texte und Untersuchungen zur Geschichte der Altchristlichen Literatur* 92], 159–69.

——(1960), *From Shadows to Reality: Studies in the Biblical Typology of the Fathers*, tr. W. Hibberd. London.

——(1965), 'Grégoire de Nysse à travers les lettres de Saint Basile et de Saint Grégoire de Nazianze', *Vigiliae Christianae* 19, 31–41.

Dawson, D. (1992), *Allegorical Readers and Cultural Revision in Ancient Alexandria*. Berkeley and Los Angeles.

de Certeau, M. (1975), *The Writing of History*, tr. T. Conley. New York.

de Lacheval, L. (1995), *Spolia: uso e riempiego dell'antico dal III al XIV secolo*. Milan.

Delehaye, H. (1998), *The Legends of the Saints*, tr. D. Attwater. 2nd edn. Dublin.

de Lubac, H. (1947), '"Typologie" et "allegorisme"', *Recherches de science religieuse* 34, 180–226.

de Lubac, H. (1949), '"Sens spirituel"', *Recherches de science religieuse* 36, 542–76.

de Lubac, H. (1959), *Exégèse médiévale: Les quatre sens de l'écriture*. Paris.

de Vogüé, A. (1980), 'Foreword', tr. D. Lavigne, in A. Veilleux (ed. and tr.), *Pachomian Koinonia: The Lives, Rules, and Other Writings of Saint Pachomius and his Disciples, vol I*, vii–xxiii. Kalamazoo, MI.

(1989), 'Introduction', in de Vogüé (ed.), *Saint Athanase: Antoine le grand, père des moines: sa vie*. Paris.

De Vooght, D. P. (1934), 'Les miracles dans la vie de saint Augustin', *Récherches de Théologie Ancienne et Médiévale* 11, 5–16.

Dihle, A. (1983), 'Die Evangelien und die griechische Biographie', in P. Stuhlmacher (ed.), *Das Evangelium und die Evangelien: Vorträge vom Tübinger Symposium 1982 (WUNT 28)*, 383–411. Tübingen.

Dillon, J. (1983), 'The formal structure of Philo's allegorical exegesis', in Dillon and D. Winston (eds.), *Two Treatises of Philo of Alexandria: A Commentary on De Gigantibus and Quod Deus Sit Immutabilis*, 77–87. Chico, CA.

Drake, H. A. (1975), *In Praise of Constantine: A Historical Study and New Translation of Eusebius' Tricennial Orations*. Berkeley and Los Angeles.

(1985), 'Suggestions of date in Constantine's "Oration to the Saints"', *American Journal of Philology* 106, 335–49.

(1988), 'What Eusebius knew: the genesis of the *Vita Constantini*', *Classical Philology* 83, 20–38.

(2000), *Constantine and the Bishops: the Politics of Intolerance*. Baltimore, MD.

(2006), 'The impact of Constantine on Christianity', in Lenski (2006a) 111–36.

Drijvers, J. W. (1992), *Helena Augusta: The Mother of Constantine the Great and the Legend of her Finding of the True Cross*. Leiden and New York.

Duff, T. (1999), *Plutarch's Lives: Exploring Virtue and Vice*. Oxford.

DuQuesnay, I. M. Le M. (1976), 'Virgil's Fourth Eclogue', *Papers of the Liverpool Latin Seminar* I, 25–100; repr. in P. Hardie (ed.), *Virgil: Critical Assessments* (4 vols., London, 1999) I, 283–350.

Duval, Y.-M. (1977), 'Formes profanes et formes bibliques dans les oraisons funèbres de Saint Ambroise', in M. Furhmann (ed.), *Christianisme et formes littéraires de l'Antiquité tardive en Occident*, 235–301. Geneva.

Eck, W. (2003), *The Age of Augustus*, tr. D. L. Schneider. Oxford.

Edwards, M. J. (1997), 'Biography and the biographic', in Edwards and Swain (1997) 227–34.

(2003), 'Introduction', in M. J. Edwards (ed.), *Constantine and Christendom: the Oration to the Saints; the Greek and Latin Accounts of the Discovery of the Cross; the Edict of Constantine to Pope Sylvester*, i–xlvii. Liverpool.

Edwards, M. J., and S. Swain (1997) (eds.), *Portraits: Biographical Representation in the Greek and Latin Literature of the Roman Empire*. Oxford.

Eliade, M. (1965), *The Myth of the Eternal Return: or Cosmos and History*, tr. W. Trask. New York.

245

Elliott, A. G. (1987), *Roads to Paradise: Reading the Lives of the Early Saints*. Hanover and London.

Elliott, E. (1977), 'From father to son: the evolution of typology in Puritan New England', in Miner (1977) 204–27.

Elliott, J. K. (1993), *The Apocryphal New Testament: a Collection of Apocryphal Christian Literature in an English Translation based on M. R. James*. Oxford.

Elliott, T. G. (1987), 'Constantine's conversion: do we really need it?', *Phoenix* 41, 420–38.

(1996), *The Christianity of Constantine the Great*. Scranton, PA.

Elm, S. (1994), '*Virgins of God': the Making of Asceticism in Late Antiquity*. Oxford.

(1998), 'Introduction [to the discussion of Peter Brown]', *Journal of Early Christian Studies* 6, 343–51.

Elsner, J. (1998), *Imperial Rome and Christian Triumph*. Oxford.

(2000a), 'From the culture of *Spolia* to the cult of relics: the Arch of Constantine and the genesis of late antique forms', *Papers of the British School at Rome* 68, 149–84.

(2000b), 'The *Itinerarium Burdigalense*: politics and salvation in the geography of Constantine's empire', *Journal of Roman Studies* 110, 181–96.

(2005), 'Piety and passion: contest and consensus in the audiences for early christian pilgrimage', in J. Elsner and I. Rutherford (eds.), *Pilgrimage in Graeco-Roman and Early Christian Antiquity: Seeing the Gods*, 411–34. Oxford.

(2006), 'Perspectives in art', in Lenski (2006a) 255–77.

Evers, C. (1991), 'Remarques sur l'iconographie de Constantin', *Mélanges de l'École Française à Rome: Antiquité* 103, 785–806.

Fabiny, T. (1992), *The Lion and the Lamb: Figuralism and Fulfilment in the Bible, Art and Literature*. London.

Ferguson, E. (1976), 'Progress in perfection: Gregory of Nyssa's *Vita Moysis*', *Studia Patristica* 14, 307–14.

Finley, M. I. (1967), 'Utopianism ancient and modern', in K. H. Wolff and B. Moore (eds.), *The Critical Spirit: Essays in Honour of Herbert Marcuse*, 1–20. Boston.

Fishbane, M. (1985), *Biblical Interpretation in Ancient Israel*. Oxford.

Fontaine, J. (1963), 'Une clé littéraire de la *Vita Martini* de Sulpice Sévère: la typologie prophétique', in L. J. Engels *et al.* (eds.), *Mélanges offerts à Mademoiselle Christine Mohrmann*, 84–95. Utrecht.

(1967), 'Introduction', in Fontaine (ed. and tr.), *Sulpice Sévère: Vie de Saint Martin* vol. I, 17–243. Paris.

Fox, M. (2000), 'Vitae', *Classical Review* n.s. 50, 95–7.

Frank, G. (2000), *The Memory of the Eyes: Pilgrims to Living Saints in Christian Antiquity*. Berkeley.

Frankfurter, D. (1993), *Elijah in Upper Egypt: the Apocalypse of Elijah and Early Egyptian Christianity*. Minneapolis.

Fredriksen, P. (1986), 'Paul and Augustine: conversion narratives', *Journal of Theological Studies* 37, 3–34.

Frei, H. W. (1974), *The Eclipse of Biblical Narrative: a Study in Eighteenth and Nineteenth Century Hermeneutics*. New Haven.

Froehlich, K. (1977), '"Always to keep the literal sense in Scripture means to kill one's soul": the state of biblical hermeneutics at the beginning of the fifteenth century', in Miner (1977) 20–48.

Frye, N. (1982), *The Great Code: The Bible and Literature*. London.

Fuhrmann, M. (1977), 'Die Mönchsgeschichten des Hieronymus. Form-experimente in erzählender Literatur', in Fuhrmann (ed.), *Christianisme et formes littéraires de l'Antiquité tardive en Occident*, 41–99. Geneva.

Gellrich, J. M. (1996), '*Figura*, allegory and the question of history', in S. Lerer (ed.), *Literary History and the Challenge of Philology: The Legacy of Erich Auerbach*, 107–23. Stanford, CA.

Gibbon, E. (1994), *The History of the Decline and Fall of the Roman Empire*, ed. D. Womersley. London.

Goehring, J. E. (1986), *The Letter of Ammon and Pachomian Monasticism*. Berlin and New York.

Goehring, J. E. (1993), 'The encroaching desert: literary production and ascetic space in early Christian Egypt', *Journal of Early Christian Studies* 1 (1993) 281–96; repr. in Goehring (1999) 73–88.

Goehring, J. E. (1999), *Ascetics, Society and the Desert: Studies in Early Egyptian Monasticism*. Harrisburg, PA.

Goldberg, M. (1981), *Theology and Narrative: a Critical Introduction*. Nashville, TN.

Gould, G. (1993), *The Desert Fathers on Monastic Community*. Oxford.

(1997), 'Pachomian sources revisited', *Studia Patristica* 30, 202–17.

Goulder, M. D. (1964), *Type and History in Acts*. London.

Green, G. (1987), *Scriptural Authority and Narrative Interpretation*. Philadelphia, PA.

Gregg, R. C. (1980), 'Introduction', in Gregg (ed.), *Athanasius: The Life of Antony and the Letter to Marcellinus*, 1–26. New York.

Grégoire, R. (1987), *Manuale di agiologia: Introduzione alla letteratura agiografica*. Monastero San Silvestro Abate.

Grig, L. (2004), *Making Martyrs in Late Antiquity*. London.

Haas, C. (1997), *Alexandria in Late Antiquity: Topography and Social Conflict*. Baltimore, MD and London.

Hackel, S. (1981) (ed.), *The Byzantine Saint: University of Birmingham Four-teenth Spring Symposium of Byzantine Studies*. London.

Hadas, M. and M. Smith (1965), *Heroes and Gods: Spiritual Biographies in Late Antiquity*. New York.

Hägg, T. and P. Rousseau (2000) (eds.), *Greek Biography and Panegyric in Late Antiquity*. Berkeley.

Hall, L. J. (1998), 'Cicero's *Instinctu divino* and Constantine's *Instinctu divinitatis*: the evidence of the Arch of Constantine for the senatorial view of the "Vision" of Constantine', *Journal of Early Christian Studies* 6, 647–71.

Hall, S. G. (1991), *Doctrine and Practice in the Early Church*. London.

Hamblenne, P. (1993), 'Traces de biographies grecques "païennes" dans la *Vita Pauli* de Jérôme?', in *Cristianesimo Latino e cultura Greca sino al sec. IV*: Atti del congresso, 209–34. Rome.

Hanson, R. P. C. (1959), *Allegory and Event: A Study of the Sources and Significance of Origen's Interpretation of Scripture*. Richmond, VA.

(1988), *The Search for the Christian Doctrine of God: The Arian Controversy*, 318–381. Edinburgh.

Harl, M. (1966), Review of H. Musurillo (ed.), *Gregorii Nysseni Opera vol. 7.1: De Vita Moysis*, *Gnomon* 38, 554–7.

(1967), 'Les trois quarantaines de Moïse', *Revue des études grecques* 80, 407–12.

(1984), 'Moïse figure de l'évêque dans l'Eloge de Basile de Grégoire de Nysse (381). Un plaidoyer pour l'autorité épiscopale', in A. Spira (ed.), *The Biographical Works of Gregory of Nyssa: Proceedings of the Fifth International Colloquium on Gregory of Nyssa [Mainz, 6–10 September 1982]*, 71–119. Cambridge, MA.

Harpham, G. G. (1987), *The Ascetic Imperative in Culture and Criticism*. Chicago and London.

Harrison, C. (2000), *Augustine: Christian Truth and Fractured Humanity*. Oxford.

Hartley, E. (2006), (ed.), *Constantine the Great: York's Roman Emperor*. Aldershot.

Harvey, P. B. Jr. (1998), 'Saints and satyrs: Jerome the scholar at work', *Athenaeum: Studi di Letteratura e Storia dell'Antichità* 86, 35–56.

(2005), 'Jerome dedicates his *Vita Hilarionis*', *Vigiliae Christianae* 59, 286–97.

Hayward, P. A. (1999), 'Demistifying the role of sanctity in Western Christendom', in *Hayward and Howard-Johnston* (1999), 115–42.

Hayward, P. A. and J. Howard-Johnston (1999) (eds.), *The Cult of Saints in Late Antiquity and the Middle Ages: Essays on the Contribution of Peter Brown*. Oxford.

Heffernan, T. J. (1988), *Sacred Biography: Saints and their Biographers in the Middle Ages*. Oxford.

Heim, F. (1992), *La Théologie de la victoire de Constantin à Théodose*. Paris.

Heisenberg, A. (1908), *Grabeskirche und Apostelkirche*. 2 vols. Leipzig.

Hollander, R. (1977), 'Typology and secular literature: some medieval problems and examples', in Miner (1977) 3–19.

Hollerich, M. (1989), 'The comparison of Moses and Constantine in Eusebius of Caesarea's *Life of Constantine*', *Studia Patristica* 19, 80–95.

(1990), 'Religion and politics in the writings of Eusebius: reassessing the first "court theologian"', *Church History* 59, 309–25.

(1999), *Eusebius of Caesarea's Commentary on Isaiah: Christian Exegesis in the Age of Constantine*. Oxford.

Holum, K. G. (1990), 'Hadrian and St Helena: imperial travel and the origins of Christian Holy Land pilgrimage', in Ousterhout (1990) 66–81.

Hopkins, K. (1999), *A World Full of Gods: Pagans, Jews and Christians in the Roman Empire*. London.

Huber-Rebenich, G. (1999), 'Hagiographic fiction as entertainment', in H. Hofmann (ed.), *Latin Fiction: the Latin Novel in Context*, 187–212. London and New York.

Humphries, M. (1996), *Communities of the Blessed: Social Environment and Religious Change in Northern Italy, AD 200–400*. Oxford.

Huxley, A. (1936), *The Olive Tree*. London.

Inglebert, H. (1996), *Les Romains chrétiens face à l'Histoire de Rome: Histoire, Christianisme et Romanités en Occident dans l'Antiquité tardive (IIIe–Ve siècles)*. Paris.

(2001), *Interpretatio Christiana: Les mutations des savoirs (cosmographie, géographie, ethnographie, histoire) dans l'Antiquité chrétienne (30–630 après J. C.)*. Paris.

Irvine, M. (1994), *The Making of Textual Culture: 'Grammatica' and Literary Theory, 350–1100*. Cambridge.

Jaeger, W. (1965), *Two Rediscovered Works of Ancient Christian Literature: Gregory of Nyssa and Macarius*. Leiden.

James, E. (1991), 'Introduction', in James (ed.), *Gregory of Tours: Life of the Fathers*, ix–xxv. 2nd edn. Liverpool.

Johnson, M. J. (2006), 'Architecture of empire', in Lenski (2006a) 278–97.

Josipovici, G. (1971), *The World and the Book: A Study of Modern Fiction*. London.

Kaufman, P. I. (1997), 'Diehard Homoians and the election of Ambrose', *Journal of Early Christian Studies* 5, 421–40.

Kech, H. (1977), *Hagiographie als christliche Unterhaltungsliteratur. Studien zum Phänomen des Erbaulichen anhand der Mönchsviten des hl. Hieronymus*. Göppingen.

Kee, A. (1982), *Constantine Versus Christ*. London.

Kelly, G. (2004), 'Ammianus and the Great Tsunami', *Journal of Roman Studies* 94, 141–67.

Kelly, J. N. D. (1975), *Jerome: His Life, Writings, and Controversies*. London.

Kermode, F. (1968), *The Sense of an Ending: Studies in the Theory of Fiction*. Oxford.

Keyes. C. F. (1982), 'Introduction: Charisma. from social life to sacred biography', in M. A. Williams (ed.), *Charisma and Sacred Biography*, 1–22. Philadelphia.

Kierkegaard, S. (1983), *Repetition*, ed. and tr. H. V. and E. H. Hong. Princeton.

Kinney, D. (1997), 'Spolia, damnatio and renovatio memoriae', *Memoirs of the American Academy in Rome* 42, 117–48.

Kirwan, C. (1989), *Augustine*. London.

Kitzinger, E (1977), *Byzantine Art in the Making: Main Lines of Stylistic Development in Mediterranean Art, 3rd–7th Century*. London.

Kleiner, F. S. (2001), 'Who really built the Arch of Constantine?', *Journal of Roman Archeology* 14, 661–3.

Knox, J. (1942), *Marcion and the New Testament: an Essay in the Early History of the Canon*. Chicago.

Kofsky, A. (2000), *Eusebius of Caesarea against Paganism*. Leiden, Boston and Cologne.

Konstan, D. (2000), 'How to praise a friend: St Gregory of Nazianzus's funeral oration on St Basil the Great', in Hägg and Rousseau (2000) 160–79.

Koortbojian, M. (1995), *Myth, Meaning and Memory on Roman Sarcophagi*. Berkeley.

Krautheimer, R. (1983), *Three Christian Capitals: Topography and Politics*. Berkeley.

(1986), *Early Christian and Byzantine Architecture*. Fourth edition, revised by Krautheimer and S. Curcic. New Haven and London.

Krueger, D. (1997), 'Typological figuration in Theodoret of Cyrrhus's *Religious History* and the art of postbiblical narrative', *Journal of Early Christian Studies* 5, 393–419.

(2004) *Writing and Holiness: the Practice of Authorship in the Early Christian East*. Philadelphia, PA.

Kyrtatis, D. (1989), 'The transformations of the text: the reception of John's Revelation', in Av. Cameron (ed.), *History as Text: the Writing of Ancient History*, 144–62. London.

Ladner, G. B. (1959), *The Idea of Reform: Its Impact on Christian Thought and Action in the Age of the Fathers*. New York.

Laird, A. (1993), 'Fiction, bewilderment and story worlds: the implications of claims to truth in Apuleius', in C. Gill and T. P. Wiseman (eds.), *Lies and Fiction in the Ancient World*, 147–74. Exeter.

Lampe, G. W. H. (1957), 'The reasonableness of typology', in Lampe and K. J. Woolcombe (eds.), *Essays in Typology*, 9–38. London.

Lane Fox, R. (1986), *Pagans and Christians*. London.

Leclerc, P. (1988), 'Antoine et Paul: Métamorphose d'un héros', in Y.-M. Duval (ed.), *Jérôme entre l'occident et l'orient*, 257–65. Paris.

Leeb, R. (1992), *Konstantin und Christus: Die Verchristlichung der imperialen Repraesentation unter Konstantin dem Grossen ab Spiegel seiner Kirchenpolitik und seiner Selbsterverstaendnisses als christlicher Kaiser*. Berlin.

Lenski, N. (2002), *Failure of Empire: Valens and the Roman State in the Fourth Century AD*. Berkeley and Los Angeles.

(2006a) (ed.), *The Cambridge Companion to the Age of Constantine*. Cambridge.

(2006b), 'The reign of Constantine', in Lenski (2006a) 59–90.

Lim, R. (1995), *Public Disputation, Power and Social Order in Late Antiquity*. Berkeley and Los Angeles.

(2003), Review of Urbainczyk (2002), *Biography* 26, 463–6.

Louth, A. (1981), *Origins of the Christian Mystical Tradition: from Plato to Denys*. Oxford.

(1983), *Discerning the Mystery: an Essay on the Nature of Theology*. Oxford.

(1988), 'St Athanasius and the Greek life of Antony', *Journal of Theological Studies* n.s. 39, 504–9.

Lowance, M. I. (1977), 'Typology and millennial eschatology in early New England', in Miner (1977) 228–73.

Lucchesi, E. (1977), *L'usage de Philon dans l'ouevre exegetique d'Ambrose de Milan*. Leiden.

Luneau, A. (1964), *L'Histoire de Salut chez les Pères de l'Église: La doctrine des âges du monde*. Paris.

MacCormack, S. G. (1975), 'Latin prose panegyrics', in T. A. Dorey (ed.), *Empire and Aftermath: Silver Latin II*, 143–205. London and Boston, MA.

(1981), *Art and Ceremony in Late Antiquity*. Berkeley and Los Angeles.

(1990), 'Loca sancta: the organisation of sacred topography in late antiquity', in Ousterhout (1990) 7–40.

(1998), *The Shadows of Poetry: Vergil in the Mind of Augustine*. Berkeley and Los Angeles.

McClendon, J. W. Jr. (1990), *Biography as Theology*. Philadelphia, PA.

MacLeod, C. (1971), 'Allegory and mysticism in Origen and Gregory of Nyssa', *Journal of Theological Studies* n.s. 23, 362–79; repr. in MacLeod, *Collected Essays* (Oxford, 1983) 309–26.

(1982), 'The preface to Gregory of Nyssa's Life of Moses', *Journal of Theological Studies* n.s. 33, 183–91; repr. in MacLeod, *Collected Essays* (Oxford, 1983) 329–38.

McGuckin, J. A. (2001), *St Gregory of Nazianzus: an Intellectual Biography*. Crestwood, NY.

McLynn, N. B. (1998a), 'A self-made holy man: the case of Gregory Nazianzen', *Journal of Early Christian Studies* 6, 463–83.

(1998b), 'The other Olympias: Gregory Nazianzen and the family of Vitalianus', *Zeitschrift für Antikes Christentum* 2, 227–46.

(2001), 'Gregory Nazianzen's Basil: the literary construction of a Christian friendship', *Studia Patristica* 37, 178–93.

(2003), 'Seeing and believing: aspects of conversion from Antoninus Pius to Louis the Pious', in K. Mills and A. Grafton (eds.), *Conversion in Late Antiquity and the Early Middle Ages: Seeing and Believing*, 224–70. Rochester, NY.

McMahon, R. (1989), *Augustine's Prayerful Ascent: An Essay on the Literary Form of the Confessions*. Athens, GA.

251

Madec, G. (1970), 'Une lecture de *Confessions* VII: IX,13–XXI,27 (notes critiques à propos d'une thèse de R. J. O'Connell)', *Revue des Études Augustiniennes* 16, 79–137.

(1996), *Saint Augustin et la Philosophie: Notes critiques*. Paris.

Magdalino, P. (1994) (ed.), *New Constantines: The Rhythm of Imperial Renewal in Byzantium, 4th–15th Centuries*. Aldershot.

Malbon, E. S. (1990), *The Iconography of the Sarcophagus of Junius Bassus*. Princeton.

Malherbe, A. J. and E. Ferguson (1978), 'Introduction', in Malherbe and Ferguson (trs.), *Gregory of Nyssa: The Life of Moses*, 1–24. New York.

Mandouze, A. (1968), *Saint Augustin: L'aventure du raison et de la grâce*. Paris.

Mango, C. (1990), 'Constantine's mausoleum and the translation of relics', *Byzantinische Zeitschrift* 83, 51–62; repr. in Mango, *Studies on Constantinople*. Variorum Collected Studies: Aldershot.

Manning, S. (1972), 'Scriptural exegesis and the literary critic', in Bercovitch (1972) 47–66.

Maraval, P. (1988), 'La date de la mort de Basile', *Revue des Études Augustiniennes* 34, 25–38.

Maraval, P. (1990), 'Introduction', in Maraval (ed. and tr.), *Grégoire de Nysse: Lettres*, 15–78. Paris.

Markus, R. A. (1957), 'Presuppositions of the typological approach to Scripture', *Church Quarterly Review* 158, 442–51.

(1963), 'The Roman empire in early Christian historiography', *The Downside Review* 81, 340–53; repr. in Markus, *From Augustine to Gregory the Great: History and Christianity in Late Antiquity*. Variorum Collected Studies: Aldershot.

(1988), *Saeculum: History and Society in the Theology of St Augustine*. Cambridge.

(1990), *The End of Ancient Christianity*. Cambridge.

(1996), *Signs and Meanings: World and Text in Ancient Christianity*. Liverpool.

(2000), 'Tempora christiana revisited', in R. Dodano and G. Lawless (eds.), *Augustine and his Critics: Essays in Honour of Gerald Bonner*, 201–13. London.

Mather, Cotton (1692) *Wonders of the Invisible World*. Boston.

Matthews, J. F. (1990), *Western Aristocracies and Imperial Court, AD 364–425*. 2nd edn. Oxford.

Mellucco Vaccaro, A. and A. M. Ferroni (1996), 'Chi costrui l'arco di Costantino? Un interrogativo ancora attuale', *Rendiconti della Pontificia Accademia Romana di Archeologia* 66, 1–60.

Menestò, E. and F. S. Barcellona (1994), 'Presentazione', *Hagiographica* I, vii–xii.

Meredith, A. (1995), *The Cappadocians*. London.

(1997), 'Gregory of Nazianzus and Gregory of Nyssa on Basil', *Studia Patristica* 32, 163–9.

(1999), *Gregory of Nyssa*. London.

Merrills, A. H. (2004), 'Monks, monsters and barbarians: redefining the African periphery in late antiquity', *Journal of Early Christian Studies* 12, 217–44.

Miles, M. R. (1982), 'Infancy, parenting and nourishment in Augustine's *Confessions*', *Journal of the American Academy of Religion* 50, 349–64.

Miner, E. (1977) (ed.), *Literary Uses of Typology from the Late Middle Ages to the Present*. Princeton.

Momigliano, A. (1963), 'Pagan and Christian historiography in the fourth century AD', in Momigliano (ed.), *The Conflict Between Paganism and Christianity in the Fourth Century*, 79–99. Oxford; repr. in Momigliano, *Terzo Contributo alla storia degli studi classici e del mondo antico*, 87–109. Rome.

(1966), 'Time in ancient historiography', in *History and Theory Beiheft 6: History and the Concept of Time*, 1–23; repr. in Momigliano, *Quarto Contributo alla storia degli studi classici e del mondo antico*, 13–41. Rome.

(1985a), 'The life of St Macrina by Gregory of Nyssa', in J. W. Eadie and J. Ober (eds.), *The Craft of the Ancient Historian: Essays in Honor of Chester G. Starr*, 443–58. Lanham, MD; repr. in Momigliano, *Ottavo Contributo alla storia degli studi classici e del mondo antico*, 333–47. Rome.

(1985b), 'Marcel Mauss and the quest for the person in Greek biography and autobiography', in M. Carrithers, S. Collins and S. Lukes (eds.), *The Category of the Person: Anthropology, Philosophy, History*, 83–92. Cambridge; repr. in Momigliano, *Ottavo Contributo alla storia degli studi classici e del mondo antico*, 179–90. Rome.

(1986), 'Ancient biography and the study of religion in the Roman empire', *Annali della Scuola Normale Superiore di Pisa, serie III* 16, 25–44; repr. in Momigliano, *Ottavo Contributo alla storia degli studi classici e del mondo antico*, 193–210. Rome.

(1993), *The Development of Greek Biography*. Expanded edn. Cambridge, MA.

Monceaux, P. (1931), 'Saint Augustine et Saint Antoine: contribution à l'histoire du monachisme', *Miscellanea Agostiniana* 2, 61–89.

Moorhead, J. (1999), *Ambrose: Church and Society in the Late Roman World*. Edinburgh.

Morison, S. E. (1952), 'Introduction', in *Bradford* (1952) xviii–xliii.

Morrison, K. F. (1992), *Conversion and Text: The Cases of Augustine of Hippo, Herman-Judah, and Constantine Tsatsos*. Charlottesville, VA.

Mortley, R. (1986), *From Word to Silence*. 2 vols. Bonn.

(1990), 'The Hellenistic foundations of ecclesiastical historiography', in G. Clarke (ed.), *Reading the Past in Late Antiquity*, 225–50. Rushcutters Bay, NSW.

(1996), *The Idea of Universal History from Hellenistic Philosophy to Early Christian Historiography*. Lewiston, NY.

Morton, T. (1637), *New English Canaan*. Amsterdam.

Moutsoulas, E. (1997), 'Le problème de la date de la mort de Saint Basile de Césarée', *Studia Patristica* 32, 196–200.

Müller-Wiener, W. (1977), *Bildlexicon zur Topographie Istanbuls*. Tübingen.

Nadel, I. B. (1984), *Biography: Fiction, Fact and Form*. London.

Nicholson, O. (1989), 'Flight from persecution as imitation of Christ: Lactantius' *Divine Institutes* IV.18.1–2', *Journal of Theological Studies* n.s. 40, 45–65.

Nickelsburg, G. W. (1973) (ed.), *Studies on the Testament of Moses*. Chicago.

Nixon, C. E. V. and B. S. Rodgers (1994), *In Praise of Later Roman Emperors: The Panegyrici Latini*. Berkeley and Los Angeles.

Noble, T. F. X. and T. Head (1995), *Soldiers of Christ: Saints and Saints' Lives from Late Antiquity and the Early Middle Ages*. London.

Nock, A. D. (1952), *Conversion: the Old and the New in Religion From Alexander the Great to Augustine of Hippo*. 2nd edn. Oxford.

Norris, F. W. (2000), '"Your honor, my reputation": Gregory of Nazianzus' funeral oration on St. Basil the Great', in Hägg and Rousseau (2000) 140–59.

O'Connell, R. J. (1996), *Images of Conversion in St Augustine's Confessions*. New York.

O'Daly, G. (1999), *Augustine's City of God: A Reader's Guide*. Oxford.

O'Donnell, J. J. (1991), 'The authority of Augustine', *Augustinian Studies* 22, 7–35.

(1992), *Augustine: Confessions*. 3 vols. Oxford.

(2005), *Augustine, Sinner and Saint: a New Biography*. London.

O'Meara, J. J. (1959), *Porphyry's Philosophy from Oracles in Augustine*. Paris.

(1997), *Understanding Augustine*. Dublin.

(2001), *The Young Augustine: An Introduction to the Confessions of St Augustine*. 2nd edn. London.

Oden, R. A. (1983), 'Jacob as father, husband and nephew: kinship studies and the patriarchal narrative', *Journal of Biblical Literature* 102, 189–205.

Olson, P. A. (1995), *The Journey to Wisdom: Self-Education in Patristic and Medieval Literature*. Lincoln, NB.

Otis, B. (1976), 'Gregory of Nyssa and the Cappadocian conception of time', *Studia Patristica* 14, 327–57.

Ousterhout, R. (1990) (ed.), *The Blessings of Pilgrimage*. Urbana, IL and Chicago.

Pasquali, G. (1910), 'Die composition der Vita Constantini des Eusebius', *Hermes* 45, 368–86.

Patlagean, E. (1983), 'Ancient Byzantine hagiography and social history', tr. J. Hodgkin in S. Wilson (ed.), *Saints and their Cults: Studies in Religious Sociology, Folklore and History*, 101–21. Cambridge.

Pegon, J. (1982) (ed.), *Oeuvres de Saint Augustine, vol. 8: La foi chrétienne: De uera religione, De utilitate credendi, De fide rerum quae non uidentur, De fide et operibus*. Paris.

Peirce, P. (1989), 'The Arch of Constantine: propaganda and ideology in Late Roman art', *Art History* 12, 387–418.

Pelling, C. (1997), 'Biographical history? Cassius Dio on the early Principate', in Edwards and Swain (1997) 17–44.

Penco, G. (1968), 'Le figure bibliche del *Vir Dei* nell'agiografia monastica', *Benedictina* 15, 1–13.

Pensabene, P. and C. Panella (1996), 'Riempiego e progettazione architettonica nei monumenti tardo-antichi di Roma', *Rendiconti della Pontificia Accademia Romana di Archeologia* 66, 111–283.

(1999) (eds), *Arco di Costantino: tra archeologia e archeometria*. Rome.

Peri, C. (1974), 'La *Vita di Mosè* di Gregorio di Nissa: un viaggio verso l'arete cristiana', *Vetera Christianorum* 11, 313–32.

Pettersen, A. (1995), *Athanasius*. Harrisburg, PA.

Portalié, E. (1960), *A Guide to the Thought of Saint Augustine*. Chicago.

Pullan, W. (2005), '"Intermingled until the end of time": ambiguity as a central condition of early Christian pilgrimage', in J. Elsner and I. Rutherford (eds.), *Pilgrimage in Graeco-Roman and Early Christian Antiquity: Seeing the Gods*, 387–410. Oxford.

Rajak, T. (1997), 'Dying for the law: the martyr's portrait in Jewish-Greek literature', in Edwards and Swain (1997), 39–68.

Rapp, C. (1998), 'Comparison, paradigm and the case of Moses in panegyric and hagiography', in Mary Whitby (ed.), *The Propaganda of Power: the Role of Panegyric in Late Antiquity*, 277–98. Leiden.

(2005), *Holy Bishops in Late Antiquity: The Nature of Christian Leadership in an Age of Transition*. Berkeley and Los Angeles.

Rebenich, S. (2000a), *Jerome*. London and New York.

(2000b), 'Der Kirchenvater Hieronymus als Hagiograph: Die *Vita s. Pauli primi eremitae*', in K. Elm (ed.), *Beiträge zur Geschichte des Paulinerordens*, 23–40. Berlin.

(2000c), 'Vom dreizehnten Gott zum dreizehnten Apostel? Der tote Kaiser in der Spätantike', *Zeitschrift für Antikes Christentum* 4, 300–24.

Reeves, M. (1991), 'The Bible and literary authorship in the Middle Ages', in S. Prickett (ed.), *Reading the Text: Biblical Criticism and Literary Theory*, 12–63. Cambridge, MA.

Reinhard Lupton, J. (1996), *Afterlives of the Saints: Hagiography and Renaissance Literature*. Stanford.

Reydellet, M. (1985), 'La Bible miroir des princes, du ive au viie siècle', in J. Fontaine and C. Pietri (eds.), *Le Monde latin antique et la Bible*, 431–53. Paris.

Richardson, L. Jr. (1975), 'The date and program of the Arch of Constantine', *Archeologia Classica* 27, 72–8.

Rosenmeier, J. (1972), '"With my owne eyes": William Bradford's *Of Plymouth Plantation*', in Bercovitch (1972) 69–105.

Roston, M. (1968), *Biblical Drama in England from the Middle Ages to the Present Day*. Evanston, IL.

Rouché, C. (1988), 'Theodosius II, the cities, and the date of the *Church History* of Sozomen', *Journal of Theological Studies* 37, 130–2.

Rousseau, P. (1978), *Ascetics, Authority and the Church in the Age of Jerome and Cassian*. Oxford.

(1990), 'Basil of Caesarea: choosing a past', in G. Clarke (ed.), *Reading the Past in Late Antiquity*, 37–42. Rushcutters Bay, NSW.

(1994), *Basil of Caesarea*. Berkeley and Los Angeles.

(1999), *Pachomius: the Making of a Community in Fourth-century Egypt*. Revised edn. Berkeley and Los Angeles.

(2000), 'Antony as teacher in the Greek *Life*', in Hägg and Rousseau (2000) 89–109.

Rubenson, S. (1995), *The Letters of St Antony: Monasticism and the Making of a Saint*. Minneapolis, MN.

(2000), 'Philosophy and simplicity: the problem of a classical education in Early Christian biography', in Hägg and Rousseau (2000) 110–39.

Ruether, R. R. (1969), *Gregory of Nazianzus, Rhetor and Philosopher*. Oxford.

Runia, D. (1993), *Philo in Early Christian Literature: a Survey*. Minneapolis, MN.

Russell, D. A. and N. G. Wilson (1981) (eds.), *Menander Rhetor*. Oxford.

Satran, D. (1995), *Biblical Prophets in Byzantine Palestine: Reassessing the Lives of the Prophets*. Leiden.

Savon, H. (1977), *Saint Ambroise devant l'exégèse de Philon le Juif*. 2 vols. in 1. Paris.

Scourfield, J. N. D. (1993), *Consoling Heliodorus: A Commentary on Jerome Letter 60*. Oxford.

Shuger, D. K. (1990), *Habits of Thought in the English Renaissance: Religion, Politics and the Dominant Culture*. Berkeley and Los Angeles.

Singleton, C. S. (1977), *Dante's Commedia: Elements of Structure*. Baltimore, MD and London.

Sly, D. (1996), *Philo's Alexandria*. London.

Smith, M. (1971), 'Prologomena to a discussion of aretalogies, divine men, the Gospels, and Jesus', *Journal of Biblical Literature* 90, 174–99.

Smith, R. (1995), *Julian's Gods: Religion and Philosophy in the Thought and Action of Julian the Apostate*. London.

Solignac, A. (1962) (ed.), *Les Confessions*. Paris.

Stancliffe, C. (1983), *St Martin and his Hagiographer: History and Miracle in Sulpicius Severus*. Oxford.

Stein, J. A. (1928), 'Introduction', in Stein (ed.), *Encomium of Saint Gregory, Bishop of Nyssa, on his Brother Saint Basil, Archbishop of Cappadocian Caesarea*, xvii–xcvi. Washington DC.

Sterk, A. (1998), 'On Basil, Moses, and the model bishop: the Cappadocian legacy of leadership', *Church History* 67, 227–53.

(2004), *Renouncing the World Yet Leading the Church: the Monk-Bishop in Late Antiquity*. Cambridge, MA.

Stock, B. (1996), *Augustine the Reader: Meditation, Self-knowledge, and the Ethics of Interpretation*. Cambridge, MA.

—— (2001), *After Augustine: the Meditative Reader and the Text*. Philadelphia, PA.

Storch, R. H. (1971), 'The "Eusebian Constantine"', *Church History* 40, 145–55.

Sturrock, J. (1993), *The Language of Autobiography: Studies in the First Person Singular*. Cambridge.

Swain, S. (1997), 'Biography and biographic in the literature of the Roman empire', in Edwards and Swain (1997) 1–38.

Syme, R. (1974), 'The ancestry of Constantine', in J. Von Straub (ed.), *Bonner Historia-Augusta-Colloquium* 1971, 237–53. Bonn; repr. in Syme, *Historia Augusta Papers* (Oxford, 1983) 63–79.

Tartaglia, L. (1984) (ed.), *Eusebio di Cesarea: Sulla Vita di Costantino*. Naples.

Theiler, W. (1953), Review of first edn of Courcelle (1968), *Gnomon* 25, 113–22.

Thélamon, F. (1981), *Païens et chrétiens au IVe siècle. L'apport de l'* Histoire Ecclesiastique *de Rufin d'Aquilée*. Paris.

Tilley, M. A. (1997), *The Bible in Christian North Africa: The Donatist World*. Minneapolis, MN.

Urbainczyk, T. (2002), *Theodoret of Cyrrhus: the Bishop and the Holy Man*. Ann Arbor, MI.

Van Dam, R. (1982), 'Hagiography and history: the life of Gregory Thaumaturgus', *Classical Antiquity* 1, 272–308.

—— (1986), 'Emperors, bishops, and friends in late antique Cappadocia', *Journal of Theological Studies* n.s. 37, 53–76.

—— (1993), *Saints and their Miracles in Late-Antique Gaul*. Princeton, NJ.

—— (2002), *Kingdom of Snow: Roman Rule and Greek Culture in Cappadocia*. Philadelphia, PA.

—— (2003a), *Becoming Christian: The Conversion of Roman Cappadocia*. Philadelphia, PA.

—— (2003b), *Families and Friends in Late Roman Cappadocia*. Philadelphia, PA.

Van Der Meer, F. (1961), *Augustine the Bishop: the Life and Work of a Father of the Church*, tr. B. Battershaw and G. R. Lamb. London.

Vanhoozer, K. J. (1990), *Biblical Narrative in the Philosophy of Paul Ricoeur: A Study in Hermeneutics and Theology*. Cambridge.

Van Sickle, J. B. (1992), *A Reading of Vergil's Messianic Eclogue*. New York.

Van Uytfanghe, M. (1985), 'L'Empreinte biblique sur la plus ancienne hagiographie occidentale', in J. Fontaine and C. Pietri (eds.), *Le Monde latin antique et la Bible*, 565–610. Paris.

Van Uytfanghe, M. (1987), *Stylisation biblique et condition humaine dans l'hagiographie Mérovingienne [600–750]*. Brussels.

—— (1993), 'L'hagiographie: un "genre" chrétien ou antique tardif?', *Analecta Bollandiana* 111, 135–88.

Vessey, M. (1998), 'The demise of the Christian writer and the remaking of "Late Antiquity": from H.-I. Marrou's Saint Augustine (1938) to Peter Brown's Holy Man (1983)', *Journal of Early Christian Studies* 6, 377–411.

(2004), 'Introduction', in Vessey (ed.) and J. Halporn (tr.), *Cassiodorus: Institutions of Divine and Secular Learning and On the Soul*, 1–101. Liverpool.

(2005), 'History, fiction and figuralism in Book 8 of Augustine's *Confessions*', in D. B. Martin and P. Cox Miller (eds.), *The Cultural Turn in Late Ancient Studies*, 237–57. Durham, NC.

Vessey, M. and K. Pollmann (1999), 'Introduction', in M. Vessey, K. Pollmann and A. D. Fitzgerald (eds.), *History, Apocalypse, and the Secular Imagination: New Essays on Augustine's City of God*, 1–26. Bowling Green, OH. [= *Augustinian Studies* 30:2]

Veyne, P. (1988), *Did the Ancient Greeks Believe in their Myths?*, tr. P. Wissing. Chicago.

Vikan, G. (1990), 'Pilgrims in Magi's clothing: the impact of mimesis on Early Byzantine pilgrimage art', in *Ousterhout* (1990) 97–107.

Vivian, T. (2003), 'Introduction', in Vivian and Athanassakis (2003) XXIII–LXVI.

Vivian, T. and A. N. Athanassakis (2003) (eds.), *The Life of Antony: by Athanasius of Alexandria*. Kalamazoo, MI.

Ward, B. (1981), 'Introduction', in N. Russell (ed.), *The Lives of the Desert Fathers*, 1–46. London and Oxford.

(1982), '"Signs and wonders": miracles in the desert tradition', *Studia Patristica* 18, 539–42.

Ward-Perkins, B. (1999), 'Re-using the architectural legacy of the past, *entre idéologie et pragmatisme*', in Ward-Perkins and G. Brogiolo (eds.), *The Idea and Ideal of the Town Between Late Antiquity and the Early Middle Ages*, 225–44. Leiden.

Warmington, B. (1986), 'The sources of some Constantinian documents in Eusebius' *Ecclesiastical History* and *Life of Constantine*', *Studia Patristica* 18, 93–8.

Weingarten, S. (2005), *The Saint's Saints: Hagiography and Geography in Jerome*. Leiden.

Whitby, Michael (1994), 'Images for emperors in late antiquity: a search for New Constantine', in *Magdalino* (1994) 83–94.

White, C. (1998) (ed.), *Early Christian Lives*. Harmondsworth.

Whitman, J. (1987), *Allegory: The Dynamics of an Ancient and Medieval Technique*. Oxford.

Wiesen, D. S. (1964), *Saint Jerome as Satirist: a Study in Christian Latin Thought and Letters*. Ithaca, NY.

Williams, D. H. (1995), *Ambrose of Milan and the End of the Arian-Nicene Conflicts*. Oxford.

(1997), 'Politically correct in Milan: a reply to "Diehard Homoians and the Election of Ambrose"', *Journal of Early Christian Studies* 5, 441–6.

Williams, M. A. (1982), 'The *Life of Antony* and the domestication of charismatic wisdom', in Williams (ed.), *Charisma and Sacred Biography*, 23–45. Philadelphia, PA.

Williams, M. S. (2003), 'Biography and the re-enactment of Scripture in late antiquity'. Unpublished Cambridge Ph.D. thesis.

Williams, S. (1985), *Diocletian and the Roman Recovery*. London.

Wilson, A. (1988), 'Biographical models: the Constantinian period and beyond', in S. N. C. Lieu and D. Montserrat (eds.), *Constantine: History, Historiography and Legend*, 107–35. London.

(1990), 'Reason and rhetoric in the conversion accounts of the Cappadocians and Augustine', *Augustiniana* 40, 259–78.

Wilson-Jones, M. (1999), 'La progettazione architettonica: riflessioni su misure, proporzioni e geometrie', in Pensabene and Panella (1999), 75–100.

(2000), 'Genesis and mimesis: the design of the Arch of Constantine in Rome', *Journal of the Society of Architectural Historians* 59, 50–77.

Wimbush, V. L. and R. Valantasis (2002) (eds.), *Asceticism*. Oxford.

Winkelmann, F. (1975) (ed.), *Eusebius: Über das Leben des Kaisers Konstantin*. Berlin.

Wiseman, T. P. (1993), 'Lying historians in the ancient world: seven types of mendacity', in Wiseman and C. Gill (eds.), *Lies and Fiction in the Ancient World*, 122–46. Exeter.

Witakowski, W. (1987), *The Syriac Chronicle of Pseudo-Dionysius of Tel-Mahré: A Study in the History of Historiography*. Uppsala.

Wolterstorff, N. (1995), *Divine Discourse: Philosophical Reflections on the Claim that God Speaks*. Cambridge.

Woolcombe, K. J. (1957), 'The biblical origins and patristic development of typology', in G. W. H. Lampe and Woolcombe (eds.), *Essays in Typology*, 39–75. London.

Wyschogrod, E. (1999), *Saints and Postmodernism: Revisioning Moral Philosophy*. Chicago and London.

Young, F. M. (1989), 'The rhetorical schools and their influence on patristic exegesis', in R. Williams (ed.), *The Making of Orthodoxy: Essays in Honour of Henry Chadwick*, 182–99. Cambridge.

Zwicker, S. (1977), 'Politics and panegyric: the figural mode from Marvell to Pope', in *Miner* (1977) 115–48.

GENERAL INDEX